Making Films Your Business

Making Films
Your Business

MOLLIE GREGORY

SCHOCKEN BOOKS • NEW YORK

— '80 0 2 9 3 6

12.62

First published by Schocken Books 1979

10 9 8 7 6 5 4 3 2 1   79 80 81 82

Copyright ©1979 by Mollie Gregory

Library of Congress Cataloging in Publication Data

Gregory, Mollie.
  Making films your business.

  Bibliography: p.
  Includes index.
  1. Moving-picture industry—Vocational guidance.
2. Moving-picture authorship. I. Title.
PN1995.9.P75G7   791.43′02′3   79-14428

Manufactured in the United States of America

Main

To
J
My best partner

TABLE OF CONTENTS

Preface

After my first lecture on the economics of the film business to a group of students—a lecture that necessarily cascaded through the rigors of financing, budgets, contracts, and distribution—one student approached me timidly and whispered: "But what about our ideals?" Like so many others, he felt that art and ideals, business and reality cannot coexist.

Making the acquaintance of reality in filmmaking does not mean you automatically shed all your ideals. Neither does it imply that a filmmaker should meekly accept the ways other people work or what other people advise: that could be as damaging as accepting the first contract handed to you. It is easier to learn the principles of business and adapt them to the dollars and cents of your own films than to learn the craft of making films.

Being aware of reality is to acknowledge that film-making is a colossal means of communication set upon an uncompromising industrial base. No field that readily comes to mind combines the discrete disciplines of both "business" and "art" to the extent they are demanded in film and forces expertise in both on the maker. The passionate, often heard argument that film is either an art or a business is pointless: it is both, and no matter what kind of film one makes, a 15-minute industrial or a 90-minute theatrical, it is still a film that requires money, talent, technique, and a form of promotion, distribution, and exhibition to nurture it to the marketplace.

It seemed time to place a lot of disparate and often hard-to-get information all relating to the same endeavor under one roof, along with some of the experiences and perceptions of filmmakers at work in the field. Also, in the last few years very significant changes have taken place, such as alteration in the tax laws and the copyright act, the development of video cassettes, satellites, videodiscs, and superstations. All have direct and far-reaching effects on film producers.

This book does not describe "how to work within the system." There are no lasting rules, anyway. But some guideposts are presented here as ways to have more control over the direction of your professional life, bolstered by the experiences of other filmmakers to give you a wider view, perhaps, of the field in which the unexpected should be expected daily.

This book springs from my conviction that if filmmakers knew more about the realities of our field, if we were better prepared for it as most other professionals are in theirs, and if those already in films could see the connections instead of the differences between facets of our field, we could produce more and better films, and have more fun doing it. For ultimately, the filmmakers who survive are those who find a way to combine the exigencies of the creative drive with the practices of the business.

M.G.
Los Angeles, 1979

Acknowledgments

Though I did not realize it when I began, writing a book is as collaborative as making a film. I have always found the filmmaking profession crowded with generous, helpful, energetic people. Many people contributed unstintingly to the making of this book, and on many levels. I am extremely grateful to the filmmakers for their willingness to take time and share their experiences with me; to the distributors who gave me their candid evaluations; and to my family and friends, who always seemed to be there when I needed them, whether it was to read various versions of the manuscript, or sit patiently through my recitations of how hard it is to write a book compared to making a film, or simply to say, press on.

Certain contributions demand special recognition: Keith Merrill, Richard J. Goggin, Peter Adair, Greg Morrison, Barbara Legg, H. B. Dave Butler, Robert Bell, Carl Lenz, David M. Kaplan, and J. English Smith. These people did more in various ways than anyone has a right to expect. They helped with hours of interviews relating personal experiences, providing counsel, critical assistance or suggestions, and perceptions of our field, drawn, in many cases, from long professional careers. I am indebted to all of you.

There were many others whose contributions whether in time, counsel, or the sharing of professional experiences broadened and deepened this book. They are Barbara Alexander; Joe Arnold, Arnold Pictures, New Jersey; Terry Bailey; Bruce Baillie; Lee Bobker, Vision Associates, New York; Bill Burch, Universal Pictures; Bari Burke; William Castleman, William Castleman Productions; Coe Film Associates; Jim Culp; Knut-Jorgen Ericksen, Ernest G. Mortensens Forlag, Norway; Graeme Fraser, Crawley Films Ltd., Canada; Ann Hassett; Pedro Hatheyer, Helicon Films, Brazil; John J. Hennessey Motion Pictures; Ann Hershey; Jean and Cliff Hoelscher, Hoelscher Productions; Walter J. Klein Company, Ltd; Lynne Litteman; William Luce; Richard

Moyer, CBS, Los Angeles; Modern Talking Pictures (Ed Swanson, and Jack Whalen); Mary Millman, attorney; Caroline and Frank Mourris; Dr. Georg Munch, Leonaris Film, Germany; Joaquin Padro, Magus Film, Inc.; Ralph Pasek, Communico, St. Louis, Mo.; Georges Pessis, Filmedia, France; V. L. Price, World Wide Pictures, London; Pyramid Films; Sheldon Renan, Renan Productions, Santa Monica, Calif.; Erik Ryge, Laterna Films, Inc., Denmark; Noreen St. Pierre; John F. Schaefer, Audiovisual Services, Washington, D.C.; Bill Schweitzer, Warner Cable; David Stewart, Director's Guild of America; Hack Swain Productions, Florida; Cesare Taurelli, Recta Films, Rome; Wim Wenders; Lowell Wentworth, The Film Group, Cambridge, Mass.; Mary Williams Music Clearing House, Los Angeles; and the following organizations: International Quorum of Motion Picture Producers; Information Film Producers of America; Association of Independent Video and Filmmakers; and Independent Cinema Artists and Producers.

And finally, I would like to thank my editor, Léon King, whose skill, courtesy, and interest, as we wended our way over a terrain new to me, was invaluable.

> *"T'was brillig, and the slithy toves*
> *Did gyre and gimble in the wabe;*
> *All momsy were the borough groves,*
> *And the mome raths outgrabe."*

With thanks to Lewis Carroll:
No one's ever summed the business up better.

CHAPTER 1

Starting Out

HOW OTHERS BEGAN

If "survival of the fittest" were a phrase relating only to the making of films, it would be apt—the people who make films are survivors. Their durability may be attributed to the enormity of their talent or the degree of their persistence; in most cases, it is both and more.

Though most people in film agree on the qualities one needs to survive, no one agrees on the best way to begin.

In truth, there are as many ways to start out to be a filmmaker as there are people who want to make films. Though apprenticeships exist to some extent, filmmaking has not developed codified, recognized routes of "residency," perhaps because the field is still not perceived as a profession. Many excellent filmmakers simply stumble into the field or turn to it from other disciplines, but others are infected with an early and consuming fascination. For instance, a California producer* of short films (who is now making his first feature) said: "I was early involved as a film viewer—sometimes seeing four or five features on a Saturday in grade school. My parents say that I tried to go up on the screen during *Bambi* when I was 3 or 4." By mistake, he was overdosed with a strong tranquilizer while in a college infirmary. After that he found it difficult to feel complex emotions for some time, except in movie theaters. "I became addicted to movies as a kind of iron lung for feeling. I had to see movies practically every day to live....This obsession has decreased with the years, moderated by the ability to

---

*There are many gradations of filmmakers and producers. In this book "producer" will be used to refer to those people who make the financing, selling, and distribution of a film possible, who exercise some creative control but hire others to do the writing, cinematography, etc. A "filmmaker" may do all the tasks of a producer (raising money, etc.) and may also write the script, or direct, or (in 16mm short films) actually shoot the film.

make films. But I remain wired to the medium in a special way—an organic connection that is perhaps beyond anything else in my life, except for love of my children and a sense of personal honor."

Another American short-film producer and writer confessed that on Sundays, when she was sent off to attend church as an adolescent, supplied with a quarter for the collection plate, she went instead to the 11 A.M. movie. "The deception was necessary, I guess, because I spent most Saturdays, all day, at the movies. My parents did not think that seeing more movies on Sunday was healthy. We were 'literary' people."

The admission of such compulsions is not uncommon and the urge to sit there in a dark room watching movies may be one of those irrational motivations that makes it easier later on to take the obstacles in stride when one starts to make films.

It is therefore not surprising that similar fascinations are reported from producers of other countries. "I am told," said a French producer of many information films, "that at 10 I was 'projecting' (with a battery lamp) newspaper cartoons of Mickey Mouse stuck on a long ribbon through the bars of an old chair, hoping to see the drawings start moving." And from Brazil, another short film producer started to work in a camera shop as a teenager: he "fell in love" with the cameras, and from there "it was easy to fall in love with films."

Yet very few "always knew" they would be filmmakers, and even fewer speak of the urge in terms of art: "I was born to be an artist and knew it," said one famous American experimental filmmaker. "I looked for my tools for a long time, painting and writing in the meantime. By 30, I was off into cinema with tremendous built-up energy. Each film became for me—as I look back on it—a stepping stone toward self-discovery."

Though many film producers speak of growing up as movie buffs, wanting to create something, the answer to that desire did not reside with a typewriter or an easel in a garret, and the reasons are not self-discovery. For one producer, who wanted to create—but not alone—a single, shocking event as a teenager gave him the impetus. He told of the sudden death of his father, at the age of 40. "It was a great shock because one day he was alive—planning, working, dreaming—and the next day he was nothing. It taught me to live each day fully and to do exactly what I wanted to do—and that was to make films."

An early appetite for movies may have something to do with becoming a filmmaker, but an amazing number of people, such as art, literature, or engineering majors in college, take an elective in photography or cinema, and they are hooked.

For information film producers, the route has been through advertising, public relations, or the Armed Forces. A respected industrial film producer got a Bachelor's degree in chemistry, a Master's in English and another in Business Administration. This background could be construed by some to be the "perfect" education for an industrial or information filmmaker: science, business, and writing. Working in public relations for a large corporation, he recommended that the firm make a safety film as part of that year's (1950) program. When they agreed, he was faced with producing a film! But instead of just plunging in, he investigated every film in the field at that time, evaluating each to determine what made it successful or faulty. On the basis of that analysis, he developed a concept for the film to be produced, and then hired a professional scriptwriter. When the script was completed, he took it to a production house. The film was an enormous success. A few years later he had to make up his mind whether he was a public relations counsel or a film producer. Naturally, he chose the latter.

This producer did not take university courses or apply for apprenticeships or learn all the basic operations of the camera. He hires the appropriate people to accomplish the tasks of the film, relying on his knowledge of what films his clients need and how to deliver the best film for the expressed need.

But many others simply leap in and learn every facet

themselves—by themselves. One such producer was a national sports broadcaster. When television arrived, he received several offers to join the networks in New York. "I realized that television was a mass medium that could never be controlled by me, that the economic forces were such that one would always be catering to some sort of alleged mass taste. I decided that if I had anything worthwhile to say, I wanted to say it in a medium I could control. The only medium I thought I could control was film—which was naive, but I believed it. So in 1950, I turned down the television offers, quit radio, and with $200 I decided I was going to make films!"

Through his work in radio, he had become acquainted with an East Coast industrialist who was developing a program in career guidance for high school students. The neophyte producer suggested a film to explain the goals and uses of the program—a rather unusual use of film in those days. When he got the $5,000 he asked for, "I started to learn how to make films."

Another producer decided to learn filmmaking to document a family safari around the world. For two years, he subscribed to every technical journal and film magazine he could find, purchased a library of books, and "reread them until I had a thorough *academic* knowledge of the art, craft and technology of film." The world trip failed to materialize. "Disconsolate, my wife and I decided to go back to finish college. Before we left San Francisco, I drove to the camera store to take one last look at the beautiful Bolex I had so set my heart upon. It was raining when we returned to the car. We sat there in silence for a long, long time. Broken dreams and youthful idealism are never comfortable companions.

"If there are critical moments in a career, this was one for us. Somehow we both knew what had to be. I walked slowly back unaware of the rain. I bought the camera, the lenses, the meters and tripods and from my total worldly fortune of $5,000 for school, I wrote a check for $1,800. Then I started to learn to make films."

This is the juncture that every filmmaker who begins in

this way remembers so clearly: the money or the gear or both in hand—no easy feat—an intense journey of discovery about to begin—without rules, guidelines, or teachers. It is recalled with exhilaration and agony, as a constellation of anxieties: "I never worked so hard on any film since," or "I put everything I knew or ever thought into that first spot." As one filmmaker said, "I had convinced a nonprofit organization to give me $6,000 to produce my first 30-minute documentary. I'd never run a camera before, I wasn't completely sure what a one-lite workprint was! When the first rolls came back from the lab, my hands were shaking so much I could hardly get the film threaded up. What if there were no pictures there? What would I say to those people who had given me the $6,000? The first ten feet of the roll was black, and I was seized with terror. Then suddenly—unforgettably—brilliantly colored, sharp focus, moving pictures bounced out of the screen!"

These are some of the beginnings of documentary and short film producers, but what about those people who want to start out in features? They usually begin in low budget, non-union pictures, and there are various suggestions about how to do this, the most useful and common being to get involved in someone else's production: it is the only way to see how it is done, and it is practically the only way to meet people doing it. A great many people who move into features have made several good short films that have won recognition, proving the ability, taste, and talent of the maker. The low-budget feature that such filmmakers move into is frequently funded by American Film Institute grants, the filmmaker's family, and deferred payments to actors and even, in some cases, to the labs.

A third way is to write an outstanding and unusual script that is suitable for a low-budget production and take it to a producer with credentials. The script becomes the young filmmaker's ticket into the production, though this does not mean that the inexperienced filmmaker/scriptwriter will be asked to direct it.

Though more people are preparing themselves by going

to film school, the profession itself is so varied that almost any kind of background is useful. What these backgrounds and beginnings point up is that very few people learn the art, craft, and the business in an orderly, professional manner, yet all, for whatever reasons, become involved by doing. As one international filmmaker says, "Don't wish—do it."

SURVIVAL QUALITIES

Talent

The first requisite. This involves the ability to see an approach to a film that is different, inventive, expressive. Talent is also connected to the ability to control the shape of a film as it passes through its various phases from idea to screen. Talent is related to taste—which is rather like an instinctive awareness of which cut or shot or framing or actor or music is right for the film, and which is not right.

Talent is the grammatical "you understood" in filmmaking, the base on which all films are built. There is no substitute for it, but it is not enough. As one producer said: "In a specialized or artistic area of film, such as creative animation, a filmmaker who has only this gift can go a long way. But for most of us who must compete with many other very talented producers, this quality is not enough in itself."

A Sense of Reality

This quality is related to but not synonymous with a business sense and the ability to analyze. The major ingredient here is that any filmmaker—especially those starting out—must evaluate the cards he or she holds and willfully compensate for the missing ones. The card most often missing is money. A poet needs a sheet of paper and a pencil or typewriter to produce a finished poem. A filmmaker, on the other hand, needs other people, a multiplicity of costly equipment, and access to expensive lab processes to produce a finished film. No one can produce a film with a pencil and a tablet. Since this profession requires the use of money, and since most filmmakers don't have money or powerful banking contacts, they can compensate by having talent, great energy, determination, and intriguing, timely film concepts.

For women who want to be filmmakers, the missing card is being male and having access to what is still a man's field. "The way our social system is set up," said one producer, "it's extremely difficult for any new filmmaker—especially women—to cut into what is essentially an 'old boy's' network. If a filmmaker does not have independent means, he or she must have nerve, brains and guts because the job is one of persuading other people to give you their money."

Every filmmaker starting out shares the initial problem of how to convince other people to give the money with which to make the film. For minorities, and for women this problem is exacerbated. The client or foundation or backers need to be convinced to look beyond their own images of women or minorities and see the filmmaker, to make decisions to fund or not to fund on the basis of talent or experience. There is a real reluctance to "trust" a woman with a large budget to the same degree a man will be trusted with exactly the same credentials.

There are no easy solutions to what is a social problem. Many backers or clients seem to feel that for women filmmaking is still essentially a hobby—not a profession or livelihood—and therefore she does not need as much money because someone else is supporting her somewhere. Filmmakers must dispel that fiction at the outset, as well as the fiction that women do not command or organize people as well as men.

For minority filmmakers, the fiction often lies not in doubt of innate capacity but in limiting minority producers to films that appeal only to minorities. Until avenues of distribution open up (thereby "discovering" diverse and neglected audiences),* women and minority filmmakers still must face the reality of greater problems and working harder to overcome them.

*See Chapter 10.

Therefore, having a sense of reality is realizing where the obstacles will lie, how many there may be, and planning ways to get over them. Generally, if a filmmaker has no awards, few contacts, and no money, that person is well advised to put aside favorite themes and, instead, rationally evaluate film concepts that can be financed or marketed and those that cannot be (see Chapter 3). After that analysis, the filmmaker with a strong pragmatic sense might choose to produce the one concept that has an appeal to a steady market and, from that success (let us assume), spring into more specialized concepts or more ambitious films. The point is that filmmakers need to perceive the world of filmmaking realistically and then perceive themselves as clearly as possible, and from those analyses strike out in a promising direction.

Honesty is necessary for the sense of reality. The producers who survive are those who have a good idea of where they stand in the business and are honest with themselves, other filmmakers, and their clients or sponsors. This is harder than it sounds.

"Everyone occasionally gets into conflicted situations where it is very tempting to fabricate a bit. Examples: telling a client that the lab is responsible for the lateness of the prints when actually the filmmaker was late turning in the print order; blaming faulty equipment for what was really a technical error on someone's part. Usually no harm is done, but once the bond of trust is broken between producer and client, it will never be repaired. Early in my career I learned this lesson. The end shot of a television spot I was shooting was hand held. Consequently, it moved a bit—unnoticeable by itself, but when a super was placed over it, the super, of course, seemed to "shake" slightly. Now, the client (an advertising agency) had a representative with whom I'd been working who had been a complete pain in the neck throughout the production. I wanted nothing more than to get the job over with just to get this person out of my hair. At the screening of the answer print, he asks, 'Why is the super jiggling?'

"It would have been so simple to have said honestly, 'Because it's a hand-held shot behind it.' But I didn't. I blamed it on a 'laboratory technical process,' thinking that no more would be heard about it. (It was a very slight jiggle.)

"Later that day the rep showed the spot to his superior, who promptly noticed the jiggle, asked about it, and was dutifully given my answer. Another savvy person said, 'By God, no, that's because it's a hand-held shot.' Caroomba! The producer lied! Result: embarrassment for the rep before his superior. Result for me: no more business from that agency— ever."

A producer who has been making award-winning films for 40 years said: "Be honest—there's less competition that way."

Business Sense

Business sense means different things to different film-makers. To a producer of information or documentary films, it is the ability to understand and analyze communication problems that films can help solve or explain, and the sales ability to convince the buyer of the film program's worth. The first is knowing how films work, being aware of the relation-ship between a film's objective and intended audience, plus the ability to translate the information by film. Without this analytical capacity, a filmmaker's chances for survival in the information part of the field are slim.

Once the initial analysis is finished, sales ability is a vital component. This is, at its base, the self-confidence "that you are," as one person put it, "as good as you say you are." But it is also the ability to communicate in a persuasive manner the results of the analysis to people untutored in film or video: it's the ability to convince people of the merits of a story or a communication program.

In a larger framework, every filmmaker needs a sense of business. It is an administrative or managerial capacity, a pragmatic sense of priorities, the ability to read and under-stand a contract and to analyze options, problems, and goals. If a filmmaker does not have business acumen, then the only move is to get a partner who does. One filmmaker spent two years working for his father-in-law, who was trying to make a "businessman" out of him. Though the filmmaker resented the years at the time, "that man succeeded in teaching me things about budgets, cash flow, project management, and organization which made the difference between the success and failure of our film enterprise.

"In retrospect, I give him tremendous credit for the pleasant success we have enjoyed in the ten years of our film business. Most of the things which angered me and which I resisted most were the qualities I so desperately needed to 'make it' out there in the real world of filmmaking."

Balance

The best filmmakers cultivate a natural duality: one side is creative and communicative and impressionable; the other side is assertive and pragmatic. Contrary to popular belief, nurturing the pragmatic side does not destroy the creative; each helps the other to survive. One film producer described well this necessary "sense of balance between what is right and wrong, the useful and the beautiful, the content and the aesthetics, the image and the sound, subject and length, the matter (money) and the mind (creation)."

Another filmmaker expressed it as "toughness versus innocence," but it all relates to the blend of a sense of art and a sense of business, which this profession demands in equal parts. People who may be good enough technically and creatively often leave the field because they were not sufficiently competent as administrators. On the other hand, it is by no means enough simply to be good at economics. "In a nutshell," said one producer with thirty years' experience, "the film business needs universal geniuses."

Education

Opposing views about the efficacy of film schools really come down to how the filmmaker wishes to be introduced to the subject—through structured classes or chaotic on-the-job training. The problem with the former is that film courses often are far removed from the real world and are comprised of history, theory, and some "hands-on" classes with camera and sound gear. The problem with on-the-job training is that all too few people get that chance—without previous experience.

Students believe that a degree in cinema will help them get a job, but in fact it does nothing of the kind. The big film schools in cities like New York and Los Angeles can help students make contacts, and many students' first jobs have come from making the acquaintance of a producer who lectured at the school.

Most of us learn filmmaking haphazardly. But in casting back, the professionals with the track records invariably cite the usefulness of a broad liberal arts education. "The best filmmakers have had an eclectic, catholic education—that is, music, arts, literature, and science. They have a genuine desire to learn, as well as a love of the creative arts." The "desire to learn" and an innate curiosity find their fulfillment in filmmaking: "I don't know of another field where you can learn something new every day! Today a film on Cambodia, tomorrow one on plastics or prisons. Each day is an adventure!"

In terms of education, most producers add that ideally, students should minor in law or business, while majoring in film, if that were possible. Anyone who wants to prepare to enter the feature film battleground could not be better served than to put together if not a full law degree—at least a solid background in management and legal affairs. The business has become an amazing jungle of legalities. Having a grasp of that world is now essential.

But the fact remains that no film departments of any school demand of filmmakers what will be required of them in the field. The producer of the first U.S. sound and color industrial film (1932) said: "Reading and learning about everything connected with art is essential. Otherwise, how can a person develop conception, execution, imagination, taste? Films are probably the toughest of all art forms, and we simply do not teach the basics needed. The British Broadcasting Corporation people really know how to do their homework, and they do it. I think that is why many of their films are superior."

Initiative

Filmmakers often have to make their own opportunities or must seize them boldly when they occur by chance. This is one of the reasons so many filmmakers have said that the ability to "self-start" is a paramount quality. Here is the way one award-winning filmmaker began his career. It is a good example of "making it happen":

"One night, driving home from my brother's (and I could mark the spot on the freeway to this day), my wife simply asked me what I wanted. *'I want to make films!'* She replied, 'Then from this moment we will not let one day pass without taking a significant step towards that goal.'

"The next day I approached my employer and suggested that I make a 25-minute film for a pending stockholders' meeting. He agreed. I worked as I had never worked in my life and learned more about making films during those long days and nights than in a six years' master's program. At the end of the meeting my employer apologetically announced that I had shot a few movies of the project, which would now be shown. The lights went down, and the film began. The chairman came right out of his seat. He had expected nothing—always a tremendous advantage!

"For all the errors, flash frames and pops on the track, which neither budget nor time had allowed to be corrected, the film was professional enough to capture the audience. I was a filmmaker.

"Following the meeting, a partner of the firm approached me about making a similar film on a project in Australia. Not bad for a second assignment. It was while crawling about in the outback of northern Australia filming lizards, and domesticated Asian buffalo that I knew I would never do anything but make films again."

An excellent first or second film gives the filmmaker

instant credibility. When a filmmaker finally lands an opportunity to make a film with someone else's money (whether it's foundation grant money or a contract with a utility company), that early film must reflect all the effort and skill that the maker is capable of at that time. The film should do what it set out to do, imaginatively, but on time and on budget. The chance, in other words, must be seized like a lifeline and played for all it is worth.

Staying Power

This is endurance, tenacity, persistence, determination. Without these qualities, no filmmaker can succeed. Staying power is also the ability to tolerate rejection, to salvage, to go on.

To get a production funded, filmmakers spend many hours preparing outlines, treatments, and budget estimates and calling on people who might invest in or fund the film. The ratio of sales calls or presentations to success is at least 20 to one, and that guess may be generous. Most proposals, presentations, or ideas will be rejected for one reason or another. Taking rejection of one's film concepts personally is suicidal. In most instances, the rejection has little to do with the filmmaker; it is the cost, the approach, the subject, the length—even the title. Filmmakers who cannot deal with rejection should go into less psychologically risky lines of work.

Specializing in a kind of film or film use is the ticket to many people's staying power. As one distributor said: "You carve out some ground that you understand better than anyone else. One filmmaker may produce films on thermo-dynamics and related fields but wouldn't know what to do with a film on dance."

A California feature filmmaker (who has made many industrial and documentary films) stressed an interesting tension between two planes of performance. He said that his "staying power" came from the ability to sell himself, manage money, budget properly, stay within budget, and do practically everything in the filmmaking process. But on another level, a key to survival is his "refusal to accept personal limitations, and the realization that immortality is not a great film, that the purpose of life is not success measured by the standards of the world: this allows me to be comfortably philosophical about the rise and fall of the business....It is a tremendous advantage."

"Total support from my wife and family" came at the head of his survival list. This recognition is perhaps one of the major reasons few women so far have been prestigious filmmakers. Anyone can see from these pages what sort of mad commitment a person must make in order to have even a gambler's chance to parlay the making of one film into a lifetime profession. It is hard to imagine a woman combining the business of filmmaking with running a house and raising a family. One California woman who formed her own film company in the late 1960s said: "I was calling on potential clients, writing proposals, acting as my own secretary, scripting, editing, budgeting—*clawing* to make it work. In the evenings, I'd cook dinner and occasionally my husband wondered out loud why the house was so dusty, and like Boxer, I'd say, 'I will work harder.' When I went back to the office at night to, say, edit a film, I actually felt guilty about leaving the dishes in the sink until I got home at midnight. Needless to say the marriage collapsed. But as I look back I am struck by how much easier it would have been had I had a partner in the way men automatically do—not just someone who takes your clothes to the cleaners, or fixes meals—though, God knows, that's a help—but someone who is totally committed to the success of your endeavor, and will do anything to help make it happen. What a gift that must be."

The definition of "staying power" in features, says one observer, depends on a filmmaker's resilience: "The people who shoot 1,000 feet of film of a rock with a zipper behind it and try to use that kind of art film to get into this business will end up so compromised that they won't last in the grind of the business, which is a requirement of the industry."

Surviving the grind depends upon a person's ability to take unusual punishment and bounce back. "Let's say someone fresh out of New York University writes a screenplay which a producer in Hollywood options—or buys. 'Sensational!' says the producer. 'Do you have any ideas about who should be in it?' And the filmmaker says, 'George C. Scott and Jane Fonda.' The producer agrees, so some rewrites are done and they send the script to George C. Scott, who says, 'I think it's terrific', and the producer sends it to Jane Fonda who says, 'No, the only way I would possibly do it would be total rewrite.' But the young writer says, 'Fonda's part is much more important than Scott's and I'd much rather lose him than her.' The producer says, 'Screw you, kid, get back in your bin.' See, the producer is obligated to the _deal_ at this point. Now Scott says, 'Listen, I want to do it with Faye Dunaway.' The kid says, 'Faye Dunaway isn't right for the part! I'll walk off!' The producer says, 'Get lost.' But the kid thinks it over and finally gets his mind around Faye Dunaway, to whom the producer has already taken the script. She doesn't want to do it. By this time, Scott has another film to do, and he says, 'I'll only do it if you get Walter Bernstein to rewrite it because this kid's young and he doesn't know.' At that point, not only has the kid had about four life crises but he's about to be thrown out the window. He can either say to the producer, 'Let me hang around—I'll work with Bernstein' or he can listen to his ego and tell the producer to stuff it. At some point, the producer is going to say, 'I'm sorry, kid, here's the option money I promised you, I'm out of the deal.'

"That whole process can take a year and it can be so demoralizing you'd rather be running a soldering gun at General Motors. The losers are the young writers or filmmakers dedicated to a principle or a story, who say, 'The story of Robert E. Lee has not been truthfully told and the film that I'm going to do on him will cut through if I can just get Robert Redford.' Those people will sink without a trace. But the person who enters into the center ring with openness and a 'circus' outlook, saying, 'If I can't get the high wire act I'm going to bring out the bears.' That's the kind of mentality or at least the positioning of oneself, that allows one to survive—be it as a producer, filmmaker, writer."

The division between the jugglers who survive and those

filmmakers committed to the vision of a single film is acute. The schism exists in both feature and short film worlds. Not everyone wants to be a juggler.

"If it was between making sponsored films or *no* films, I would choose no films," said one producer who had just completed a feature-length documentary. "Even though I adore films, saying something through them is more important to me than simply working in film." Everyone makes a choice; it's most important to know what one's choice is.

Passion

Above all, filmmakers share a compulsion to create moving images in time and space. "Making movies for me is the most important thing in my life. My passion remains unchanged, but I seem to be increasingly interested in making films of social commitment. In my darker moments, I sometimes think the reason for this is atonement to rationalize the expense and self-indulgence of my monolithic obsession." A Brazilian filmmaker said, "If you do not *love* cinema, forget it."

With the passion comes the work: "The key is commitment to a way of life centered around filmmaking and then a willingness to work your ass off, holding nothing back." But the work is still a passion: "I used to imagine the worst thing that could happen, if I failed in film, was going to work. With countless 18-hour days and 100-hour work weeks behind me I'm certainly glad I never had to go to work."

THE IDEAL FILMMAKER

Filmmakers must have an easy mastery of the fine and performing arts, social and political history, psychology and human behavior, mathematics, business practices, lighting and photography techniques, a grasp of the principles of physics and optics, history of architecture, knowledge of film emulsions, fascination with and understanding of sophisticated equipment such as Nagras and Arriflexes; a filmmaker knows the plays of Racine, the paintings of Rubens and Pollack, the notebooks of da Vinci, Mycenean and Boeing designs, and the poetry of Sexton and Dante and can speak with equal interest on the Peloponnesian Wars and the evolution of the United Nations charter. A filmmaker needs to be conversant with the history of cinema (foreign and domestic), and patterns of criticism on current film genres, directors, and techniques (foreign and domestic); at the same time, a filmmaker must keep up with technological developments such as videodisc, optical fiber, and the potential of cable television. Besides having a vivid sense of visual design—color, composition, and movement, as in dance—they can see a single flash frame go by in a 16mm print. Filmmakers are acquainted with mechanical and electrical engineering, the function of F stops and three-color separations and can bring the same intense focus to discussions of the musical principles of a Bach fugue, the sociopolitical implications of child-care centers as they exercise during an eight-channel dub, selecting one cut over another, or coaching a terrified, arrogant actor. Not only that, while shooting, filmmakers can instantly visualize the dramatic or narrative results of reverse shots, POV, cutaways, inserts, ELS over ECU and match cuts—all as they will appear in the finished film. At home anywhere, filmmakers are extroverts who delight in and can communicate with winos, board members of large multinational corporations, gay community leaders, and sculptors; they also appear at ease with two disparate groups of surly often rebellious people with whom they work: the technically oriented craftspeople and the aesthetically emotional artists.

But to be a filmmaker is to live on a tightrope, for she or he also needs to develop and cherish the characteristics of an introvert: writing scripts for long lonely hours, plotting shooting plans, figuring budgets. For this reason, the filmmaker is also a skillful writer, enjoys the quiet practice of language arts, has a strong sense of plot, story, character, and an excellent ear for dialogue. Nonetheless, a filmmaker cannot hide behind written words, but must be a highly articulate storyteller so that anyone listening can "see" the movie and is convinced of its worth, either educationally or commercially.

In addition, filmmakers should not be so far ahead of the popular tides of thought that no one can recognize the film's merit but not so far behind that the idea lacks timeliness. Filmmakers, then, are persuasive salespeople, able to convince others to pour their money down a theatrical investment rathole (where the odds are one in ten of making their money back). These filmmakers know all about the Paramount Decree, arm's-length agreements, what distributors and publicists do, the blockages in the avenues of gross and net from box office to backers, changes in the U.S. tax shelter and copyright laws, and the resulting effects one or the other may eventually have on financing and distribution. A filmmaker understands limited partnership agreements, recognizes the value of promotion and advertising, what a 90-10 percent agreement with an exhibitor means compared to a 60-40 percent with a 75 percent floor, and what constitutes the house nut, icing, palming, and four-walling. Aside from knowing when to use a Tyler mount, filmmakers are compassionate, diplomatic people with the organizing abilities of Bismarck, the financial acumen of J. P. Morgan, the spiritual tolerance of St. Francis, all of which they are called upon to exhibit regularly. They are so familiar with the elements of a budget they can quote various costs from memory, such as the going union rate of best boys or recordists, or the per-foot costs for a color reversal intermediate, as well as outline when it is best to get an electroprinted sound track instead of rushing into an optical transfer. Filmmakers know which elements of a script will automatically raise the budget (such as rain scenes, stunts, or trained seals), but they also have the artistic judgment to know which may be abandoned without harm to the picture's concept and style.

Filmmakers are jugglers able to keep one film in production while scripting and selling a second, dreaming of a third as they attend the preview screening of the fourth, made the previous year. They know what money can and cannot do, where it can be found, how it can be used, and when money alone will not solve aesthetic or technical problems. Filmmakers deal well with rejection, thrive on 18-hour work days, enjoy the conflicting sides of their personalities. Creatively, they are compelled to communicate through film in a cohesive, if simplified fashion for the education or delight of millions of people. A filmmaker is a masochist, warrior, scientist, artisan, market analyst, storyteller, athlete, magician.

CHAPTER 2

Writing Skills

GOOD FILMMAKERS ARE GOOD WRITERS

Even though the genesis of a film is an image or idea, the successful culmination of that idea on film often depends on the ability of the filmmaker to communicate the idea clearly and powerfully on paper. Filmmakers who sharpen their basic writing skills enjoy a distinct advantage over those who have failed to realize the significance that competent writing plays in the field.

There are a number of stages between the original idea for a film and the final screening of that film before an audience. These stages vary, depending on the film's length and whether it is a feature, documentary, or animated short. Generally, the process starts with a written statement of the core concept, usually a single paragraph or page and moves on from that to an outline of the film.[1]

There are all kinds of films, and they have been given all kinds of names—industrials, documentaries, feature-length documentaries, shorts, sponsored films, experimental, features, and so on. Some people refer to all films by breaking them rather cavalierly into two giant groups, such as fiction and non-fiction, or theatrical and nontheatrical. Of course, any definition of a film category that has a "non" in front of it does not define what the category encompasses, but only what it is not. It is just as inaccurate to refer to all "nontheatrical" films as documentaries. There are a lot of "non-theatrical" films that are not documentaries either, such as industrials or experimental shorts.

To simplify the following discussions, the categories of films will be divided into *information* (which will include documentaries, industrials, and educational films), *shorts* (experimental or animated films of an unusual character, sometimes fictional, sometimes not), and *features* (fictional films 90 minutes or more in length for theatrical release). When differences within one of the categories need to be pointed out, the exact sort of film will be named so that there is no confusion.

OUTLINES AND TREATMENTS

Information and Short Films

Before writing any proposal or outline, the filmmaker needs to separate the elements of the film idea or program and analyze them: what quality about the proposed film is so appealing that people will be excited about it even as they read it? How does this approach to the concept differ from similar films already produced on the subject? Who is the audience for the film? In other words, who will care and why?

Just because the final result is to be a film—not a book— does not mean a filmmaker can ignore the discipline of testing concepts or searching for the best words to explain them. It's amazing how many proposal outlines—even from "old pros"—ignore the discipline of editing and often founder on poor analysis of the film and its use. One must be willing to rewrite, cut, polish, judge every sentence critically. Is the meaning clear? Does it express exactly what the filmmaker has in mind? Are there other unstated aspects of the proposed film that would augment the original premise?

If the initial or core concept for the film has been approved in some manner (either by contract with a client or acceptance by a foundation or backer), the next stage is an outline of three to five pages. The length of the outline depends upon the length of the film; a three-page outline is suitable for a 20-minute film, but not quite enough for a 60-minute film. The outline contains the film's objective or goal, the subject or content of the film, the audience, a budget estimate, and plans for distribution (a sentence or two). Depending on the nature of the film, it may include a clarifying note on the style of the film. The outline stage of the film may be written up in the form of a letter between the producer and the client or sponsoring agent, or it may form the crux of a proposal.

From the outline, a treatment is developed. Unlike the proposal or the outline, the treatment should read like a short story, giving a sense of immediacy, a sense of seeing the film unfold on paper. It tells the film story in narrative form without cinematic gimmicks. It may contain sample narration or dialogue. Most of the major research is completed in this stage. Major transitions, characters (if any), settings, blocks of information—all are solved and presented. For films 30 minutes long or less, a treatment may run 5-12 pages. Twenty-page treatments for 60-minute films are not unusual. When the treatment is approved, the writer (or writer/producer) progresses to the script.

Feature Films

The emphasis of this chapter is on information and short films, but we should take a brief look at the steps between idea and script for feature films.

The idea and outline stages are similar to those for short films except for length: an outline for a 90-minute feature film may run up to 15 pages. It highlights characters, plot, story, locations, theme. Well-known writers may present an outline to agents or studios, backing it up with verbal descriptions of the action or even specific scenes with dialogue, along with all the reasons why audiences everywhere will love it if a certain actor or actress plays the lead. Unknown writers, however, almost always need a full script. The next step: a brisk, punchy, complete treatment. Average length: 40 pages.

Either treatment or outline (synopsis) or both may be included in a financing package to give investors an idea of the film's story and characters. The script—from 90 to 120 pages, depending on length—is a cinematic translation of the treatment.

THE ORGANIZATION OF A PROPOSAL

Techniques of Writing

Good Beginnings

In many instances, a written proposal introduces the filmmaker. Therefore, it should reflect clear thinking, creative approaches, a sense of form, attention to detail, and organizing ability.

The first paragraph of a proposal or a bid for a film sets the tone for all the pages to come; it should encourage the reader to continue. Spend extra time polishing the first page or paragraph, because a strong, commanding opening that involves the reader is well worth the extra effort.

Do not start with "I hope to produce a film about teenage pregnancy...." Nobody cares about the filmmaker's hopes. The originality of the film's approach to a well-known subject, the new effects of a subject or the film's goal—are all better openings than hopes. A potential sponsor of an information or documentary film is really only concerned with the quality of the concept and how the idea relates to his or her organization, or why the film is needed. "The rate of teenage pregnancy has risen to epidemic proportions in the United States," is a far stronger beginning.

Aesthetics

A proposal, outline, or written presentation of any kind should attract the reader at first glance. The words should be as carefully and attractively placed on the page as a film director frames a shot. Use generous margins, large or pica type, and double-space it. The components or sections should be separated and headlined so that each page has "breathing space." A proposal whose pages are too thickly covered with words daunts the reader and tends to bore in advance. Such a proposal becomes antithetical to its primary purpose, which is to communicate as fully as possible.

Strong Writing

Writing proposal outlines requires a quiet, dignified,

clear, unpretentious use of language. Nothing sabotages the meaning or dissipates the impact of a proposal as much as passive sentences. "The reason this film should be made is that it would show the plight of the sea otters." Active sentences compel the reader forward and help maintain interest. For example, "Sea otters live on the brink of extinction."

The use of "would" or "will" in proposals is perhaps a matter of taste, but look at the difference:

"This film would make an impact on prejudice in America."

"This film will make an impact on prejudice in America."

The tone of the second sentence is much stronger. Also, by writing "will" all the way through a proposal, the reader senses the producer's strong belief in and commitment to the film concept.

The Word "Project"

"Project" is widely used in this field as a synonym for "film," and its use should be critically reexamined.

"The project is a film about Navajo art," or "I am working on a project with Warners." "Project" sounds like volunteer work connected with a charity bazaar; "project" is amateur, and its use tends to degrade the complexity and difficulty of getting a film off the ground. Do surgeons refer to their 7 A.M. "projects" in O.R. 4? Do lawyers talk about their antitrust "projects"? Do conductors work on their Beethoven "projects"? Filmmaking is not a hobby—it is a profession; our language should reflect recognition of that fact.

Repetition

First-drafts for proposals are usually full of repetition; they need to be shaved—sometimes axed. Even the most experienced producers, working against deadlines, can fail to catch the same thought written in three different ways in three separate parts of the proposal. A proposal for a film should be lean; to make it so takes discipline. Keep in mind that the paramount idea is communication—not self-expression.

Format

The basic format for an information or short-film proposal covers the objective, theme, audience, film description, and distribution plans. (Proposals to foundations are slightly different and are dealt with later in the chapter.) Before tackling the separate parts analytically, it is best to try to see the proposal as a whole. This gives the writer a needed sense of direction.

Length of proposals depends on the subject of the film and the funding agency or client to which the outline is directed. Though a film producer must describe the vision or idea of the film completely, proposals are no longer judged by the pound: brevity is best. An estimated budget for the production and a short paragraph suggesting the distribution plan should accompany each proposal. (See Chapter 5.)

Purpose

This is a statement or paragraph describing the fundamental reason for the film. It defines the problem to be solved, or the goal of the film, or the attitude the film sets out to challenge, or the information gap it is intended to fill.

Theme

Many producers and sponsors think a documentary does not need to have a stated theme if its purpose is clear, but good films, no matter what kind, always have an underlying thematic statement. For example, the objective of a film may be to show the varying effects of poverty on the elderly. The film may also quietly imply that it is a rude, harsh, ungrateful country that treats the elderly in this fashion. On the other hand, the film's objective may be to show the benefits of the Social Security system; the underlying theme might be to show that the U.S. government cares about and respects its elderly citizens. Clearly defining the theme of the film as well as the objective often will lead filmmakers to discover innovative organizations of the material in scripting, and later, when filming, dictate the choice of one camera angle over another, of composition, of use of light, or of optical effects. Guided by a known theme, such choices invariably deepen the quality of any film.

Audience

For whom is this film primarily created, and to whom might it also appeal? Be specific. "General audience" is an immediate giveaway that this section (as well as the first two) have not been well conceived or analyzed.

A film created for a grade school audience, ages 6–9, will contain language, music, and visual choices quite different from one created for an audience of middle-class adults, ages 35–65. Knowing the audience for whom the film is created before scripting and shooting leads to creative cinematic decisions that will ultimately sharpen the focus of the film. One filmmaker told of her experience regarding audience. The purpose of the film was to rebut myths about and prejudices against welfare recipients. The filmmaker chose the music on the basis of the narrative content of the lyrics; in effect, the music track became a second narrator. Having made this exciting creative choice, the filmmaker failed to keep the audience in mind, many of whom said they didn't understand some parts of the film, but commented that their teenage children did. Why? Most adults don't listen to the lyrics of rock or even some folk songs; most teenagers do. Consequently, the white middle-class adults (who formed the primary audience) missed about one-third of the narration.

The Need for the Film

Need strongly relates to purpose, and a statement of need may be covered in conjunction with that section. If the need for a film can be clearly shown, its value will be readily perceived, and the film will be easier to finance and distribute.

The need may be to rectify a widespread misunderstanding or ignorance on a certain subject or supply a lack of current information or explain an emerging social crisis or attitude. For instance, at one time a need existed for films on abused children, and that need was filled by several producers and distributors. Later a need existed for a film about battered wives, and a few films on that subject have been made. In 1979, there was a need for films on such problems as incest, teenage pregnancy, and alcoholism.

The Description of the Film

The description of the film is more than just a glance at the subject matter; it plunges into the heart of the film-to-be, describing the approach to the subject, the story, people, and locations of the film.) If one person personifies the film's subject, such as a teenage mother, then this section tells her story: the challenges, agonies, frustrations, loneliness, resolutions. If the film is ten minutes long and it doesn't really have a "story," the filmmaker writes what he or she sees. The reader will finish this section, if it is skillfully focused, with a sense of having actually seen the film.

In the previous sections of the proposal, the filmmaker writes objectively—standing outside the film. At this point, the writer steps inside, telling the story succinctly, strongly, and with feeling. This part of the film proposal reflects not only the filmmaker's grasp of the subject but his or her commitment to it.

Style and Approach

This part may be included with the description of the film or in a section by itself. There's a film on nearly every subject, and many, such as ecology, off-shore oil development, and rape have been filmed dozens of times. This section describes the filmmaker's different emphasis or completely original approach to the subject and by what filmic means the idea will be translated from the prose of the proposal to celluloid. Animation? Cinéma verité? Scripted documentary? Will it have a narrator, actors, special effects?

The description of style should not bristle with technical jargon. Constant references to "wipes," "SFX," "supers," "rack focus," minute descriptions of frame composition, annoy readers and obscure the film story. A film writer can also get into trouble in this section when the film treatment is so innovative that few people can understand how it is to be produced. The risk is, naturally, that the writer/filmmaker will leave the sponsor/funder far behind, buried in complex technical concepts.

As for approach, here is the filmmaker's opportunity to show that she or he has researched other films on the subject and how this film differs from them, if that is the case.[2] But it also refers to the filmmaker's grasp of the subject and whether the selected approach to a film about, for instance, U.S. campaign spending practices, is filmically viable and sustaining. This section is one of the most revealing—for those who read it in terms of whether the subject or story will really make a film, and for the filmmaker in terms of analyzing all the various ways of approaching a film on the subject proposed.

The Budget

Since, in most cases, the script has not been written, budgets at this point can only be estimates. But even estimates, if done realistically and carefully, can be surprisingly close to the mark. The standard way of estimating this in 1979 was to budget $1,500 to $2,500 per finished minute of film (more if animation was used) and divide it into three sections (pre-, during, and post-production), the bulk of the money allotted to the latter two sections. (See Chapter 4.)

Distribution

No filmmaker should ever propose a film without having a plan for its distribution. In most cases, this will mean (1) learning about the various kinds of distribution available, (2) selecting the method most applicable, and (3) sending a letter of inquiry to distributors and going to see those who respond. In some cases, this is the first and last stop a filmmaker has to make since distributors sometimes finance films they know they can market.

In any case, distribution should be sought before any film is made. For this proposal, the distribution marketing plans may be drawn from such diverse avenues as commercial or educational TV (national and local); transfer to video cassettes or reduction to super 8 for desk top use; sponsored or commercial educational distribution, cable or pay-TV, or videodisc. Whatever the plan, it needs to be specific and keyed to the primary and secondary audiences. Attach to it an estimated cost for distribution and prints or cassettes. These costs are additions to the estimated production budget. For sponsored distribution of industrial films, these costs are usually divided: one-third for the cost of production, one-third for prints, one-third for the distribution fees.[3] Often, prints and distribution are handled as a separate contract so that the production budget covers only those costs up to release print.

Credentials

Prize-winning filmmakers have no problem writing this crucial section, but even award-winning producers sometimes miss the hidden question here: Why should you especially make this film? To answer the question well, filmmakers need (1) to be sensitive to their special interest in the film subject and (2) to analyze objectively those professional and personal strengths that uniquely suit them to create the proposed film. Personal or professional strength is not merely technical expertise; it is often an ability to draw on an area of experience or understanding that bears directly on the proposed film that will make the measurable difference between one filmmaker and another, even though both competitors may have similar credentials and awards.

This section should include a full résumé of the filmmaker and may also contain cinematographer's and writer's credits, as well as those of planned consultants.

WRITING PROPOSALS TO FOUNDATIONS

Two major sources of grant money are available: (1) government grants: federal, such as the National Endowment

.for the Arts, which includes the American Film Institute, and the National Endowment for the Humanities, and state, such as the state arts commissions; and (2) private foundations.

The First Steps

Private Foundations

Of the literally thousands of private foundations, few support films, though there are more foundations today that view films and videotapes as valid artistic or educational endeavors than there were even a few years ago. The subject of the proposed film should match a foundation's major area of interest. It's a waste of time to propose a film on urban murals to a foundation with a history of granting in the mental health area. Researching foundations is a monumental but essential task. Most libraries contain a fat volume called *The Foundation Directory*, which lists every U.S. foundation and its area of interest, the *Annual Register of Grant Support*, or current issues of *The Foundation News*.

The Foundation Center in New York City can be used for researching those foundations with a record of funding films. If you are not in New York, you can write for a copy of their publication "Films, Documentaries, Media and Audiovisuals," 888 7th Ave., New York, N.Y. 10019. Also check the *National Directory of Grants and Aid to Individuals in the Arts*, Washington Arts Letter, Box 90005, Washington, D.C. 20003. The American Council on the Arts has a new book on 359 major U.S. corporations funding practices in the arts, which is available from the Council, 570 7th Avenue, New York, N.Y. 10018.*

For private foundations, the filmmaker must write a solid, clear, strong letter of inquiry, which should include the following:

• a brief statement of the purpose of the proposed film;

---

*Also used occasionally in contacting nonprofit organizations, agencies, and corporations, but primarily for use with private foundations.

- why the organization (or foundation) to whom you are writing will be interested in such a film;
- the filmmaker's previous work on the subject and other credentials;
- a capsule description of the film and the audience for whom it is intended;
- experts or advisers knowledgeable in the field or subject of the film who support it, or consultants who will work on the film;
- the amount of budget money requested; and
- the distribution plans.

The purpose of the letter of inquiry is to discover if a foundation has any interest in the film, and whether the concept for the film falls within their granting guidelines for the current period. If so, most foundations respond promptly with application forms and instructions. Though a letter of inquiry should not be longer than two pages, it must represent the filmmaker and film to the prospective funder completely. Considerable time and concentration should be invested in them. Jotting down a few casual ideas and sending them to a dozen foundations or organizations will not usually result in enthusiastic responses.

Public Foundations

Initial inquiries to the National Endowment for the Arts, the American Film Institute, and the National Endowment for the Humanities are much simpler. Drop them a note requesting a copy of their brochures. This will present the categories under which individuals (and organizations) are eligible for funding, the application forms, instructions, and the schedule of deadlines. Read the material they send very carefully to determine which category the film is most suited for.

For either private and public foundations, it is a good idea to try to make personal contact by telephone, or in person if possible, in order to clarify any questions the filmmaker might have and to establish some kind of personal rapport. When this is possible, the filmmaker-applicant often receives first rate information and guidance.

The Proposal

Proposals to foundations do not differ radically from writing film proposals generally, but the format differs enough to deserve special mention. As can clearly be seen by now, writing any proposal is a skill, and not everyone has it, though almost anyone can learn to be competent with practice. Filmmakers who feel that the kind of films they wish to produce are best funded by foundations (rather than by industry, for example) need to learn how to write proposals.

Those who do not feel capable of writing proposals, or who "cannot face it," must get someone else to do it—preferably, of course, someone whose proposals have been funded.

Generally, foundation applications include the following:

- the film's goals;
- the work (or production) plan and schedule;
- the film's significance, which should include a strong rationale for the funding;
- description of the film's content;
- the distribution plan;
- applicant's credentials, and those of other key people, including consultants;
- the budget; and
- the evaluation plan.

The significance of the film can be included in sections that deal with the audience or the purpose, but for many foundations, this is an aspect of the film that should be dealt with in a separate section. The question is, of course: Will this film make a difference? What, if anything, is so special about it, or so radical? Will it result in something important—for instance, an instant grasp of some basic principle, such as an economic theory or Mendelian genetics? What sets this film apart? What contributions will the film make to the audience? How are we made better having seen it?

The term "Evaluation Plans" usually confuses film-makers, yet foundations invariably ask the filmmaker to describe these plans in some detail. Filmmakers tend to believe that if everyone likes the picture and the distribution is wide, then the film is a success. But this is not necessarily so.

Evaluation usually involves a plan created by the film-maker to test the film and confirm whether it has met the goals originally set for it. For instance, evaluation of a short film on schizophrenia might include a screening for a panel of psychiatrists who specialize in that disease. Informed of the stated use proposed for the film, the panel might even act as a review committee at scripting and interlock stages. At any rate, a plan to evaluate the film must exist, for it will indicate that the filmmaker is aware of his or her responsibility to make the film perform as promised. But more impor-tant, the salient question for information films is, Does the film do the job? Finished films that do not perform the task for which they were created constitute an industrywide complaint. If a film's purpose is to create in the audience a willingness to contribute to the protection of porpoises, the audience should learn something they did not know about porpoises, and should be given strong reasons why a world without porpoises is undesirable.

Foundations ask for evaluation plans with the written proposal, but the whole issue of whether the film does its intended job should be a matter of real concern to all filmmakers whether or not they are receiving grant money. If, upon completion, the film is found deficient or muddy or inconclusive, that result can be traced directly to how well the filmmaker matched objective with audience with subject and how clearly the filmmaker, client, or granting agency analyzed the major elements of the proposed film. According to one filmmaker, "Some technically mediocre films may be brilliantly successful in reaching their audience, while an innovative artistic creation may float gently over the aver-age viewer.... Hence the supposed justification for all the corporate intervention in 'creative process'....The biggest problem is getting the people who need to see the film in front of the screen."

Biographies, Letters of Support, Advisers

People in the business of giving grants appear to have a conservative, academic appreciation for those applications bolstered by experts' curricula vitae. This is not a section where less is better. Gather up letters of support from the most renowned experts in the subject of the film. List advisers and consultants in the field and give their credentials. Include letters from distributors stating their interest in screening the film, citing its potential distribution possibilities. New filmmakers may want to pull in someone with a fine film reputation, who, acting as a kind of executive producer, might give the foundation a feeling of confidence.

The filmmaker's résumé should be full, listing every pertinent award, scholarship, article written, work experience, and degree.

The foundation's criteria upon which proposals are often judged include the following:

• Creativity: nobody's defined that and ideas of what it is vary from foundation to foundation. But most agree that it includes an innovative idea and an exciting or original approach to the subject.

• How well the proposer has communicated the purpose or goal of the film and the potential significance of the end result.

• The design of the "project" (as films are invariably described by foundations!) and the feasibility of the total plan. It should be well conceived, complete, clearly set down.

• They like to see that an applicant has a specific audience in mind that will derive certain identifiable benefits from the film.

• And finally, they want to know why the applicant is the best person to do this particular job. This is even more difficult than writing one's own résumé. Filmmakers must be really clear on the reasons they wish to and are capable of creating the film in the first place. Otherwise, it is almost impossible to convince someone else of the proposer's fitness.

The question-and-answer method is an alternative approach to proposal writing. This is another way to attack the proposal, peeling away all the extraneous ideas to get down to the essential elements. (This method can also be adapted for film proposal outlines for industrial and educational sponsors.) At a film conference[4] a few years ago a sheet was passed around that offered some startlingly good questions for any proposal writer to consider. Answer each question with a short paragraph, and the proposal is written.

A. _The idea. What do I want to do?_ Write the goal or purpose of the film. _What do I expect to accomplish?_ State the problem to be solved or the issue to be raised. _Whom am I aiming at?_ The audience. _Who am I?_ Credentials of the filmmaker.

B. _The plan. How am I going to go about it?_ The program, the design, the schedule. _Who's going to do this?_ People chosen to make this movie and why: writer, director, consultants, cameraperson, perhaps the composer—whoever is special, integral to the project. _What will they do?_ Describe the jobs they will perform, why the film cannot be made without them (which could justify the excessive budget you have requested).

C. The cost: _How much is it going to cost?_ The budget. _Are you going to have in-kind contributions?_ List them.

D. The evaluation: _Did you do it or how will you know you did what you said you were going to do?_ Also consider on what level the film will be evaluated and whether that level is sufficient evaluation for the film.

Though each foundation handles its flood of proposals differently, it is wise, in all cases, to submit applications well before the deadline. Granting periods usually run once or twice a year. Proposals are numbered consecutively, as they come in, and then turned over to staff, who usually read them in numerical order. They read proposals for days on end. Who wants to be the last one read?

A proposal for a film is like good tapestry: it has an intriguing and cohesive design; the purpose, theme, and audience are as entwined and mutually supportive as the elements of need, significance, and style.

When first conceived, an idea most closely resembles a film: it moves in the filmmaker's head, it's visual. The filmed result of the idea is visual, too. But the pathway between idea and film is strewn with letters, proposals, presentations, treatments, scripts—in short, words. Good filmmakers are good writers.

NOTES

1. Good sources for the writing of feature and documentary or information films are Constance Nash and Virginia Oakey, *The Screenwriter's Handbook*, New York: Harper and Row, 1978; Dwight V. Swain, *Film Scriptwriting*, New York: Hastings House, 1976; *Teleplay, Screenplay Format*, New York: Writers Guild of America, 1978; Lee R. Bobker, *Making Movies: From Script to Screen*, New York: Harcourt, Brace, Jovanovitch, 1973. All filmmakers should own and use the trusty guide to grammar and writing, William Strunk, Jr., and E.B. White, *The Elements of Style*, New York: Macmillan, 1959.

2. Researching previously made films on various subjects can be done by referring to the NICEM Directory, published by the University of Southern California (copies available in most libraries). The directory lists films by subject, gives running length, date, title, maker, and distributor. The Educational Film Library Association (EFLA) in New York City is also a good source on films that have already been produced, as is the Landers Film Review, published in Los Angeles.

3. Forms of distribution are discussed in Chapter 5.

4. First Western Women's Film and Video Conference, Los Angeles, 1975.

CHAPTER 3

Selling and Financing Information* Films

Films are expensive collaborations: a person can spend a year at Harvard or Stanford for what it costs to make one ten-minute 16mm color and sound film. It is hard to convince anyone to spend many thousands of dollars on a film, given all the alternate uses of the money. Moreover, because the effects of the finished film are usually ephemeral and intangible, no one can point to the film and say "See? That was useful!"

All filmmakers are faced with the problem of financing: how does one make one's own films on other people's money? One does not. With rare exceptions, one makes *other* people's films on other people's money. Even grant money is not without limitations, for all foundations have guidelines (within which the film subject must fall), and they inevitably approve or disapprove the idea before handing over the money.

The film subject, the approach to that subject, and the source of money are inextricably linked. Standard Oil of California would be unlikely to fund an experimental, animated film on women's liberation, though it might consider a history of the suffragette movement or a documentary on Susan B. Anthony. Large corporations are more likely to make films that fill a corporate need—such as training films—or those that have some effect on the community or that enhance their images.

But filmmakers have it within their power to increase or decrease the sources of the money available to them since the availability and the variety of sources of that money depend upon the film's concept and approach. A film about the ravages of drought has more potential available sources of funding than a film about the filmmaker's cousin or a 90-minute documentary on social issues, which is the most difficult of all to finance.

*Documentary, industrial, educational, experimental, etc.

This is not to be confused with tailoring a film idea to a specific client's need or to a distribution market. In those cases, a specific need already exists for a known audience from which an outline of the film emerges.

Concept, then, is integrally related to the availability of financing. Below are the traditional sources of film money in the United States (business, government, education, foundations, investors, and so on) and approaches to those sources. Those who make their living making films develop their own creative mixture of approaches to the various sources available.

ABOUT SELLING FILMS

Selling films to other people takes confidence in one's capabilities, an utter belief in the film concept, strong motivation, the ability to convince others that one can deliver, and a good sample film or films.

There are no easy rules to follow that, if used, will convince a client or sponsor to spend thousands of dollars on a medium whose effects are ephemeral and not necessarily practical. But here are some guidelines.

1. Film is basically a means of communicating something to an audience. Therefore, no producer "sells a film" for its own sake. Instead, the approach is to sell a need, or a way to raise funds, to describe a service or education program, to provide a new understanding or perception. The producer sells a film as a way to fulfill these assignments. It just happens to be a film because a film can do the best job.[1]

2. Most sponsors or clients are not interested in a filmmaker's special ways of doing things or in a showy array of bewildering technical expertise. They are interested in the filmmaker's creative perceptions as they apply to a problem or objective. For that reason, filmmakers need to know the prospective sponsor's needs and goals nearly as well as they know film.

3. Don't get hung up on the cost of the budget; break it down and talk about benefits. Crawley Films in Canada produced *Picture Canada* for Eastman Kodak. It has been telecast 2,000 times and programmed live by 20,000 community audiences, world wide, at a cost of less than 1¢ per person reached—less than one cent for a half hour of attention and with the combined impact of picture, motion, color, sound, and drama.

4. Be an expert: filmmakers should be knowledgeable enough to educate sponsors on the many ways film can be used today: it doesn't just come on a reel in a can. Once the answer print in 16mm is made, the film can be transferred to tape and video cassettes; reduced to super 8 for table top display; or blown up to 35mm for theatrical release. Radio spots can be made from the track and TV spots cut from the outs. The film can be sold to cable and pay TV and eventually can be produced in videodisc form. It can be distributed in a variety of ways and promoted. Videotape is now widely used in schools, universities, and business; Kodak has developed raw stocks in 16mm that film excellently by the light of one candle—unheard-of capacity just a few years ago. It's the producer's job to communicate to the sponsor the enormous and constantly increasing expansion in the field. U.S. production of films has tripled in 20 years, and expenditures on equipment may have exceeded $4 billion in 1978.[2] One filmmaker said, "I subscribe to about 25 journals, trade magazines and news magazines. I keep them in a box by my bed and when the stack gets about a foot high, I start going through them, clipping and marking. So much is going on it's the only way I can keep informed."

5. When selling films to business, a filmmaker has to communicate, translate, solve problems; in some ways, the relationship with a client requires the filmmaker to be a sort of "film shrink" or film doctor. The filmmaker is saying, "This is what your problem is and this is how it can be solved." When a producer veers away from standard film treatments into more imaginative film

territory, he or she must bring more energy and more facts to the teacher/doctor role to overcome resistance.

6. It is with inexperienced buyers that most of the problems occur. They cannot conceptualize a film; they are most comfortable with print and haven't the faintest idea what the final filmed result will look like. The producer is put in the role of teacher, but the producer cannot spend all her or his time teaching people because in the end all any producer has is time and ideas; and these cannot be given away for free. This classic dilemma haunts all film producers, and, as one distributor said, somewhere in between, the business of making films is done.

7. Each film has an optimal length. It's almost impossible to sell anyone a 45-minute film: not only is it costly to make, it's too long to receive wide distribution. With rare exceptions, a film of this length indicates the filmmaker has not judiciously perceived the core concept.

8. The people who keep on making films are generally extroverts who enjoy a wide acquaintanceship. They are genuinely interested in all sorts of people, places, problems, spheres of thought, action, and behavior. They are not snobs. Filmmakers who shun meeting a variety of new people will find themselves limited—both in film content, funding sources, and lines of communication. This is perfectly all right, of course, as long as the filmmaker has independent income to support the costs and knows the ultimate result in terms of what sorts of films he or she may make.

What else does it take to sell (or fund) a film? Persistence. One letter, one call, one appointment, one grant application is only a beginning.

A Note on Speculative Treatments

The core of the issue is that any speculative treatment for bidding purposes cannot be very well thought out for any specific film. This is especially true if a producer speculates several times a year without having the appropriate research materials available. It has been called immoral, unethical, and unreasonable, and the practice is not in the best interests of anyone. If a filmmaker takes a speculative treatment to a corporation or organization, the latter is under no obligation to pay the filmmaker for the treatment—unless the film program is purchased. If, however, a corporation or organization requires a specific treatment and requests one, that organization does have an obligation to pay for the filmmaker's work. The charge can be anywhere between $500 and $2,500. Almost no corporation buys speculative film ideas initiated by the filmmaker. In order to turn that speculative treatment into a contract, the filmmaker really has to know the corporation as well as it itself does, and that's impossible.

No producer should mind talking over a client's needs or problems and how film might help solve them. "It is the specific act of being asked to provide a written treatment which, in a sense, is the guts of a picture—the creative genesis, the work on which the picture will rise or fall, that I object to giving away."[3] Consultation, on the other hand, is to the producer's advantage.

TRADITIONAL SOURCES OF FINANCING INFORMATION FILMS

Business and Industry

Industry is the largest single buyer and user of films and videotapes in the United States. Film subjects for these clients are not just coal or pipes or corporate public relations, but run a broad gamut from public service programs and training films to documentaries and educational series.

Nowhere is the division between art and business more apparent than in this sector of the filmmaking world. Many producers and clients really feel that art has no place in industrial films; they want just the facts. A minority feel that art, or creative imagination, has a very real place in these films. The lack of communication between the two groups stems from a basic assumption: if industrial films are "creative," they will miss the informational mark set for them—they will fail to do their job. But films for business have a multiplicity of jobs to do, and the one thing they must *not* do is bore the audience. The best business films are as enjoyable, imaginative, dramatic, and informative in their own way as the most searing documentaries or the fluffiest musicals are in their way.

Films for business generally fail to do a good job because of the way they are sold. As one producer notes, they are "poorly conceived, poorly used, poorly executed." Producers are not educating clients, and they themselves often fail to see the point of innovative or dramatic film techniques in industrial films. Wall-to-wall narration is still used, along with canned music, old-fashioned lighting, and unexciting editing.

One reason for this is that there seems to be an unspoken agreement between filmmaker and sponsor that business films should be "different" from entertainment films, should be conservative, logical—even dull—made to a formula that disappeared in every other type of film long ago. Typical business films, showing only what is good in the business, lack reality and hence impact.

A lack of boldness on the part of the buyer is another reason for the poor state of the art: "Most information films are made by committee. The corporate advertising department gets in the act, the vice president of public relations has a lot to say, everyone in middle management fights for involvement in the 'company plum', the legal people always want to review it, and usually the president not only wants to be asked for a cameo, he bothers to request 'meaningful input' from every department. State of the art as far as techniques, innovation, daring visual expressions is all thwarted by this procedure," said a film producer.

It *is* true that corporate public relations departments often prevent an original film concept from reaching a dynamic or creative conclusion. Any producer can recall an experience in which fear of what is different or expressive has dominated a corporate film conference. But the same hesitations occur with clients in nonprofit associations or federal or state government: It is the instinct to produce something safe; the result as one producer called it is a "celluloid manual."

"If I could wave my magic wand and change anything in our business," says the vice president of one large film-producing corporation, "I would ask that all communicators in industry, governments, associations and institutions be blasted out of their print-oriented stance.

"I would ask that they pause in their eternal war of paper to realize that a third of all North Americans are functionally illiterate, that business people are getting more to read than ever before and reading less, that it is television and film that now guides our purchases, our votes, our perceptions, and our convictions."

Arising not only from a fear of risk, this attitude also stems from a lack of trust in the producer, lack of basic film knowledge on the part of the client, and lack of respect for the capabilities of film.

Clients distrust producers who describe the proposed film as having big-name talent or an original music score—promises that are rarely fulfilled. Promises are also often made by producers that the film will turn the world around or bring untold profits to the corporate purchaser. Films do not supply a quick return on money, and it is often hard to see any return at all. Buyers are used to seeing quick returns on their money. Moreover, films do not readily fit into overall marketing plans, and many do not perform well for clients because the producer did not back up the proposal with concrete reasons for making a film along with solid distribution plans.

Corporations that make successful films look on them as an investment, source of information, their community responsibility, good public relations, or a combination of these. The major criteria in selecting a producer and a film approach should be creativity, quality, and audience impact.

"I have rarely met a client who knew exactly what he wanted—outside of the general film purpose—who wasn't receptive to whatever idea that could seriously achieve that goal, no matter how 'wild' that idea was. I think that producers are often lazy, or too tired, or ignorant. This kind of creative inertia doesn't do the industry any good, nor does it encourage bright people to get into it," said a producer.

Filmmakers who want to make films for business but find themselves blocked in that effort often do not understand what it is they are really selling and then, even more tragically, how to sell it. Says one distributor, "Most producers approach clients with, 'Here's what I did for so and so, and here's what I can do for you.' They rely on the client to decide when a film is needed, rather than doing their homework, analyzing the needs and selling solutions. Most do not produce communications programs—they produce communications experiences." This major distributor, who works with producers every day, says that the buyer of the film must completely understand how the goals and objectives are going to be met by the film. The way for a producer to accomplish that is to do the necessary preparation before proposing the film program. "There's no question but that I've sold more productions as a distributor than I ever did as a producer. Because as a distributor I sell the results. Producers do not do that," said a large distributor.

What should producers do? First, identify the problem. Second, analyze the audience. Third, analyze the approaches that will present the problem effectively to the audience. Fourth, present the audiovisual concept as a complete package with the concept, the budget, the objective, the audience, and the distributor. The producer, then, is not selling an idea so much as a program, built on a logical progression of these steps, which justify the use of the medium.

Identifying the problem: it is really up to producers to determine what the needs are and what the industry's response should be. How does one discover a need? First of all, to make films for business, one must read the business section of newspapers, and the *Wall Street Journal* and *Fortune* Magazine. In some instances, discovering a need is as simple as opening up a newspaper or magazine to see that an organization has a communication problem. The idea, the need, and the source of the funding may all be contained in a single article. While vacationing in a neighboring state, I once picked up a local paper to find that the Department of Rehabilitation had just been awarded a substantial federal grant to improve relations and communications with the community it served. After doing some research, I paid a call on the state director and proposed a film and a series of spots to accomplish that objective. I got the contract.

Analyzing which films are actually needed—films that will increase understanding or knowledge—is the filmmaker's key to survival. For business, those areas might be conservation of energy and resources, economics, political and government education, or, in fact, almost any other subject. If one determines that a need exists, it is still essential to do a careful analysis of the company's problem and set out the objective of the film or videotape program that will fill the need and then a program design that will achieve it. Film sponsors from business, government, and education hire producers who have a knowledge of their problems and offer communications solutions.

One industrial producer reported that shortly after incorporating, he got his first film in competition with three other producers. He asked his new client on what basis he had been selected: "You were the only one of the four who discussed a business problem that I had, not the making of a motion picture. You talked of motivation, recognized that we have a problem of quality control..." This producer also says that if a pamphlet would have done a better job for that client, he would have suggested that route.

Corporations tend to select producers on whether or not the client's objectives are realized. Here again is a place where talent is not enough; the filmmaker must exhibit a genuine interest in the client's needs.

Research and analysis extend to people within the

corporation, too. Talking to the wrong organization, or the wrong person within the right organization, will only waste time. About four years ago, I optioned a nonfiction book on the subject of dealing with and understanding money, believing that a bank could be found to sponsor a film based on that book. I took it to a banking organization, with an introduction to the wrong person: he had no control over the audiovisual budget and no authority to approve the concept's sponsorship, but he felt good talking to a film producer and pretending that he did. "We're going to do it," he said. What else is he going to say after talking to me all that time? We are *not* going to do it? So, for about two months, I walked down a dead-end street. Better research on the corporation and the people within it would have saved a great deal of time and money.

Distribution plans are of crucial importance to this source of money. Whenever possible, producers should work with distributors on a film, since the distributor is the logical extension of the producer. This is especially true of industrial films.

Leaving film production for teaching, one distinguished producer said that retrospectively, he began to form questions which, ironically, would have made him a more successful filmmaker. The filmmaker's concern has traditionally been *how* to make films; that is different from being conscious of how films are made and how they affect the audience. Answering the latter questions can assist filmmakers to sell films.

For example, "When we all start out to make films," he said, "we only know the model of the films to which we have been exposed. So what we are engaged in is an imitation of what has already been made. As craftspeople, we are embellishing, introducing modifications, nuances, or embroidery in existing forms of practice. If we are unconscious, all we know is what *is*; we don't know *how* meaning is produced by the cultural and cinematic codes. Every one of the craft practices, from writing to film editing, involves the manipulation of cultural, cinematic, and filmic codes. If we are *not* conscious that we are dealing with a code system, and don't know what the codes are, then we simply repeat them automatically. It's only by being conscious of the codes, and trying to extend them without losing the audience that one can be aware of what one is doing. In reality we're operating in a closed system, and the codes are part of the expectations of the audience. The audience responds well to a film when that film meets those expectations; nothing unique happens except that the audience is held in thrall and the circle is closed. Not recognizing the nature of film can limit a filmmaker's productivity."

Unaware of the film codes, corporations are rightly concerned with content. They are also looking for the attention-getting devices in film that will continue to excite, surprise, or focus the audience on the film's content. He continued, "Our company succeeded precisely because we manipulated the codes better than many other filmmakers. Our films looked different—which gave us the advantage— but they weren't so outrageous that the audience was left behind or disoriented."

This producer suggests that filmmakers struggle to understand why film is such a powerful medium, and what the experience and relationship are between screen and audience. He has thrown out a tantalizing intellectual puzzle, and, as well, an economic lifeline to filmmakers. It sounds theoretical, but it is a practical point of view for anyone who wants to become a filmmaker. "When I ran my film corporations," he says, "I was always looking for filmmakers who practiced the craft in a conscious way, who intuitively realized the limitations and tried to extend them. That is what made our films look different and accounted for so much of our success. I would urge new filmmakers not just to imitate or to be craftspeople doing what everyone else is doing—but to extend themselves and their consciousness of their medium."

One of the major problems of selling films is the cost of the effort: "We have a problem educating our clients as to the cost of making motion pictures," says a producer with a very large communications firm. "We should educate clients to appreciate a responsible producer's role in recommending film solutions to their problems in a fair manner. Just because some film companies are rip-offs doesn't absolve clients from their responsibilities, which is to pay enough for the film to be made correctly and to pay on time. Our receivable accounts are terrible. Some of the largest corporations in the world are delinquent by as much as five and six months...on completed and approved work! They could put a small producer, with limited financial strength, out of business within a few months." When proposing films, producers should speak in terms not of "$50,000 to make this film" but in cost per thousand or cost over the ten-year life of the film—which is realistic.[4]

"I always sold above my experience," said one producer. "The films I would describe to clients in the selling process were always over my head. I would tell them all the incredible things I was going to do for them, then go out and dedicate my life to delivering all that I had promised. Apparently, I came close enough to retain credibility client to client."

Each producer sells films in a different way, and each must find his or her own way of doing it, taking what is useful from other people's experiences, discarding what is not. Some people sell on the basis of past films, letting "the films speak for themselves." But for most, the sample reel is not really that useful. One industrial producer says it is a personal business. "I have sold more films by having people look at me and believe in me than by showing them something nice I have done for someone else."

Not everyone can or even wants to sell films to business. "The business of American film business is business—it just happens to be the production of films" said a former producer of information films. "I stopped producing because the quality of life that had any meaning for me stopped in relation to making films within that system. We produced films for The World Bank, the *Wall Street Journal*, and other major corporations. Our idealized notion was that we could become so good that people would come with their money and say, 'Do what you want. We have confidence in you—you know better what we need than we do.' We had as much freedom as one could ever expect. Finally we faced the fact that we were actually dealing with social, political and economic issues that conflicted with the interests of the people who were supplying the money. That conflict developed into a basic antagonism—which I can understand now but did not then. We finally realized that in this system when you are spending someone else's money, eventually the power resides with them."

Some filmmakers are not good at making business films, while others understand what these films require. They can inspire confidence in the management of large numbers of people and large amounts of money and make clients understand the creative endeavor. However one views it—as a lifetime profession or a stepping-stone to other kinds of films or a learning process—the selling and making of films for business takes analytical ability and a view of film as a communication process, from concept to ultimate distribution.

Education

Just as business and industry *make* more films than other institutions in this country, so schools, colleges, universities, and libraries *use* more 16mm films than other markets. But since schools and colleges do not generally finance films, a variety of other funding sources, such as business, associations, distributors, and the government produce films for this market.

Educational films cover an extremely broad range of topics and uses: health, safety, social studies, humanities and arts, to name only a few. It is this market to which young filmmakers turn for distribution once they have completed a student or independent film. And it is this market as it is currently constituted that often determines the approach and content of short films in the United States—whether "educational" in nature or "documentary." Aside from sponsored distribution (see Chapter 5), the educational film market is the only user of short information films that is supplied by an organized system of distribution.

Test film ideas on educational distributors before making the film. Distributors know which films are currently needed, and they will suggest specific uses, approaches, lengths, subjects. For example, a few years ago, before the issue became one of concern, a distributor, for whom I had made several films, indicated he needed a 15-minute film on child abuse. He also had a sound suggestion as to whom to contact for sponsorship: the local sheriff's department. Filmmakers can also go to the local and state educational audiovisual departments to research what sort of films those departments wish they had.

Occasionally, educational distributors will advance a low-budget amount to a filmmaker on the basis of a script. But more and more distributors are setting up their own modest production arms—to make films they know they can market widely.

The films in this area that bring the greatest financial and professional rewards to the filmmaker and have the longest lives, are those that can be used equally well for a variety of classes. *Occurrence At Owl Creek Bridge* (1962) is a famous example. Adapted from a short story by Ambrose Bierce, produced by Robert Enrico, it is still shown widely in social studies, literature, history, creative writing, and film-making courses and theatrically to film societies. Classic films such as this one cross educational curricula with ease.

For the educational market, then, the basic concept needs to be as broad as possible. If the subject is architecture, take the time to find out which aspects of the field are taught widely and what sort of films are currently unavailable. Consider enlarging the original concept: how could the film be made so it would also apply to sociology or history, music or psychology? To some extent, films made for specialized audiences, such as grade school children, are economically feasible, but the film that appeals to a large audience still has the best chance of making back its production costs and earning a small profit for the filmmaker. Though films made for educational use must frequently suffer from low budgets —unlike films made for business—this market allows film-makers a traditional training ground to test and refine their techniques while making films on practically any subject.

Two for the Price of One

It is often possible, while making a film for one purpose, to create a second film at one-tenth cost, suitable for educational use, from a rearrangement of the outs or a little additional shooting during the main production. I made a 15-minute film on an artist, describing in a rather abstract, rapidly cut fashion the artist's particular creative approach, his environment, and the art he produced. As in any film, there were a lot of outs after shooting and taping. The result, though pleasing and useful to the sponsor, was practically undistributable. The audience for films on art and artists is limited. While there are hundreds of art departments in the country, unlike athletic programs, most suffer from budget crunches. Moreover, students and/or teachers often appear to be more interested in films that show a "how-to" process— not one artist's creative experience. From the outs of the first film, I could have created a second, more practical film for a broader audience.

The professional benefits and personal satisfactions of making films for the educational market spring from the filmmaker's chance to initiate original film ideas that can be distributed. Films that truly contribute to the understanding of an issue, or have broad curricula application, are the real winners in this field.

Government—Federal, State, Local

The government as a film sponsor can bring on a producer's longest nightmare.

Since each government agency controls a separate audio-visual budget, no one knows how many films the government as a whole sponsors or produces per year because no master lists exist. Estimates of the money spent vary. For 1977, according to congressional testimony, one of the guesses was $500 million for about 2,300–3,000 films and tapes. By no means does all this money pour forth to independent film producers. Much of it is spent on in-house productions— making the government a direct competitor to filmmakers. The government also spends about $2 billion annually to buy audiovisual equipment, and another $55 million to upgrade audiovisual machinery. Agencies such as the National Institutes of Health and the departments of Health, Education and Welfare, the Treasury, Defense, and the Interior sponsor films and videotapes for a dazzling array of uses. Each agency, moreover, has used its own forms, bid procedures, and criteria for selecting producers. Budgets run from a few thousand to hundreds of thousands, and no one seems to know exactly what sort of distribution government-made films receive or if, in fact, anyone sees most of the films produced.

The government has made films since 1908, including such classics as *The River*, by Pare Lorenz, made in 1937 for the Farm Security Administration, and, more recently, the U.S. Information Agency's *John F. Kennedy: Years of Lightning, Days of Drums*.[5] Criticism of federal audiovisual practices was first stated publicly by Barry Goldwater, Jr., a California congressman, who issued a report in 1972 on the high rate of waste in the government's film operations. A chorus of complaints ensued, culminating in hearings at which the audiovisual practices were called "monstrous, wasteful, duplicative and growing."[6]

The House Government Operations Subcommittee held hearings in the fall of 1978 in an effort to unravel the government's audiovisual procurement, production, and distribution procedures. Here are some of the problems that have confronted producers when dealing with government agencies:

1. The bidding procedures are exceedingly complex and defy comprehension.

2. The sheer volume of paperwork required for a single film is ridiculous and wasteful.

3. Some invitations to bid are made after a producer has already been secretly selected; the subsequent bids are requested only to satisfy regulations. Some bids are put up on such short notice for preparation that it is evident a successful "bidder" has already been chosen. This is called a "wired" film.

4. To prepare a bid, producers are often asked to perform expensive research that may require travel and the purchase of reference materials; since large numbers of producers bid, this effort represents hundreds of thousands of wasted hours and dollars to the film production as a whole. As one producer said, "Being solicited speculatively for a creative concept and bid is, I believe, immoral, unethical, illegal...Unfortunately, even civilian procurement is beginning to be done this way."

5. Many government agencies ask for elaborate treatments as part of a bid—treatments that require professional writers hired at considerable expense, but these filmmakers are not usually recompensed for the treatments. Accusations have been made by some producers that this free brain-picking has resulted in ideas being "borrowed" for use in the film up for bid, or in subsequent films by the same agency.

6. Producers in the private industry sector are asked to bid on production work in direct competition with bidders in publicly supported institutions.[7]

Speculative proposals often require producers to create bids that may include a general technical approach, a lengthy treatment, a shooting outline, a proposed production schedule, a background of personnel and how each will relate to the film under consideration, and an elaborate cost breakdown. All of this material was required, and all of it was on speculation. [The new federal audiovisual procurement guidelines indicate that producers should be paid for the treatments they prepare.]

A producer who has been making films since the 1930s told this story about his frequent work for the U.S. Navy:

"The Navy people knew that certain producers were better than others for certain jobs. Therefore, some producers who had proved themselves to the Navy were put on a special list for bids. There were six or seven of us in this one area. By law, three bids were required—so the Navy sent bids to the one on the list who they wanted and to two others (also on the list). When I'd get a request for a bid, I'd call the Navy to ask if I needed to meet with them and survey locations. If the Navy said, 'Don't bother,' I knew the bid was not for me, so I merely guessed very high. If I got a warning call that I had 'overlooked' some expensive elements, I would submit a new, higher bid. One other bidder would do the same so the low bidder (the one the Navy wanted) got the job. The Navy was hard boiled but very fair. They did not want a producer to lose money. They tried to avoid low bidders who bid just to get a job."

Most producers whose primary client is the government would like to see (1) the government cease its in-house production business (except for national security subjects); (2) the labs cease giving better price breaks to the government agencies than they do to independent producers; and (3) the government get out of the distribution business.

It is estimated that only a third of government television, film, and tape work is contracted out to independent producers. Clearly, the government competes with independent producers, and its advantage is even greater because of the low prices labs give it on high volume. (The standard contract between a lab and the government states that the lab is prevented from giving any independent producer a lower price.) Therefore, though the government requests a producer's bid on heads and tails and prints, no bid in reality can match the price the government is assured from the labs.

One producer's representative who has served as a liaison between producers and post production services for fifteen years said: "I can understand virtually all classified film work conducted by the government being handled by their own facilities and I think the commercial labs would agree with me that they would like nothing better than to get out from under security-type work. Most of the large labs today will not accept government classified work. The net return is simply too small to put up with the government gobbledegook that accompanies handling these films."

In April 1978, a study of federal audiovisual activities, conducted by Robert Lissit for the Office of Telecommunications Policy, surveyed all government filmmaking procedures (which he characterized as "an audiovisual monster") and made recommendations for change.

The overall goals listed in the Lissit report are to make government more efficient and stop the waste in government filmmaking. "What is needed," he reports, "is to make certain that all government audiovisual production is subjected to rigorous justification procedures, to assure that the recommended format is appropriate for the material, to make certain that a specific audience is targeted, to carefully monitor costs, to assure adequate distribution, and to assure the taxpayer that all government audiovisual communication is effective."[8]

A uniform government procurement system has been adopted by the government, under which all "private-sector" audiovisual contracts will be issued, evaluated, and administered by the Office of Federal Procurement Policy's (OFPP) Directorate for Audiovisual Activities. This office will also supply a central source of information on government motion pictures. The DAVA office has compiled a Qualified Film Producer's List (QFPL), which is used by all agencies seeking proposals from independent producers. No producer may be considered for a government film if he or she is _not_ on the government QFPL roster.

To be eligible for the QFPL, all a filmmaker need do is submit a film to the Inter-Agency Audiovisual Review Board (IARB), which is composed of members of the Federal Audiovisual Committee (FAC, an interagency committee chaired by the office of Federal Procurement Policy). FAC includes representatives from over 20 government agencies.

Criteria for evaluating each film is as follows:

1. Achievement of Purpose(s):
Did the film accomplish its stated purpose(s)?

Was it appropriate for its intended audience?
Was the manner of presentation appropriate?
What were the reviewers' impressions of the film?

0-20 points

2. Creativity:
Did the film provide a fresh or innovative way of conveying the message?

0-25 points

3. Continuity:
Did the subject develop in a logical or understandable manner?

0-15 points

4. Technical Quality:
Did the following qualities in the film exhibit technical competence?
Direction
Writing
Photography
Editing
Artwork/Animation
Narration
Music and Sound
Special Effects

0-40 points

Producers whose films receive an average composite score of 70 points or more and who enter into a contract with the Executive Agent of IARB will be placed on the Qualified Producer's List. Producers whose first submitted film fails to win 70 points may submit until they either get 70 points or run out of films.*

In future, when an agency needs to have a film produced, the procuring officer will contact the executive agent of IARB. For short, less expensive films, the executive agent

---

*Excerpted from a memorandum from the Office of Management and Budget, Office of Federal Procurement Policy, 9/29/78.

will provide the agency with the names of the five firms at the top of the rotating list. The agency procurement officer may, in addition, choose two more producers at random from the list. For films over $100,000, ten names on the list will be supplied the procurement officer who may choose an additional four. No more than fourteen producers will be competing for any bid. After being chosen, all seven or fourteen firms' names will be placed at the bottom of the list.

Having centralized the bidding procedure and created a test for producer competency, the government has moved to correct some of the more flagrantly wasteful practices of the past. But it is still in the production and distribution business and will probably remain in it, though production units operating at less than 30 percent capacity have been ordered to shut down.[9]

It should be noted that there *are* ways to work comfortably with the government—especially when starting out in the film game—and that's at the local or state level. State agencies need, use, and sponsor films and should not be overlooked. Since local and state agencies are service oriented, the *raison d'être* of the film should be made absolutely clear and concrete. February is the best time to begin proposing film ideas: agency budgets come up for annual review in April and May. The fiscal year starts in July. Therefore, what is not spent in June must be returned, and the next fiscal budget may be cut down by the surplus amount. Filmmakers should be aware that agencies have been known to contract for films at the last minute, seeing a surplus in the present fiscal year's budget and wishing to spend it so that they get the same amount next year. More appropriately, the cost of the proposed film may be built into the following year's budget to be produced on an orderly basis. This is best accomplished in the spring when the next fiscal budget application is being prepared.

One problem making films for state agencies is that the filmmaker may be persuaded to accept a committee as the "technical assistant." It is as true in short films as in features that one person should be responsible, over all, for the direction a picture takes. It is collaborative, but it is not a committee function.

Few good films come out of committee arrangements. Ideally, a filmmaker should work with one sympathetic, knowledgeable person within the agency who represents the agency's point of view and has the authority to approve or disapprove the various stages of production.

Story boards are a terrific asset with any client but are especially helpful with government agencies. Since they have little or no training in films and are far more print than visually oriented, story boards can vitalize a film concept for them. Many filmmakers feel they are essential to show how planned animated sections of the film will look, as special effects.

The budgets for films at the state level are generally lower than at the federal level, but not as low as in the educational field. The patient producer can put together a film, partly funded by a local or state agency and the remainder by industry for distribution by an educational distributor primarily for, say, high schools. It's a collaborative business.

Foundations, Public and Private[10]

There are two ways to apply for foundation money in America: the first is to apply directly, as an individual; the second is to apply indirectly through a nonprofit organization or institution, using it as an umbrella.

Applying as an Individual

A filmmaker wishes to make a film on sculpture. He or she writes a letter of inquiry (Chapter 2) to private foundations, after doing the necessary research, and asks the State Arts Commission, or the National Endowment for the Arts for applications and quidelines. If a private or state or federal foundation sees merit in the idea, the filmmaker then writes a preliminary proposal, and a budget for submission. Here personal contact within the foundation is useful—for feedback on the proposal's development, distribution plans, budget or any other aspect. A final proposal is written and then a period of usually several months goes by before grants are announced.

Financing films from grant monies is a slow, tortuous route through an often bleak landscape. It was recently estimated that the average annual income to independent filmmakers from grants may only amount to less than a thousand dollars. Compared to the cost of most other creative endeavors, films are extremely expensive, making the amount of money allocated by public and private foundations seem even smaller. It is conceivable that a foundation grant of $6,000 can support a painter for a year (not in riches but above the poverty line) during which time he/she may turn out a completed work; but the same grant would not technically produce a fifteen-minute film and would go no distance at all toward supporting the filmmaker.

Not only is the money inadequate, the filmmaker often waits a long time for the funds only to see them arrive heavy with excessive paperwork. Most foundations do not make grants for films; of those that do, most do not grant to individuals—only to organizations. Nonetheless, there are individuals whose films were partially made on granted funds (Kopple and Cox and Weill, to name just three of the better known), but the agonizing delays and the obstacles, only briefly alleviated by small grants, point up the unhappy absence of appropriate funding for all kinds of films in this country. As one well-known experimental filmmaker said: "There is virtually *no* film financing in the United States for independent creative filmmakers. A little bit from AFI; occasionally, in times past, from Guggenheim—but *never* for unknown, upcoming artists in film. Funds should be given to establish apprenticeships, but it's an all or nothing, success-oriented system, which seemingly cannot contribute seriously to the *development* of people working in the most impressive medium of communication the world has ever known."

However, once armed with an individual grant, the

filmmaker may progress with a rare independence, exploring his or her personal vision or film assignment in comparative freedom.

Applying Through an Organization

Here the filmmaker sees the need for a film that coincides with the stated objectives of a nonprofit agency, group, school, or organization. Armed with an outline, a budget and a distribution plan, the filmmaker takes his ideas to that organization, which hopefully has a known track record of service and reliability. The organization—not the filmmaker —applies for the grant money. If the grant is approved, the organization takes a percentage for administrative costs and channels the bulk of the funds back to the filmmaker.

With grant funds received under the umbrella of a nonprofit organization, one has less freedom, and the working relationship more closely resembles that of producer-client (the relationship is one of give and take to reach a mutually desired goal.) But nonprofit institutions offer filmmakers tangible advantages: they endorse the filmmaker's concept and provide an aegis for the proposal's progress to foundations. Most nonprofit institutions such as museums, health institutions, or environmental organizations, have excellent reputations and recognized goals, which redound to the filmmaker's credit and ease the film's introduction to foundations.

In many cases, nonprofit organizations may not have recognized the need for a film until the filmmaker points it out. Once the approach and objective are agreed upon, the organization may assign a staff member who, with assistance from the filmmaker, writes a proposal, which goes out under the organization's name, guided to logical funding sources known to it. Or the organization may allow the filmmaker to use its official letterhead and the credibility of its reputation but will not always assist in either the writing of the proposal or the search for the funding. In either case, the filmmaker is usually often better off—even with institutional restrictions—than going it alone.

Advice on Foundation Film Proposals

The quality of the initial film concept and its suitability to the specific foundation cannot be overemphasized. Foundations are inundated with requests for film grants that do not fit their specific guidelines. Always check the foundation research sources (listed on page 30) before writing a proposal.

The way the filmmaker presents himself or herself on paper is nearly as important as the quality of the film idea. The filmmaker should appear competent and committed. Honesty and sincerity have a way of shining through. Foundation people read applications all the time—the phony, ill conceived, or condescending are quickly spotted.

A film proposal of any kind must include a distribution plan; anyone who funds a film has every right to know how the filmmaker intends to reach the audience. The plan presented may be only letters of interest from distributors or libraries or schools, but, no matter how sketchy, it must indicate the filmmaker has given careful thought to this aspect of the film. In many cases, if the film shows a profit, the filmmaker is expected to repay the grant to the foundation from that profit, so that the funds can be recycled to other filmmakers.

If one foundation rejects your proposal, ask it to suggest other foundations (and the names of people to contact) that might consider the film concept.

Always try to meet and talk with the people who make the decisions at the foundation to which you are applying. In large organizations this is all but impossible but well worth the effort in smaller ones.

More and more filmmakers are setting up their own nonprofit, tax-exempt organizations (with a board of directors) in order to find grant money. This procedure, if successfully accomplished, obviates the necessity of going through other nonprofit organizations.

For any proposal, the budget represents the filmmaker's expertise in the field.[11] Budgets should receive rigorous attention; underestimating costs can be as harmful as overestimating. (1) A budget is measured in feet or hours or days or miles. There is only one grey area—"acts of God" (unforeseen delays or disasters)—that often comes under a budget heading of "contingency," a category that no foundation will allow. Therefore, it is even more important that the numbers be accurate. (2) Most foundations will not allow switching from one line item to another, so if the filmmaker has budgeted too much money under research and too little under lab costs, the monies cannot be moved around to accommodate actual expenses. (3) Filmmakers often omit sales tax; omission can create a staggering deficit of at least 6 percent on some costs in some states for the hapless filmmaker. Be sure to put it in. (4) Foundations are not in the business of purchasing equipment for the filmmaker; budgets should reflect rental costs for the gear. (5) Travel costs should be held to a minimum and must be absolutely necessary to the success of the production. Accommodations and meals on location are usually assigned a per-diem cost ranging from $40 to $75 per person.

In-kind contributions: The cost of loans or gifts in equipment or space made to the project may be subtracted from the total budget. Such contributions reflect that people other than the filmmaker are interested enough to make a dollar investment.

Matching funds: many foundations stipulate they will give, say, $5,000 *if* the filmmaker can match the $5,000 with an equal sum from another organization or individual.

Direct costs: production expenses such as film processing or salaries.

Indirect costs: money the nonprofit organization receives for supervising the "project," usually indicated by a percentage of the total budget—an amount that is subtracted from the grant's total. Therefore, if a grant of $50,000 is awarded, the sponsoring organization may take 15 percent of that off the top. The percentages range all the way from 10 percent to 50 percent.

Television

This section would not be complete without a mention of financing information and documentary films through television.* Watch television for a week and count the number of documentary productions on the air: this avenue inevitably means applying for grant money from the Corporation for Public Broadcasting, or the Public Broadcasting Service, since the networks (ABC, CBS, and NBC) finance their own documentaries, and only occasionally purchase already finished work from independent filmmakers.

The Independent Documentary Fund of the Television Lab at WNET in New York City funds independent films. There is no restriction on subject or format. The Corporation for Public Broadcasting (CPB) offers the Revolving Documentary Fund along the same lines. [For notes on both these funds see the foundation list in the Appendix.[12]]

Large PBS stations in Boston, New York, Minneapolis, Los Angeles and San Francisco always look at ideas for either series or single films that come from independent filmmakers. Such concepts must have national appeal in order to be awarded development money for scripting. When the script is approved, a production plan with a director and actors is put together by the station. With this package, the station sets out to find the money to produce: CPB will only put up one-third to one-half, which means that PBS stations must go to other foundations, a government agency or a corporation for the rest of the production budget. There simply is no single source of money for PBS programming in America.

If a filmmaker is convinced he or she has a viable commercial documentary concept that belongs on one of the networks, the best way to get someone to listen to it is to take the concept (in outline form) to strong, well known television producers; they have access to the networks and unknown filmmakers do not. The filmmaker's objective would be to

_____
*See Chapter 7 for fiction film financing through television.

seek development money from the producer in order to write the script.

In the case of an information film that has already been completed, the filmmaker deals with television as a distributor/exhibitor, not as a means of financing it.

Multiple Sponsors

This is a method of funding whereby two or more entities combine their financial resources to produce a single film.

The advantage: companies or organizations with limited funds can suddenly afford a film because the producer has, in effect, augmented the corporations' limited resources by matching them from other corporations. It is the rare nonprofit organization or small corporation that can finance a $70,000 film by itself. But the film swings within reach if seven join together at $10,000 each. Since the producer couldn't begin to make a $70,000 film for $10,000, multiple sponsorship opens up groups of clients and avenues of film financing that otherwise would be unavailable: the producer now has the opportunity to sell seven organizations on the virtue of communicating by film.

The producer may also gain credibility with the sponsors as filmmaker-cum-fundraiser—not unlike the Hollywood packager, for whom Americans have a certain guarded respect. Bringing together seven people who have never met before to create a cooperative film not only gives the producer prestige, but in some cases greater control over the outcome. The credibility of the film content also improves: if the film is about home computers, and several corporations jointly sponsor the film, the results will give a more comprehensive view of models and their capacities than a single film about a single computer, which could resemble an advertisement instead of an informative film.

As one producer said, "Let's take the amateur dancing field as an example. Danskin is just about the only large company supplying children who take dancing lessons. But there are hundreds of smaller firms turning out costumes, ballet shoes, and other supplies. If we proposed a film to

Danskin, we'd have a less than 50-50 chance of closing it. But instead of dropping the idea we would look into the corporate worth of the smaller industry suppliers (who might share the budget's cost). If we found them to be generally insubstantial, we would close the file. But if we found fifty more substantial firms involved, we would look more carefully to see if there were several noncompetitive areas of interest that could constitute a sponsorship team. Without such a combination, we could not succeed in developing several sponsors for one film."[13]

The concept of multiple sponsorship does not have to be confined to commercial corporations but can apply to all sorts of associations. The proliferation of women's studies or organization—with exceedingly limited funds but similar goals—could make them likely candidates for this kind of shared funding in order to communicate a shared objective.

In most cases, though the benefits outweigh the problems, multiple sponsorship can plainly increase problems associated with any collaboration. Some producers feel that multiple sponsored films turn out poorly no matter what the producer does. The producer is working with a committee. In the beginning, each sponsor may wait "until the others sign" rather than take the first plunge. Unsolvable disagreement over the script may develop—or even, as one producer has experienced, over the order in which the sponsors' names are listed in the credits. Approval at stages along the way from script through answer print may take an inordinately long time. Having put in an equal amount of money, each sponsor wishes to receive an equal amount of time in the film. One sponsor can create very real problems if he or she feels slighted, and the producer may feel called upon to be more of a psychiatrist than filmmaker. However, if one sponsor really wants to cause trouble, for whatever reason—and this can happen to any filmmaker on any film—then the best response is to confront the problem, and work it out; ignoring it will usually make it worse.

For many producers the only good rule is simply to work with people one feels good about and with whom one can communicate easily. The working relationship between sponsor and filmmaker is very close, but its boundaries are fluid. Both parties need to pick their way carefully, guided by a mutual respect for the other's expertise. Producers who have made a number of multi-sponsored films can recall one trying experience after another. Not everyone can work this way, for multiple sponsorship requires diplomacy, patience, and a talent for finding equitable solutions. The collaboration works best when a producer has found a creative match of non-competing sponsors and a specific film concept that will fill a real need.

Associations, Organizations, Institutions

Generally, associations are devoted to the communication values of print, preferring brochures or slide programs to films—an attitude that may stem from their genuine horror at the cost of films and their notorious shortage of funds. As a group, they are unlikely sponsors except as umbrellas for foundation grants or as spokes in a multiple-sponsor wheel.

Another avenue for producers of films with associations is to find a wealthy individual who wants to contribute but also wants a tax break. That individual can donate the funds to a tax-deductible nonprofit association, earmarking the sum for the film budget. A few associations regularly produce films—for example, United Way and the United Jewish Appeal, which have made award-winning films. Filmmakers would be well advised to check an organization or association's film track record and the operating budget before spending a lot of energy on speculative proposals for this group.

Selling Shares, Incorporating, and Co-ops

A filmmaker can create a private corporation either alone or with associates and sell off 49 percent of the shares to capitalize the first film or supply the overhead expenses to sustain the filmmaker over the first difficult period. The filmmaker should, of course, retain 51 percent to assure the controlling interest in the corporation.

Incorporating is neither difficult nor expensive though

some of the federal tax paperwork can be boring and time consuming. Choosing this route has some definite tax advantages, such as liability protection and the deduction of business-related expenses. It also gives the filmmaker a certain professional status. But a filmmaker who incorporates and then risks that capital on the production of a single film had better select the film subject and approach very carefully. The film should lend prestige to the producer and be made for a broad but definable audience so that it stands a good chance of being distributed.

It is impetuous to incorporate without capital of any kind.[14] The film business is one of steep and widely spaced crests and troughs. If one has no capital, one has nothing to carry the corporation through the troughs. One way around the worst of the risks is to establish a joint venture with other filmmakers. Pooling resources, contacts, gear, energies, and disparate talents can make a corporate, creative life somewhat less uneven and much more enjoyable. The group also benefits from shared criticism, feedback, and encouragement. As one producer in his late thirties said: "I'd never incorporate alone again—the life of an independent producer demands so many varied talents and skills, it just makes good sense to start off with two or three partners—share the overhead, share the contacts, share the grief, share the joy."

Filmmakers might also consider incorporating under nonprofit, tax-exempt status. This venture also requires the services of an attorney to draw up the necessary paperwork. The producers, in effect, may become employees or officers of the corporation, in the employ, so to speak, of the board; but if the board members are well chosen, devoted to the task of raising money to produce special-interest films, the board becomes a partner to the task. Nonprofit status also gives the filmmakers access *as an organization*, to foundations and other grant money.

Investors

With or without a corporate structure, anyone can seek individual investors in a film. Approaches to such people have narrowed since the formerly enticing provisions of the tax shelter laws were revised,[15] but investments or contributions to *nonprofit* ventures still exist.

The motivations of private investors or contributors include the following:

1. The film's concept is compelling or appealing to them. It matches or in some way fulfills a personal philosophy, cause, or hobby. To contributors, the craft of filmmaking may not be crucial, but saving the whooping crane or defining a political structure is. The approach of the filmmaker becomes one of emphasizing the power of the film to motivate, influence, or inspire the audience.

2. An investor or contributor wishes to encourage the filmmaker's capacities and talents. He or she may believe in the filmmaker and usually loves the medium of film. Here the investor becomes a patron. The approach stresses the filmmaker's aspirations, creative ideas, and knowledge of the medium.

3. Investors intrigued by supporting a film no matter what it's about or who produces it, instead of sheltering their money in cattle or grain or oil, can sometimes be troublesome. They may want in on the act. Some enjoy saying they are investing in filmmaker Y's movie at cocktail parties. The best approach to such people is a businesslike one listing all the pessimistic realities about narrow or nonexistent profit margins and a firm, explicit contract. Make them limited partners so that legally they must remain in the background.

All over the country individuals are supporting the arts or ecology, wildlife or children's programs. Such people can be approached to contribute directly to the filmmaker for a specific film or to a tax-deductible, nonprofit organization, earmarking the money for the production. Usually, they are not primarily interested in making their money back or in making a profit. More frequently, they look upon the contribution as an investment to promote or communicate their own interest in a given subject or to assist a worthy aspiring filmmaker.

NOTES

1. Graeme Fraser, "How To Sell Film Production," *Quorum Quotes*, Winter, 1974.

2. Hope Reports, quoted in *Filmmakers Film & Video Monthly*, April 1974.

3. From the 1978 National Conference of Information Film Producers of America, Vail, Colo. Speaker, John J. Hennessy, producer. Transcripts of this panel discussion, "The Producers vs. The Film Buyers" are available from IFPA for a small fee.

4. See Chapter 4 for more on the question of pricing.

5. See also Alex Ward, "Star Spangled Studio," *American Film*, 1978.

6. Bill Baldwin, former President, AFTRA, U.S. Congress, House Government Operations Subcommittee Testimony, September 1978.

7. See Bob Seymour, editorial, *Backstage/Business Screen*, 1975. (Excerpted by permission.)

8. Robert Lissit, "Findings and Recommendations on Federal Audiovisual Activities: A Report Prepared for the Office of Telecommunications," April 1978.

9. See "A Different Look at Federal Audiovisual Spending," by Jack Oswald, former IFPA president, *Filmmaker's Newsletter*, December 1978, or contact Independent Media Producer's Association (IMPA), 1100 17th St., NW, Washington, DC 20036 for further information on government regulations in audiovisuals.

10. See Appendix A for list of foundations.

11. See Chapter 5 for complete film budgeting.

12. Applicants to PBS should write for their "Independent Producers' Handbook" PBS, 475 L'Enfant Plaza, SW, Washington, D.C. 20024.

13. Excerpted from a speech by Walter J. Klein, president, Walter J. Klein Co., Charlotte, N.C., an acknowledged multiple-sponsor expert.

14. Eastman Kodak's "The Business of Filmmaking" (1978) has a good section on incorporation and business practices, and also includes sample film proposals. See Mitchell Block's articles on business in AIUF's Newsletter, Spring, 1979.

15. See Chapter 7.

CHAPTER 4

The Cost of the Film

BUDGET ESTIMATES

Estimating a budget involves figuring out the cost of each facet and analyzing the plan of action as well as potential trouble spots, and it contributes substantially to the filmmaker's knowledge of every part of a proposed film. But budgets tend to overwhelm many filmmakers, who perhaps believe creativity is incompatible with numbers. Such an attitude ignores the bedrock on which film is based: money. In the film world, money is a tool, not a symbol, weapon, wish, or reward. A filmmaker courts disaster if she or he evades the dollar amounts on which a film is constructed. Confronting the real costs puts the filmmaker in control. Accurate estimates can be protections. For instance, when a filmmaker builds a budget skillfully and honestly, he or she knows what the film will cost and cannot be manipulated by unreasonable demands from clients or sponsors.

Anyone can speculate on and differ about how a script should be shot, but no such argumentative latitude is available in budgets. Nor does it require talent—just a grasp of reality, an ability to research costs, and attention to detail. Clients, sponsors, and foundations familiar with film costs know by the first line items of a budget whether the filmmaker has the necessary expertise and commitment to produce the film. Sloppy, inaccurate, or incomplete budgets usually mean (1) the filmmaker has not thought out the various processes of the craft or does not know them and, therefore, does not have the experience to do the job, (2) the filmmaker is not enough of a businessperson to learn budgeting or to delegate the task to someone else, or (3) the filmmaker has misjudged the profession, believing only "creativity" counts.

It's impossible to do a complete budget until the script is finished and broken down, but in proposing and discussing films with clients, it is necessary to give a fair estimate. If an outline or treatment exists, some details of the film can be identified: length, gauge, synch-sound and/or narration, actors or animation, and so on.

A formula to estimate the cost of a 16mm color film is to multiply the number of planned finished film minutes times $1,500-$2,500.* Therefore, if the planned film length is set at ten minutes, it may cost $20,000, depending upon the complexity of the concept. This is nothing more than a rule of thumb developed over legions of budgets and is about as accurate as a guess. The truth is that a film can be made for almost _any_ amount of money, cheaply or expensively. It all depends on how one plans to make it. If a certain concept can only be done well by shooting all over the world with actors, that film will be expensive. The formula, then, is only useful when contemplating a cost _range_ for a film that may not yet even have a treatment written for it. It is a way of saying, "You want a 20-minute film on book binding? It may cost $40,000."

Once the script is finished and the breakdown completed, the costs are finite, measured in feet, days, hours, or miles. The only "flexible" costs are some fees, such as for writer or producer or percentages for insurance or overhead costs.

In preparing a budget, the filmmaker must consider the following:**

1. For scripted films, begin with the planned finished length of the film, then list the film's components: anything that is special or unique about the production that will add distance, lab costs, time, or people: number of locations and/or sets, actors, opticals (such as split screen), aerials, animation, crew members. You now have a preview of the major expense areas.

2. Estimate the number of days; usually two to five pages of script can be shot in a day, but watch out for such simple lines as "He falls back, breaking a table, as

---

*Actors, animation, distant locations, animals, sets & children are among the categories that automatically increase the cost per minute.

**Complete budget sheets in Appendix C.

she stomps out the door and down to the crowded, cheering compound where she gets into her 747 and flies off."

3. Estimate, in days, the pre-production part of the budget: location scouting, shooting tests, hiring, and casting. This can amount to 25 percent of the total budget.

4. Some general cost estimates:

(a) Processing, raw stock, and work printing of 16mm color film can be calculated together at 35¢-50¢ per foot. Since 16mm film runs at 36 feet per minute, a ten-minute film will be 360 feet, and at a 10:1 shooting ratio, the total footage shot will be 3,600, which, at 50¢ a foot will be $1,800; at 35¢ a foot, $1,260.

(b) A five-person crew (camera, assistant, sound, gaffer, grip) will run about $1,000 a day plus $40-$75 per diem per person (meals and room) plus travel cosᴌs. Non-union crew fees are negotiable.

(c) Writer's fees are normally calculated on a percentage (10-15 percent) of the budget, or a per-minute cost ($100-$250) times the number of finished film minutes. Therefore, if the film is 20 minutes long and the writer charges $130 per minute, the cost will be $2,600.

(d) Always include a figure for a still photographer—even in low budgets. Good stills of the production can be the producer's greatest single asset (outside of the film, of course!) for film festivals, distributor's promotional materials, news releases, and publicity. Stills also form a record of each production and can be used for copyright purposes.

(e) Stock footage costs about $10 to $25 a foot, 10 foot (or $100-$250) minimum, plus dupe negative and print costs. Rare footage may cost more.

(f) An answer print, or first trial, comes from 16mm original A's and B's. It is the first composite print (track and picture married); a check print is the first release print struck from the internegative or CRI (Color Reversal Intermediate).

(g) *Music*

Cleared library music, obtained from a sound studio or music library will average $1,200-$1,500 per 30-minute film.

Original music: it is two-thirds less costly to have the score recorded by an orchestra in London or Vienna or even Manila than the United States, so, especially if a filmmaker needs a big orchestra sound, it is clearly more economical to go to these places. In the United States, a score played by even a small orchestra (ten union musicians) will cost $15,000 to $20,000. The cost elements are the composer, musicians, studio, tape, copyists, and transportation to get all the gear to the studio. A producer may sometimes negotiate a cheaper price for a score if the composer may retain rights to the music. If the producer requires ownership—that is, exclusive use of the music composed—the cost will be more. The basement price of any original score is about $100 per minute, but this, too, is negotiable depending on the size of the orchestra; if, for example, a composer is orchestrating for forty musicians, it takes more time than music written for four or five musicians.

For a short industrial, an original score can cost 10 percent of the budget, so a library of cleared music is certainly the least expensive route. Also, the quality of cleared library music is much more sophisticated than it was even a few years ago.

(h) *Animation*: simple—about $3,000 per minute; complex—about $5,000 to $7,000 per minute.

(i) *Percentages*:

1. Insurance: 2-4 percent of total budget (nonunion). (See Chapter 6.)

2. Contingency: 5-10 percent is commonly allotted for "acts of God"—unexpected occurrences. There are other ways of handling the contingency percentage, which is a safety hatch for the filmmaker. One is to state the total budget

amount, indicate areas in the script that may cost more, and if they *do*, add the itemized charge on to the final bill to the client. The beauty of this plan is that the client knows he or she will pay *what the film costs.* As one experienced producer said, "Most clients feel that a flat bid that includes a contingency percent is slanted a bit for the producer, and that the really low bidder will try to economize at the expense of the film. I leave no allowance for stupidity on my part, but if I make an honest mistake, or if something occurs that could not possibly be foreseen, I always ask for more money. I have never been refused."

3. Overhead: 5–20 percent.

4. Profit: 10–20 percent. To stay in business, producers need to make a profit because the flow of the film business is one of crests and troughs. If the producer makes nothing above the fee, the corporation cannot carry its expenses from one year to the next. Since most foundations allow neither contingencies nor profit line items, the budgeting process for them must be done even more carefully. In general, percentages of overhead and profit and even contingency may be calculated on a "cost-plus" basis: the total budget estimate *plus* a certain amount to cover these percentages.

Producers often make a mistake by sticking "profit" in under travel expenses, which is where the canny client expects to find it hidden. It's far better to be straightforward, make the client a partner to the real budget costs, and do away with exorbitant travel or contingency items.

5. Opticals: Estimate opticals at roughly 10 percent of the budget if split screens and other effects are planned, 3–5 percent for more ordinary effects. A few labs still charge for fades and dissolves; most do not.

6. Taxes: payroll, pension for union employees, plus in many states, a 6 percent sales and use tax. Estimate 10 percent to cover both.

A West Coast producer offers the following "Basic Truths": First, things will always cost more than you expect. The corollary to this is that you cannot count on getting anything free. Second, a film will take longer to complete than your first estimate to the client. Third, a key piece of equipment will always fail, so you should schedule (and budget for) back-up. And fourth, there is no substitute for competent people with well-maintained equipment.

(j) _Unions_: Union structure and rules are so complex, a recitation of them could make a book in itself. A union exists for every function of filmmaking and a union crew behind the camera plus SAG talent in front can double or triple a budget. Filmmakers who reach a point at which they must use union crews or wish to become signatory producers to the unions should make it their business to familiarize themselves with the rules and regulations and all union rates, or hire a good production manager who is fluent in this language. Not knowing the costs of overtime for the teamsters who will control a production's mobility can throw a budget wildly into the red.

Most independent filmmakers work successfully as essentially nonunion enterprises, using SAG actors or DGA directors only. If a filmmaker is not a signator and is raising the money through independent sources, there is usually no need to use unions unless the filmmaker chooses to do so. On the other hand, in certain cities, such as New York, it is almost impossible to function without certain unions. Also, studios, being union signators, may not finance non-union pictures and may not even guarantee loans for such pictures unless the filmmaker shoots a union picture. (Studios may pick up or buy outright completed non-union films for distribution.)

SAVING MONEY

Properly conceived and carefully executed, some low-budget films—documentary or feature—have a way of allowing the filmmaker's talents to shine through: there is no elaborate artwork, few if any sets or effects, no big names to carry the story—just the original power of the script and the filmmaker's talent to put it on the screen. Exciting low-budget films of all kinds have been made, but a filmmaker must know where to cut costs without harming the picture.

Time can substitute for money; thus, tight intelligent planning can take the place of a large budget. But without good production management *and* strapped by limited funds, the filmmaker may be tempted to start hacking at the script—cutting bit parts, retakes, opticals, a location here or set there—any of which will ultimately mar the finished look of the film.

The following suggestions can save the filmmaker money.

1. Rely on the strength of the concept, not on flashy effects, exotic locations, expensive animation. In other words, a simple idea can be done well for less money while a complex idea usually needs a lot of financial sustenance. Examine the concept carefully: is it the sort of film idea that easily lends itself to a low budget?

2. Pre-plan every move and every shot. It is much cheaper to plan on paper than on location while eight crew members and actors stand around waiting.

3. Variations in weather can be a real enemy—stay inside as much as possible.

4. Use a few competent people rather than trying to shoot *Quo Vadis* with amateurs and friends.

5. Use simple sets, or create a film that uses real locations, instead of sets built for it. If there is very little money, consider devising a script that can all be shot table top or studio limbo.

6. If you own stills, or if they are cleared or in public domain, you can use them to make some extremely

powerful films. Moreover, with stills there are no problems of weather, sets, highly paid actors or expensive moves from one location to another.

7. Choose locations that do not compound costs, by distance, difficulty, and involved logistics.

WHY FILMS GO OVER BUDGET

No good excuse exists for running over budget except for poor planning, or "acts of God," a flood, avalanche, fire, or a circumstance so far outside anyone's experience that the producer cannot be held responsible. For example: "I'm in Hawaii on my first picture there and I go out to look at the field operations. To my amazement, I find we can only shoot about an hour or two each day because of the frequent clouds. Light meter's 10 or 400. I had based my 30-day shooting estimate and my budget on California weather—no one had ever mentioned that awful light variation in Hawaii. I now estimated the script would take three to four months to shoot, with triple the budget. It was an honest mistake."

Films run over budget because a disaster occurred during the shooting, or the filmmaker forgot smaller budget categories that cumulatively add up, such as taxes (federal and state); costumes or props calculated for free but which always end up costing money; or the filmmaker, a foolhardy optimist, agreed to anything just to get the contract. It's the little items that usually throw a budget off, not one big budget category.

Misjudging the original film concept can also lead to underestimating costs and therefore running over budget. Some film ideas are best fulfilled by a modest approach and a modest budget; others demand expensive opticals or a star or an on-camera narrator or authentic locations in South America. It's the producer's job to know when the concept can be shot for a low price (but so the resulting film doesn't look starved) and when it cannot.

The only way to avoid going over budget is to be a complete realist: do *not* hope for the best, hedge costs, or guess at them. Plan for the worst.

BIDDING

Most producers are honest; they want to produce a good film for a fair price. Clients, however, seem to feel that any price, as first offered, will be inflated. To guard against this, the client pits one producer against another in order to get a lower price. This ceremony is called competitive bidding.

The widespread practice of bidding resembles a shell game. The client (whether an association, government agency, or corporation) knows which shell hides the amount they've set aside for the film's budget; it's the producer's job to guess that amount to win the contract. The stated purpose of bidding is to give producers an equal but competitive chance to arrive at a gross figure for the film in question. What it more frequently does is to focus everyone's attention on money instead of on concept.

Budget, value, and film content are entwined; if the film script cannot be produced adequately without name actors or exotic optical effects, there is no point in bidding low. The picture simply will not work. On the other hand, a documentary that can be shot with a small crew in one part of town can be irreparably damaged by complicated opticals or wall-to-wall orchestral scoring. Therefore, the specifications (purpose, audience, length) that the client gives the filmmaker on which to make a bid are crucial; those specs dictate the amount of the budget. But budgets, as has been pointed out, vary enormously. One producer made two films with the same running time but the budgets were $20,000 to $175,000. One was a simple training film, the other was shot on four continents with animation. So cost really depends on the specifications of the particular film. A good question for the client is: "How much do you *want* it to cost? What is it worth in relation to the communications problem to be solved?"[1]

Then, within reason, the producer can design a film to fit comfortably within the budget.

Reputable or experienced film clients give producers a range of amounts. One corporation took six bids for a film, ranging from $19,000 to $105,000. All six producers had identical information to work from. This company indicated they wouldn't ever do that again but will give a price range from which producers can work because they now believe that all six producers would have bid within about $3,000 had they been told what the allotted amount was.[2]

All filmmakers bid low at one time or another, succumbing out of happy ignorance, or contempt for the budgeting process compared to the creative process, or naked need for a contract—any contract. It is an experience they never forget. That is why ridiculously low bids come most frequently from filmmakers just starting out. It can destroy the integrity of the picture and spell disaster to the filmmaker. Ultimately it threatens the delicate fabric of trust between sponsors and filmmakers.

One famous story concerns a state health and welfare agency that hired a filmmaker in 1967 to make a 30-minute film on the range of their community services. Since they had never sponsored a film before, the agency director thought that the bid of $3,500 was high but manageable. The film-maker should have known better than to bid what amounted to about $110 per minute! The final film, in color, appeared to be a series of pans of rural communities accompanied by voiceover interviews. Needless to say, the agency, ridiculed, consigned all 20 prints of it to a shelf. It was five years before a competent producer could talk that agency into doing another film.

It can be justly argued that the first producer was simply incompetent, that no system can protect unwary clients. But any producer who's been in the business for a few years can recite the experience of making a fair bid only to be ridiculously, even criminally, underbid by a newcomer or by an incompetent. The root of the problem is that sponsors of films—be they business, government, or foundations—encourage bargain-basement cut-raters, courting ever lower prices, believing they are making a shrewd deal. What they've done is collaborated on a bad film. The embarrassed sponsor withdraws, and the sour aftermath affects everyone —marring the reputation of films and film producers.

But the producer's own yearning to make films also sets up the "low bid" trap. Such a desire blinds the filmmaker to a sense of reality. In the heat of bidding, it's "psychologically convenient," as one producer said, "to forget what has already been learned through hard experience." If a film-maker is being forced to work within a figure that is too low, it is far wiser simply to say "no" to the film.

The excessively precarious nature of the film business sets up another trap for producers while bidding: there isn't enough work to go around. At some point all filmmakers are tempted—by economic stresses—to underbid just to get cash flow, or to keep learning, to keep making. When they are coaxed, for whatever reason, to severely underbid a film, the only warning with any merit is that the effects will always show in the film. In the end, the filmmaker will have wasted time, agony, and energy because the film will probably not be a proud example of accomplished work.

A producer won a bid for a film that he knew was about $10,000 underbudgeted because the client had insisted on an animation sequence. The filmmaker did not raise the bid or inform the client of the exact amount of the budget increase. "I was pretty green and I thought I'd pick up the costs by cutting locations and throwing in the contingency, profit, and most of the overhead percentages." About halfway through the production, however, he won a bid on another film—this one for $25,000. To complete the first as contracted for, he "borrowed" from the second. Now the second was nearly 50 percent underfunded. The end of the story: the producer may still be making films but probably in a different state. What should he have done? Faced facts: this business is based on the most stringent realities. Animation cannot be added without additional costs, and if a producer cannot talk the sponsor into more money, then the animation, or the film as originally scripted must be dropped.

Even experienced film sponsors, knowing they can always find someone to do a motion picture cheaper, often request a price cut. When the filmmaker knows the proposed budget is fair, his or her answer should be that a lower price will always mean lower quality _unless_ script changes are made to scale down the initial film concept.

Pricing represents what the filmmaker thinks he or she is worth. For that reason, it is extremely difficult for many filmmakers to judge accurately and fairly the fee for the filmmaker on the production.

A filmmaker is always on safe ground when the film concept has been correctly analyzed and placed in a low, medium, or high category so that the amount of money requested will fulfill the intrinsic promise of that concept, and when the filmmaker has proceeded to develop an honest and realistic budget.

It's worth noting that low budgets do not always get the job. Some clients automatically distrust low bids; they have heard of the high cost of film and are afraid the film won't be any good unless it costs a bundle. Also, many don't have the experience to know if the film concept under consideration can actually be made well for a modest amount.

Though an inflated budget can signal a filmmaker's inexperience, deliberately kiting costs to reach an excessively high bid is just plain dishonest. Word gets around very rapidly, and such producers do not stay in the business long. But they can last a bit longer than those who bid too low, since their films will probably look better.

One cannot out-guess or out-psych all the variables of the shell game. There are two solutions: (1) the filmmaker carefully and objectively analyzes the film concept and creates the lowest, fairest bid; or (2) the client (or sponsor) states out front what figure has been budgeted for the film. "A client may see competitive bidding as cost effective, but in my experience it often leads to bad budgeting, bad products, and bad faith," said a West Coast industrial filmmaker. "One of our clients decides on the film subject he wants, sets some parameters and an informed budget figure, and then invites producers to come up with ideas within that figure. The best *idea* wins! Not the lowest bid! Which is where the emphasis ought to be—on concepts, not guessing dollars."

Members of accounting and purchasing departments are frequently the people most eager to keep the bid system going so that management cannot question the final price of the film or the judgment of signing one producer over another.

If a sponsor tells a producer that it wants a film about subject A and gives the producer no more information than that, it is probably not really interested in buying or already has a producer in mind and is simply going through the motions of a bid.

Fighting back: One answer to bidding is for a producer to get a script commitment from the client. This makes the client take the producer seriously. Second, any producer deserves to have a dollar range estimate, and clients ought to bring this fact of life home to their purchasing departments. Third, producers should know who their competition is. If the competitors are solid producers with good experience, then the bidding procedure will result in fair bids. But if the other producers are inexperienced or about to go out of business, then underbidding is likely. Fourth, find out how much research the buyer expects the producer to do prior to the interview, and whether the producer will be remunerated for that research. Many people ask for speculation bids and then never supply enough information to make the bid and the film outline worthwhile.

Ideally, the production specifications should include the film objective, purpose, or message, the target audience, the kind of film stock, the dates when the script needs to be approved and when principal photography should start, the deadline for completion, and the answer print deadline. A limited number of producers should be asked to submit sample reels for a specifically named film subject that is being planned. From those, two or three should be selected. Those remaining should each be given a day's seminar on the problem to be solved or communicated by film. They should be paid for the research and the treatments that result. In this way, the sponsor will get the best of what each producer has to offer.

NOTES

1. Graeme Fraser, Vice President, Crawley Films, Ltd., Ottawa, Canada, *Quorum Quotes*, Winter 1977.

2. The 1978 national conference of the Information Film Producers of America, Vail, Colo.

See Lee R. Bobker's book, *Making Movies: From Script to Screen*, New York: Harcourt, Brace, Jovanovich, 1973, for an excellent chapter on budgeting films.

CHAPTER 5

Distributing Information Films

THE IMPORTANCE OF DISTRIBUTION

Filmmakers often underestimate or virtually ignore distribution for their films, viewing it as "business" distinctly separate from and below the elevated art of moviemaking. Such attitudes are counterproductive and always work against the filmmakers because the quality of distribution will directly affect their reputation and economic livelihood, since some form of distribution is the only way anyone will ever see the film. Filmmakers should start investigating distribution before they begin shooting. For example, checking with a distributor, a filmmaker may find that the planned 40-minute length for his/her film on Persian rugs actually hinders distribution, but if the filmmaker will cut the proposed length by 12 minutes, distribution might be likely. (It's a maxim in the business that most films are too long, anyway.) I once took a concept for a film series on ecology to a distributor, looking for financing. The distributor agreed the idea was marketable, but only if the films were cut from 20 minutes each to 10 and the audience changed from high school to grade school. The films were made and distributed along those lines. I doubt they would have been at 20 minutes each.

Distributors are not infallible, but most know which film subjects have a market, which do not, and what the optimum length is for a given subject and audience. Many distributors gladly credit filmmakers as creative people but fault them on budgeting, preproduction planning, and failure to determine the market for a film before shooting. One distributor said that successful filmmakers in his experience "have a sense of the whole. They know that less is better (if you can say it in 15 minutes, don't use 20 minutes); they meet the budget they set, and they understand that the more money spent on production, the more prints will have to be sold to obtain a profit."

The central issues filmmakers need to be concerned with are (1) What sort of distribution and promotion does this film need? (2) How well does a particular distributor reach the intended audience? (3) Is there a relationship between distribution and ease of financing? and (4) What constitutes a fair contract between a filmmaker and a distributor?

No matter what sort of film or what kind of distribution is arranged for it, it is vital that filmmakers view what happens to their films _after_ they are made as a matter equal in importance to the production itself; it is vital that they work with distributors to make sure the film reaches its audience. Such partnerships sometimes result in better films; they almost always improve the filmmaker's opportunity to make more films.

CHOOSING A DISTRIBUTOR

Distributors differ from one to another just as filmmakers do; each has his or her limitations, special expertise, and preferences. It is extremely important that filmmakers learn the characteristics of the different distributors in just the same way they know the differences between cinematographers and film stocks.

The idea here is to find a distributor who understands the film being offered, has shown an ability to distribute that kind of film but one who is not overstocked in the subject, who is sufficiently capitalized to do a good job of marketing it, and who appears to be stable enough to maintain promotion for the life of the film, which may be up to ten years.

All distributors publish catalogs, and all of them maintain mailing lists. Get on the list: the subsequent mailings will show how well they promote their new films. Get a copy of the catalog and check it out for the kinds of films they handle, those they do not have—either because they have a hole in the list or because they are not interested in handling that sort. Size up the quality of the catalog, the layout, the design.

When talking with distributors, explain the film idea concisely, and the audience for whom it is made. The distributor may agree that the concept and audience are sound, but the film must be in color, 15 minutes shorter, and should include some facet of the subject the filmmaker ignored.

Since most distributors market films nationally, the subjects they are likely to be most interested in are those with national appeal, not regional or local events—unless the latter can point up or exemplifies a national problem, mood or interest. Public relations films made by business are not frequently seen as "educational" unless a very good working relationship with the client has been established and the concept has been tested carefully with a distributor.

Letters to distributors should cover the film's objective, description of the content, length, intended audience, and planned style of the film. The point is to determine if the proposed film is marketable. If for one reason or another it is not, the filmmaker may wish to rethink the approach.

One may write to ask distributors what types of films they need but do not have. If any subject mentioned by the distributor is appealing, the filmmaker can set about raising the money knowing a market for the film exists. Distributors occasionally advance money for films they actively wish to have if they have confidence in a filmmaker's ability.

If the film is already produced, the search for a distributor can be done by letter, describing it and requesting that it be screened. Most distributors will screen any film, especially one introduced by an intelligent letter.

TYPES OF DISTRIBUTION

Four separate systems of nontheatrical film distribution —not all of them competing—are available to film producers in the United States: educational, free loan or sponsored, nonprofit, and cooperative.

Educational

This is an unsatisfactory catch-all label for "nonfiction," nontheatrical films on practically any subject. These distributors sell prints to schools and libraries, primarily, but other submarkets exist, such as museums, churches, government, and television. Educational films are made by every sort of filmmaker, from the inexperienced to the old pro; it is through making these films that some filmmakers break into the business and move onto features.

Distributors in this category come in four sizes. The large assembly-line model may have up to 2,000 titles and depends upon a large sales staff. Because of their high overhead, a high proportion of their films must appeal to the curriculum buyers for schools and colleges, a sure and steady market. Often they either produce films themselves, to maintain a constant flow of "product," or they hire independent producers, as do medium-size distributors. Large distributors shy away from a film that needs "special handling" for they would have to adjust their "normal" marketing procedures to suit a unique film. Consequently, many filmmakers find it difficult to get experimental or unorthodox films distributed and must rely on small companies. To large distributors, films are "products," piped over well-worn paths to sprawling school districts, or to other huge, well-defined markets. It is easy for a producer's single film to be lost in these mammoth catalogs.

The middle group of smaller but distinguished houses may have between 250 and 1,000 titles for sale and rental. They use direct mail and salespeople but are still, for the most part, small enough to maintain personal contact with both filmmakers and buyers. Such medium-size houses often excell at the "special handling" of unusual films, as do the smaller houses. But unlike the latter, these houses have enough capital to market films widely and well and on a sustained basis.

Small distributors may have staffs of five to ten people, and they may handle 50 to 300 titles. These houses, like the medium-size ones, specialize in types of film or film subjects such as health and safety or documentaries or Third World films. In inverse proportion, as the size of the distributor decreases, the unconventional quality of the films increases: the films may be unusual in approach, subject, or use of the medium, compared to more pedestrian content of larger distributors' films that appeal to the greatest number of people.

Small distributors deal with both buyers and filmmakers even more personally than the medium size houses; they push new additions to their lists aggressively. Normally, they market by direct mail, though they may have a few salespeople in the field. They nearly always specialize in types of films and in certain markets. The disadvantage of a small house to the filmmaker is that it may not have the capital to market and maintain new titles adequately. Mini-houses are often run by one or two people, and their film lists rarely exceed 50 films.

Large or small, each distributor cultivates its own part of the market wherever possible. One distributor may concentrate narrowly on the grade school curriculum and in doing so will know when she or he needs a film on arithmetic for seventh graders, how long it should be to fit into the school period, and on which part of the subject. A second distributor will be expert in the short-film-as-art genre for adults and will know exactly what constitutes a distributable film of this sort plus every available way to market it. To take an idea for a curriculum film to the latter distributor would obviously be a waste of time.

It has been estimated that about 250 new educational films are released per month, or about 3,000 a year. The average running time is 21.5 minutes. The overwhelming majority are in color and live action; the subjects range from social studies, communication, literature, psychology, science, health, the arts, and commerce, in descending order of popularity. Most were made for the adult and senior high school markets,[1] though films for grade schools are becoming increasingly popular.

The following facts apply for most films and educational distributors:

1. The life span of a film is about five to ten years.
2. An educational distributor must usually sell 200 to 300 prints to break even on an initial investment of $3,000 to $12,000, which is what it costs a distributor to market a single film.
3. Five hundred to 1,000 prints sold represents a solid success for both producer and distributor; 2,000 to 5,000 prints (over ten years) represents a run-away best seller. Most films sell only 50 to 100 prints a year, but even 50 is still considered good.
4. Most distributors offer producers 17 percent to 25 percent royalties on the gross sale of the film. Percentages on rentals are usually lower since the cost to the distributor of renting films exceeds the cost of selling them. Larger companies tend to offer smaller percentages, thanks to their high overhead.
5. The pricing of a film runs between $12 to $20 per minute, short films costing more per minute than longer films, since it takes the same amount of money to promote a film, whether it is five minutes long or 30 minutes.

Educational distributors are responsible for the administration, booking, and promotion of films, and the maintenance of prints. The biggest distributors—really, corporations with large sales staffs—may gross up to $12 million annually, but most distributors are small businesses with gross incomes from $1 million to $4 million annually.

One medium-size distributor has said, "This is a highly fragmented business where everything is small and backwards. There are hundreds of distributors, thousands of producers, thousands and thousands of films sold to thousands and thousands of customers very few of whom spend thousands of bucks. The 'preview process' is an unbearable way of selling: nobody gets to take home a $250-$350 piece of furniture for a week or a month to try it out in order to decide to buy—not it but a new, unused one! It takes one or two years to get a film established, and if the film is older than three years, forget it. If it is successful, it still takes five years to get your money back."

A distributor's major job is to know the markets—this year, next year, two years from now. When a filmmaker comes in with a film, or an idea for one, the distributor should be able to say, "Yes, there is a place for this film" or "No, it's not marketable until you do this to it," or "Take it to X distributor down the street. They handle films like yours."

Major Educational Markets

The major markets include the following:

Schools: This market is normally divided into four groups: primary (grades 1-6); secondary (grades 7-12); the district school level, where most film sales occur, usually to audiovisual buyers for an entire school system; and the building (or per school) level, primarily rentals to teachers and film strip sales, but becoming year by year a more important buyer of films.

Colleges and universities: This market includes film libraries operated out of universities for public and university course use. College departments may rent films for individual classroom use direct from the distributor, but usually the university's audiovisual library contains prints bought from distributors for the use of college classes, either free to them, or for a rental fee.

Libraries: This group forms about 15 percent of the market for distributors. Included in this category are the regional film libraries (which buy for the districts in their region) and the State Film Libraries in many State Departments of Public Instruction. More recently, they have become what amounts to secondary or subdistributors (as have some university audiovisual libraries), circulating the films purchased to the public, frequently in 8mm for home viewing.

Government: This market, both federal and state, often purchases huge numbers of prints of a single film, perhaps 50 to 100 at a time, for use in employee training or other

educational programs such as motivation, vocational training, or safety.

Industrial: This group uses more video cassettes than
other markets since that mode of viewing can be done at the
employee's convenience, and playback monitors have become common pieces of industrial equipment. The market is
not large for educational films though it is a substantial user
of privately sponsored films.

Churches, institutions, and museums are a very small
part of the overall market, though churches are increasing
their use of films generally. Museums almost never buy
films and rent heavily only when "films as art" are part of a
study program or film center.

Home use: When video cassettes and videodiscs are
widely available (predicted by the mid-1980s), this area of use
promises to be large and could become the largest of all the
nontheatrical markets. (See Chapter 10.)

Some of the changes distributors foresee in these markets are that films will have to offer solutions—they can't
just take a look at a problem; films will have to apply to
many markets rather than depend on one, unless they are
made for a specific new market; and, what the federal
government legislates can create new markets for films,
such as Equal Employment Opportunity (EEO), or health and
safety standards for industry; self-help and self-education
films will probably be successful on videodisc, but too
expensive for videotape.

The problem with this kind of distribution is the low
royalty the distributors pay to filmmakers, the newer offers
by first-rate houses sliding down as far as 12.5 percent to the
filmmaker, the distributor receiving the rest. No matter how
great the success of the film, no filmmaker can get rich with
this sort of distribution. (See Contracts, this chapter, for a
fuller discussion of royalties.)

Free Loan or Sponsored

The striking difference between this kind of distribution
and the educational just described is that here the system of

payment is reversed: In this case, the client pays the distributor to market the film, but the film itself is free to the audience or television station or theater that wishes to exhibit it.

The leading distributor of sponsored films, Modern Talking Picture Service, says that with a $9,000 to $17,000 fee from the client (usually the corporation that sponsored the making of the film), plus 100 to 200 prints, the film will be shown to 150,000 to 300,000 people in the college and school audience. For additional fee, and prints, a number of television airings can be booked. In this vein, Modern indicates that it books with 95 percent of the 700-odd television stations in the United States. The average television audience per booking is 40,000; thus, 75 to 100 bookings on television per year might reach three to four million people. The higher the fee and the number of prints, the bigger the projected (and promised) audience for the film—up to a point. Only those films that have wide audience appeal or deal with subjects of social import or public service can reach those large audiences. Packages of sponsored information films are also distributed by both Modern and its runner-up, Association Films, to hundreds of cable TV systems by video cassette and satellite. The number of transmissions via satellite to receiving stations can be more controlled by either distributor or client within the limitations of the budget than by ordinary television bookings.

A hefty amount of market research conducted by Modern covers the schools, various adult audiences (community, church, industry, summer vacation, and recreation areas), commercial TV, cable and pay TV, and theatres. Newsletters, brochures and research reports published regularly give producers and buyers a chance to hear from the audiences what they would like to see, which subjects are needed, and what the optimum length of a film for a specific use ought to be. The rationale behind the research is to match needs in education (both school and adult) to what subjects the clients desire to communicate.

Unlike most educational distributors, Modern Talking

Picture Service and Association Films maintain offices and film libraries in a number of major U.S. cities. Modern is the only North American member of Inforfilm International—the international association of information film distributors (22 member countries) and can therefore offer producers international distribution links, if desired.

Sponsored film distribution particularly benefits producers of films for business because it provides print sales and, less tangibly but no less importantly, an avenue of distribution for films made by business that do not necessarily fit into school curricular or other nonfiction modes. At its best, sponsored distribution provides films such as *Of Time, Tombs and Treasures* and *American Enterprise* (Exxon and Phillips Petroleum, respectively) free of charge to schools and organizations; at its worst, it services films laden with advertisements extolling the corporate sponsor that no one would pay to see.

It is obvious at this point that the experienced filmmaker appends the cost of this distribution service (plus prints) to the price of the film production budget. These costs are usually one-third for production, one-third for prints, and one-third for distribution fees.

Free loan distribution is viewed skeptically by many producers of educational films and documentaries, who see it simply as a means of purveying dull business films. And it is true that some of the films distributed by Modern and Association tend to be self-serving commercials for the business enterprise that sponsored them. But every category of film has its dull reels and the dull, commercialized industrial film is just as difficult to distribute as the dull or condescending children's film.

If a filmmaker wishes to make films for business, the real issue is: how does a filmmaker produce quality films for the market and in which ways can the distributor assist? The quality of films for business rises in direct proportion to the cooperation between producer and distributor and how well the client is educated in film communication. The filmmaker should make the distributor a partner to the production—and this is true no matter what kind of distributor is being sought, for distributors can help a great deal. For example, when a client insists on a ten-minute talking head segment in the middle of the film (the message from the corporate president), it is frequently easier for the distributor, backed by research, to educate the client on effective films for sophisticated audiences in conjunction with the producer's expertise, than if the producer talks solely of creativity or pace. Working closely with a distributor also increases a producer's capacity to make more films: wide and successful distribution gives the producer's work visibility and affords clients the opportunity to see whether the film does the job for which it was created or if it flops. If it succeeds, that client is likely to hire that producer again.

This form of distribution also gives the producer increased print sales, which the producer orders from the lab, screens the check print, and delivers to the distributor. For this service, the filmmaker may charge a mark-up percentage on the prints or video cassettes. Recommending one distributor over another to a client sometimes results in an unethical kickback percentage of distribution billing to the producer. Therefore, though the producer does not and should not make a percentage from sponsored distribution (as producers rightly may do with educational distribution) there are many other benefits in print sales, reputation, and return business.

A good relationship between a producer and a distributor can help the producer sell more films. Such teamwork allows the producer to talk about objective, theme, and filming methods while the distributor talks audience, promotion, the impact of quality films, and the wide variety of methods developed to reach audiences, including satellite. It can be a powerful combination.

But in the end, it is the producer's job to educate clients about distribution. A lab salesman tells a classic story of a producer who sold a 30-minute film concept to a state farm agency in the West. The budget included an additional price for 100 prints, which the lab delivered to the state capital office as directed when the film was completed. A few days later, the lab salesman received a call from an angry and bewildered farm bureau chief: "What do I do with all these god-damned prints?" he yelled. The producer had never mentioned distribution to this client.

Many clients believe they can distribute their own films. Distribution is not mysterious, but it takes a lot of time, capital investment, good promotional materials, contacts, a marketing system, and people. A business that is engaged in other pursuits does not have the experience or the facilities, and its employees usually have other jobs to do. No film can be properly distributed in a back-handed, part-time, amateurish way. Corporations that have tried it usually report unhappy and expensive results.

It is in everyone's best interest to get professional distribution for a planned film. But the only person interested in making a film is the filmmaker; everyone else is only interested in the result—the film in the case, what it will do, who will see it, what they will think about it or learn from it. This is especially true of films sponsored by business, and the filmmaker who does not realize this is adding another problem to an already difficult career. As one film producer put it: "If the client could accomplish the goal with smoke signals or dixie cups, the client wouldn't make a film and couldn't care less."

Nonprofit

The largest organizations are the University of California Media Extension Center and Indiana University's Audiovisual Center, but there are some 200 nonprofit distribution outlets scattered over the United States today. Since they are nonprofit, their prices for films are below those of commercial distributors, and the percentages on royalties to filmmakers are often higher, though not always.

These organizations maintain close connections with film users, provide excellent personal service, and supply unusual, sometimes politically radical or wildly experimental films, or the work of new filmmakers that otherwise might not be distributed at all. However, their budgets are inadequate to promote films widely, they often suffer from bureaucratic or administrative restrictions, and they cannot compete with commercial distributors in the marketplace.

A special nonprofit house is the National Audiovisual Center, which is part of the National Archives system run by the U.S. Government's General Services Administration. Primarily established to distribute government audiovisual products, it has about 8,000 titles, of which about half are films. It pays no royalties. Its prices to users are cost plus 10 percent. Its marketing is nonexistent.

Cooperative

Unaffiliated with universities or libraries, this group of distributors generally gives the producer a larger percentage of sales and rentals than education or other distributors, the split reaching 40 percent to 60 percent. Many, such as Canyon Cinema Co-op in Sausalito, California, or the Women's Film Co-op in Massachusetts, provide an outlet for what used to be called underground or experimental films—an outlet that is virtually nonexistent in the commercial distribution world. Undercapitalized, to say the least, they cannot promote the films they handle with zingy brochures or a legion of salespeople trekking across the land, but the service they perform for special films is not to be ignored.

Though co-ops and nonprofit outfits offer alternatives to commercial distribution, they are not a sound choice for the filmmaker who wishes to make back the negative costs of the film. As technology develops, these forms of distribution may change, making the current process of distribution less expensive.

THE DISTRIBUTION CONTRACT

There are so many different kinds of filmmakers, films and distributors that no single standard contract invariably answers everyone's particular needs or desires at all times, but there are some guidelines all filmmakers should be familiar with. While filmmakers' jobs are to assume the obligation of raising and managing the finances for their productions, they are the last in line for repayment. And it is an extremely vulnerable position, making the filmmaker dependent upon the expertise and honesty of the distributor. This is true whether the film is *George, King of the Visigoths* in blazing Panavision or *Felix, King of the Housecats* in modest super 8. But at least in 16mm distribution the print is sold outright (in most cases), and the filmmaker's return is not measured by box office ticket counts all over the country. A fair contract can help the filmmaker "earn" back the costs of the film.

It can be said that the contract agreement a filmmaker signs with a distributor reflects the filmmaker's (1) image of him/herself, (2) the way in which he/she views the film, (3) how hungry the filmmaker is, and (4) how much he/she knows about the varying producer/distributor responsibilities regarding the marketing of the film, and the form of such agreements. The result is a bargain mutually arrived at between both parties in which both filmmaker and distributor have agreed to give up one thing in order to get something else.

To understand the meaning of a contract's terms, a filmmaker must come to grips with the terms "net" and "gross." Royalties are earned income from sales. Royalties paid on the "gross" (off the top) mean the filmmaker will get a percentage of whatever the sale price of the film is. The percentage usually runs 17-25 percent. A percentage on the "net" means that the filmmaker's royalty will be derived from the gross *minus* expenses, such as the cost of the internegatives. Gross percentages are always better than net, and new filmmakers should always contract for a percentage of the gross proceeds.

One producer says that when he started out, crashing around in the underbrush of contracts, he signed with a nontheatrical distributor for 20 percent of the net (gross *minus* cost of prints, internegatives, and foreign translation, if any), and the contract was to run "in perpetuity." An extremely poor deal. Needless to say, he never saw a dime from a modestly successful film series.

Mechanics of the process: a filmmaker has just completed a five-minute, 16mm color film that cost $9,500 to make. The distributor sells it for $100 per print and takes 75 percent of that sale price—or $75 per print—a percentage income that helps cover the printing and mailing of promotional materials, shipping, and the cost of prints. (A successful film will often carry the costs of distributing the films on the list that are not making money.) If 200 prints are sold in one year, the filmmaker may earn, from 25 percent, $5,000; the distributor will earn $15,000. To sell 200 prints of any film in a year is very good. But even at this rate, it will take the producer two years to earn back the costs of making that film *before* profit. Since the life of most information/education films is about five to ten years, any subsequent sales after two years may be a profit to the filmmaker—if the film keeps selling well.

Since most 16mm films do not sell 200 prints in three years, take a look at a bleaker, but no less realistic vista: the contract with the distributor calls for the producer to pay the cost of the internegatives, plus dubbing costs of foreign translations for the new tracks. This means the producer's percentage is on the net, not the gross. In addition, the producer will receive 20 percent—not 25 percent. If print sales still reach 200 a year, the producer will receive $4,000 in annual royalties *minus* costs—internegative, recording, transfers, and so on.

In terms of a contract with a distributor, ideally a filmmaker wants the following:

• An advance fee. There are two schools of thought about advances: one is to take it whenever you can get it; the other: it is better for both distributor and producer if the amount of the advance is spent marketing the film. If the filmmaker believes that money in hand is better than a percentage of future hopes, and takes the advance, he or she may have to settle for a slightly smaller royalty percentage. Advances are deducted from royalties.

• Control of the film's A and B rolls—the original elements. If the A and B rolls are retained, the distributor will order the internegative through the filmmaker; by this means, the filmmaker will be able to keep a rough count on the number of prints the distributor is actually selling. If the filmmaker hands over the A's and B's and the distributor turns out to have three sets of books (one for producers, one for himself, one for the IRS), a filmmaker never knows if the quarterly tally of only 14 prints sold is accurate or not.

• Length of the contract should be five to ten years with an option to renew.

• The distributor should pay for the cost of the prints. All distributors can get a better price on prints than film-makers, because of the volume of their business with labs. Since a filmmaker may only get 25 percent of the gross sale price, no one should have that percentage eaten away by print costs. Therefore, filmmakers should receive a percentage of the gross sale and rental price of the film.

• Understand what constitutes the gross receipts. Unless the filmmaker knows what the elements are on which the gross percentage is calculated, the filmmaker will have no idea how much he or she may earn. Therefore, which revenue sources will make up the gross? It can be constructed by media (8mm, video cassette, television); by geography (United States, worldwide); or by market (educational, theatrical, and so on). The larger the scope of the rights, the larger the potential royalty. Film-makers should read this part of the contract carefully. Which rights are assigned to the distributor? Does the filmmaker receive a percentage of the gross from all those rights? For example, does the filmmaker get a gross percentage on U.S. and Canadian 16mm sales and rentals, or just sales? Does the filmmaker receive a percentage on worldwide 16mm sales and rentals? Which rights is the filmmaker choosing to retain? For example, unless the distributor has a proven track record of TV syndication and international distribution, it is best to hang on to these rights and lease them to an agent who knows the territory. The royalties for television should not be calculated at the same rate as the 16mm rights, but for 40 percent-60 percent. Videodisc and video cassette markets are still largely underdeveloped; no one knows what they may bring or how they may be developed. It is best to retain those rights. The major action is that of trading certain rights for other benefits; if a filmmaker leases all rights to the distributor, the former should have a gross percentage on the revenue derived from those rights.

Other contract elements include the following:

• Promotion and advertising: Agreement between distributor and filmmaker on the primary and secondary markets is essential since it reflects a common understanding of the film. The contract should call for an adequate amount the distributor will spend on advertising and promoting the film. The filmmaker should have some idea of the kind of design for the film's announcement and where it will appear in the distributor's catalogue. Small announcements are easily lost in large catalogues.

• The royalty payment schedule: The accounting to the filmmaker of how many prints have been sold or rented usually occurs quarterly.

• Audits: The distribution contract should contain a clause giving the filmmaker the right to audit the distributor's books. The request—if it becomes necessary —is made in writing, and the cost of the audit is borne by the filmmaker.

• Exclusivity: Nearly all contracts give the distributor the exclusive right to market the film—and for good reason: the market is crazy enough without having two or three distributors marketing the same title to the same audience. However, the filmmaker should have the right to make "private" sales to associates or people who go directly to the filmmaker with a request to purchase.

TELEVISION OUTLETS

Network, Syndication, Station-to Station

The myth here is that television has an insatiable need for independently produced films and tapes, but the reality is that it "needs" films and tapes largely of its own design. Television is more a system of distribution and exhibition than it is a medium. For the most part, it produces and exhibits its own material in the same way the movie studios once controlled their products, routes, and theaters before the Paramount Consent Decree of 1948. It is lunacy for any filmmaker who values the time spent making films to take on the travail of marketing single films to television.

There are three ways to sell films to television: at the network level, through syndication, or locally, station to station. Selling a network a documentary (feature films are covered in Chapter 7) is so rare that most independents of smaller size and reputation than David Wolper will not be able to do so.

Hustling a film around the television syndication network takes enormous expenditures of energy, time, and hard-won contacts. For short, single films, it is best to sign with a distributor whose track record in this area is good or give it to a syndicator who specializes in documentaries or packages of short films to chains of stations. For instance, Coe Film Associates in New York supplies a syndication service for independent or nontheatrical distributors. They retain exclusive television rights to the film for three years; the split is 60 percent/40 percent.

Syndicators and agents have made some inroads with cable television systems. Independent Cinema Artists and Producers (ICAP) is a nonprofit organization created to promote the showing of independently produced 16mm films and ¾-inch tapes on cable TV. ICAP acts on the filmmaker's behalf as a nonexclusive agent with cable TV programmers offering packages of short films. ICAP retains 25 percent of the fees from cable for the films; the filmmakers receive 75 percent. The fees are based on film length, number of subscribers, and number of times the film is shown in a year.

Syndicating independently produced pilots for television series, either fiction or documentary, has increased, as have the syndicating outlets: there are over 200 of them, and anyone contemplating a pilot—whether for commercial network television or cable pay TV—would be wise to investigate syndication in the same way one would investigate distributors.

Cable television keeps promising to be rewarding—in terms of programming variety to the viewers, and financially to the filmmakers—but it has yet to fulfill that promise. Cable still offers little money for the lease of short-film packages, and even less for promotion, which unknown films badly need to attract viewers. However, pay TV is an increasingly significant distributor/exhibitor as far as feature films are concerned and may turn out to be important as a window to documentary filmmakers.

Airing a film on television draws attention to it and augments future sales and rentals. This is especially true if the film is about to be or is newly released to the nonfiction markets. Seeing it on television, potential school users may be inspired to order it for a class or library program. But no filmmaker with short information films should count solely on television as a way to distribute and exhibit them. At best, it is good backup display of the film's regular distribution program.

Public Broadcasting Service

PBS constitutes a patchwork quilt of 270 independent stations, licensed to colleges, public school systems, and communities. Most stations have some sort of acquisition program, but there is no pricing standard or central agency whereby one filmmaker can be assured of reaching all stations. Therefore, the filmmaker is staring at a horizon dotted with separate letters, telephone calls, and the mailing of prints to a "market" of individual stations that may pay from $1 to $5 per finished film minute. They accept only a few films a year. That's a very bleak market.

A slightly better horizon appears when the filmmaker considers regional educational networks, such as Eastern Educational Network (EEN) centered in Boston. They pay $100 a minute.

Public Broadcasting Service in Washington, D.C. is clearly the place to start since their purchases of finished films are for national consumption. Prices per minute range from $100 to $250. The money comes from the Corporation for Public Broadcasting (CPB), the administrative umbrella for PBS. (See Appendix A for various grants and funds available.)

The sale of independently produced films—especially documentaries—to either commercial or educational stations is simply not a real distribution alternative, and despite many efforts television remains a closed shop to independents. Access is extremely difficult, and access for documentaries of a controversial nature all but impossible. Unlike the commercial networks, PBS does buy packages of short films, such as the PBS series *Academy Leaders*.

The Telecommunications Financing Act (1979) may improve access for independent video and filmmakers to the public television system. This bill mandates that a "substantial portion" of CPB's programming funds be set aside for independently produced work.

But until that "substantial portion" of CPB's money is available to independents, what is a filmmaker to do? People who have had long experience in trying to open up public service television for independently made single films feel there are only two responses at present that make sense: (1) The filmmaker should become a television producer/packager of short-films series, selling the series to PBS in much the way syndicators sell pilots (and promised series) to commercial television; and (2) if a filmmaker wishes only to make documentaries to be shown primarily on television, then that filmmaker would be better advised to join a PBS station that has a strong production department. These suggestions spring from the nearly insurmountable difficulties of selling single films.[2]

Television adopted its programming concepts and time

frames from radio, and this continued lack of imagination makes it difficult for independent filmmakers to break through. Dedicated PBS watchers believe that service will invariably slide into programming not significantly different from the commercial networks, and that it is in fact already halfway down the slope.

Structural alterations are on the way to revise the 1934 Communications Act that will affect PBS through the end of this century and probably beyond. The Carnegie Commission report on public broadcasting, that appeared in early 1979, will undoubtedly have a major influence on the future shape of PBS and CPB. One of its many recommendations that may benefit producers is the establishment of a program services endowment—an organization ("notably absent from the present system," says the report) to stimulate American talent. The endowment would underwrite TV and radio productions, would fund pilots, research and productions centers, and national competitions and subsidize existing programs. The report recognizes all too well that American film and tape makers do not have access to PBS at present and that PBS has not encouraged diverse American programming. It should be remembered that the Public Broadcasting Act, which created CPB and PBS grew out of the first Carnegie Commission report on educational television in 1967. Therefore, the recommendations of the second report on a program services endowment will undoubtedly have a major influence on independent film production.

THEATRICAL DISTRIBUTION OF SHORTS

So far, this market exists as an additional exhibition outlet only for the rare short film. Traditionally, theater owners have not wanted to pay money for a 10-minute film that only added turnaround time to the evening's program and therefore decreased revenue. So what has developed are "free" films to theaters. Association Films and Modern Talking Picture Service both provide selected films that thematically tie in with the main feature, and both programs have met with success.

These two commercial outfits have recently been joined by the National Endowment for the Arts' Short Film Showcase program, in conjunction with the National Association of Theater Owners (NATO) and administered by The Foundation for Independent Video and Film. After a successful pilot program in 1978, designed to encourage the return of short films to theaters, they are now embarked upon a nationwide distribution program to theaters, with the backing of the exhibitors and favorable responses from the audiences. Films must be eligible for a G or PG rating, be made by U.S. citizens or permanent residents, and be no longer than seven minutes. Contracts with the administrator of the program, the Foundation for Independent Video and Film, Inc., are options for three years for nonexclusive use; the filmmakers are awarded $2,500.[3]

DISTRIBUTING IT YOURSELF

The 80 percent/20 percent split in royalties granted by educational distributors has forced many filmmakers seriously to consider distributing their own films. But the only way to do that well is to stop making films and devote total energy to the distribution process—or to join forces with other filmmakers to make the work of distribution worthwhile. It is as easy (or as hard) to distribute one film as it is ten films. Though self-distribution means the filmmaker receives 100 percent of the sales price, all the expenses and charges for the filmmaker's time must be deducted from that 100 percent.

The questions filmmakers might ask themselves when considering self-distribution are: Is there enough capital involved to pay for at least 50 prints, promotional materials, advertising, festival fees, shipping, and the clerical and mechanical work involved for at least one year? Will those costs deducted from the sales price amount to a better percentage than offered by the distributor in the first place and make up for the time the filmmaker lost as filmmaker?

Distributing one's own film—either alone or in concert with others—requires a full-time commitment and a willingness to learn the mechanics of distribution. No one can be a filmmaker and a distributor unless the filmmaker is in a cooperative or partnership of some sort where the work is shared, or the filmmaker has substantial capital to hire someone else to run the distribution.

Distributors buy the films that appeal to the broadest number of people. The independent film and video artists are those who suffer, and nowhere is this more apparent than in the distribution of self-expressive or personal films for which there is only a small market. When the filmmaker/ artists, who have scrounged for $11,000 over two years are offered 20 percent of the gross, they naturally turn to self-distribution. With normal sales, that 20 percent wouldn't pay off their negative costs in four years. Without wide distribution, how are they to get more money to make more films? Most learn that what is true for the distributors, however, is also true for them when they become distributors: that though the "market" for short films of a special nature may exist somewhere, no one has devised a profitable way of reaching that market. Therefore as long as the method of financing and distribution is expensive—as long as it takes $1,000-$2,000 per minute to produce, and up to $12,000 to market a film that sells for $10-$300—and as long as television continues to ignore the short experimental film, many independent filmmakers will have no means to distribute their films.

One answer is to form cooperatives both to produce and distribute that are *capitalized* to sustain the effort so that one filmmaker is not reinventing the wheel each year to distribute one film. A second answer is to hang on until the distribution of special films directed to small markets is economically feasible—for example, when the per-print price is $3, making for an instant popular "film" market just as the paperback market exists today. This rosy future will only be possible, however, when video cassettes and videodiscs become household paraphernalia as widespread and accessible as records for phonographs.

What independent video and film artists are facing is the curse of the specialized product, which is an economic disaster in mass market distribution systems. As long as the distributors aim for mass markets, self-distribution is a skimpy proposition at best, unless it is structured along the lines of a cooperative production/distribution organization whose films are directed to a new and significant audience.[4]

Film Festivals

Whether awards are indeed a standard measure of a film's excellence, or simply a ceremony whose benefits are intangible and ephemeral, film festivals cannot be ignored. They provide, at least, an environment to present one's films to a public and to distributors who regularly attend festivals.

Filmmakers should research festivals before entering them. Some festivals specialize in kinds or categories of films, some are easier to win than others (and therefore of less value), so they need to be evaluated in terms of the film to be entered and the festival's reputation.

In the United States, the festivals[5] range from the Sinking Creek Film Celebration in Tennessee for student and independent films to the Cindy Awards held by the Information Film Producers of America, and the American Film Festival, sponsored by the Educational Film Library Association, held each spring in New York and drawing large numbers of distributors—to giant international festivals, such as Chicago or New York whose major attractions are the features they present. The only government sponsored film festival in the United States is the Council on International Non-Theatrical Events (CINE). Winners of the CINE Golden Eagle award are entered in major film festivals in Europe, where showcase competitions for short films flourish.

To enter a festival a filmmaker should supply good black-and-white and/or color stills from the production, a

16mm composite print (in most cases), the entry fee ($10-$100), and an entry form. Some filmmakers fail to fill out the forms correctly, thereby dooming the film, no matter how excellent. The filmmaker is required to select the category that most aptly suits the film such as industry, arts, health, safety, or student film. If, in the opinion of the jury, the filmmaker has chosen the wrong category, the film may be disqualified. In some cases, it is possible to enter a film in two categories, such as biography and art (usually for a double entry fee).

The second crucial area is the filmmaker's synopsis of the film, its purpose and audience. This section is read aloud to the jurors before each film is screened; and the film is evaluated on, among other items such as the technical or creative, how closely it fulfills the stated purpose. Films have missed simply because what the jurors saw on the screen bore little or no relation to what the filmmaker said she or he intended. Usually this is the result of the film-maker's carelessness or simple ignorance of the fact that the films are being judged, in part, against the stated purpose.

Film festivals are one of the natural conclusions of the distribution process, as a film travels the route to a film or television screen. The point of making any film is to get it seen; if a filmmaker cannot find a distributor, a film festival can usually be found for it, it may win an award, and *then* a distributor might be interested in it. One producer made a feature-length documentary before he realized the size of the distribution problems he faced. Unable to find a single distributor for it, with élan and continued commitment, he entered it in the Academy of Motion Picture Arts and Sciences and, wonderfully, it was one of the five nominated that year for an Academy Award. Never give up.

NOTES

1. Based on 1977 information, it is likely films for that age group will be overstocked by the 1980s. For further information see

Salvatore Parlato, Jr., "Freeze Frame: The Educational Film Industry," *Sightlines*, Fall 1978.

2. On the estrangement of filmmakers from PBS: see George Storney, "We've Never Had It So Good!" *Sightlines*, Fall 1978; and David C. Stewart, "Getting It On—Public TV Markets," in Judith Trojan and Nadine Covert, *16mm Distribution*, New York: Educational Film Library Association, 1977.

3. See Appendix A.

4. See Julia Reichert, *Doing It Yourself*, New York: Association of Independent Video and Filmmakers, 1977. This is an excellent book that no filmmaker who wishes to distribute should do without.

5. American Film Institute, Kennedy Center, Washington, D.C., has a good up-to-date list of American and foreign film festivals. So does Trojan and Covert, *op. cit.*

CHAPTER 6

The Filmmaker and the Law

The risk in filmmaking is not just monetary; it involves other people's rights to privacy—to be filmed or not to be—and the legal release of that right to the filmmaker; contractural protections with clients, investors or sponsors; insurance; and the protection of one's own work by copyright. For these reasons and more, filmmakers should become well acquainted with the laws that may affect them.

COPYRIGHTS

More than any group, filmmakers deal with the entire spectrum of copyrights in other arts and media—music, dance, literature, and so on. The concept behind the original copyright law was that no matter how modest the "art" created, each person's creation had something unique, and, therefore, the work could be copyrighted. From that beginning, copyright statute has become a law more about money than about art; its purpose is to see that the rightful owners of original material are not cheated out of their rightful gain.

Though it is often difficult to separate one from the other, copyrights protect *methods* of expression, not ideas or concepts. To differentiate a method of expression from an idea: if a choreographer staged the last dance in Federico Fellini's *8½* in a park in such a way that a resonable person could say that choreographer had *copied* the last dance in *8½* and charged admission to the dance, then Fellini's copyright on the film has been infringed. The manner or mode of the infringement does not make any difference; it is the similarity of the copying.

Everyone wishes to protect his or her ideas, but an "idea" cannot be copyrighted until it has a distinct form—as a film, play, or book. It is not naive to believe that one's ideas—even fully scripted or filmed—will be stolen, but no one can afford to live under the shadow of that fear. A filmmaker's overriding objective should be to act as professionally as possible—copyright what is protectable, and, once done, to go on.

The New Copyright Law—PL #94-553

On January 1, 1978, the U.S. copyright law (created in 1909) was brought into accordance with the international standards and extensively revised. The new law, characterized as "almost as incomprehensible as the tax code,"[1] seeks to balance the rights of creators and the needs of users. The less controversial or complex changes include the following:

- Establishment of the American Television and Radio Archives to preserve radio and television programs.
- Establishment of the Copyright and Royalty Tribunal, which is a five-person board that sets royalty license fees for cable and noncommercial television systems; negotiates the fees of authors whose works appear on such systems; and arbitrates disputes. They are appointed, like the FCC, by the president, for five- to seven-year terms. It will be a position of some power.
- Extension of the period of copyright protection from the former 56 years (28 years with an option to renew for 28 years) to the life of the author plus an additional 50 years. If a copyright is owned by a corporation, the term is 75 years for publication or 100 years from the creation of work—whichever is shorter. Those copyrights in force on January 1, 1978, will extend to the first 28-year period, and then—if application is made one year before the end of the first period—the renewal will extend 47 years.
- Everything is automatically copyrighted the instant it is created, but when a work is "published" it must bear "notice of copyright," else the creator loses the protection forever.
- A U.S. copyright also secures copyright in most, but not all, foreign countries. It also extends U.S. copyright

protection to works first published in foreign nations if the nation is a party to the Universal Copyright Convention, as most are.

"Fair Use"

Other aspects of the new copyright law may be highly controversial. For instance, the owner of copyright is given exclusive but not unlimited rights to copy or sell the work created. Limitations are drawn under the "fair use" section of the new law, which provides guidelines for libraries and schools, allowing such institutions to "reproduce no more than one copy or phonorecord of a work, and to distribute such copy or phonorecord" *if* the copyright name is clearly shown, no monetary gain results, and the institution is open to the public.

Libraries and schools form the major market for nontheatrical film distribution. It has long been suspected that some schools or universities, even corporations, unscrupulously transfer preview prints of films to videotape for burgeoning video cassette libraries, only to return the preview print, with thanks but no purchase.

Sometimes, videocopying of prints is done with a cavalier innocence. In my own experience, when I inquired about a print I had sent a university for preview, I was told that they couldn't afford to buy it since it did not quite fit into their curriculum in that area, but they had duplicated it on video "in case" one department might need it later. They very kindly returned the print to me one week later.

It is feared in some quarters that the traffic in bootlegged prints may prove to be "legally" epidemic if the "fair use" guidelines are not strictly defined. Obviously, as far as ruffling the commercial seas of distribution, the issue is whether such institutions may copy material they have *not* purchased and own.

The "fair use" provision allows limited copying of copyrighted work. It is permissible to copy a few pages from a book and distribute them at a meeting, but it is an infringement of the law to make copies of an entire book because that would curtail sales.

Arguments flare about whether institutions can "Betamax" prints of films for the same nonprofit purpose, but a careful reading of the law makes this appear unlikely, for in Section 108, (h)[2] "The rights of reproduction and distribution under this ['fair use'] section do not apply to a musical work, a pictorial, graphic, or sculptural work, or a motion picture or other audiovisual work other than an audiovisual work dealing with the news ..."

Holding a copyright of a film means, in its most basic sense, that the filmmaker alone has the right to make copies (with "fair use" limitations as noted); therefore the small library that videotapes a film it does not own infringes on the filmmaker's right to protect what she or he has created. The new law tries to balance access to information against the right to control one's creation and make money from it (for example, make prints). How well the new law will provide that balance remains to be seen.

The new copyright law extends liability, for the first time, to cable and public television systems under compulsory licensing. This means that for a set fee (paid to the original broadcaster of the "primary transmission," in the case of cable TV, or to the copyright owner), these television systems may now use copyrighted material. The fee will be set by the Royalty and Copyright Tribunal; the television systems need _not_ receive the author's permission. In 1978, it was estimated that cable television paid about $6 million (1.1 percent of their gross revenues) in copyright fees—which was the first year of operation by license. That money is divided between several hundred copyright owners.[3]

"Work Made for Hire"

"Work made for hire" may prove to be as controversial to filmmakers as it has already been for some free-lance magazine writers whose magazines have required they sign agreements giving up _all_ rights to the pieces they write on assignment. The "work made for hire" concept of copyright ownership applies to that work for which a person is paid that was created within an employee's line of duty. If a staff writer for a network was assigned to write a show during her regular hours while being paid a salary, the copyright would belong to the network, not the scriptwriter. This does *not* apply to the patron or sponsor contracting with an independent filmmaker to produce a film. In that case, the copyright owner would be the filmmaker unless the contract stipulated otherwise.

From the film producer's point of view, when hiring a composer, for example, the legal concept behind "work made for hire" is that the filmmaker holds the copyright in that performance or creation for the film—unless there is an agreement to the contrary.

How to Copyright Films and Video Tapes

To copyright a film or videotape requires three acts on the filmmaker's part: notice, registration, and deposit.

Notice

The symbol© followed by the name of the maker (or entity who owns the copyright) and the year in which the work is completed ("published")

© Smith 1980
All rights reserved

constitutes "notice" when it appears on the head or tail (or both) of a film. It is a good practice to place notice on the actual title card, as in:

SHORES
© Smith 1980
All rights reserved

Publication is a slippery concept. It can mean an offer for sale or a display for the public. Publication is sometimes a matter of intent, the nature of the intent judged from the surroundings. If the film is shown to a small group of friends without any indication that the filmmaker claims any rights to the film, *that* may be publication. The filmmaker may not be behaving protectively enough for the court to believe that he or she meant to protect the rights. It is always wise to claim the earliest possible date in the copyright notice. The rule of thumb is that if a filmmaker is going to show the film no matter to whom, then treat that showing as publication and copyright the film.

Registration

After giving notice, the government requires that the filmmaker register and deposit the work. Formerly, the creator only had to place notice on the work in order to protect the right and maintain a lawsuit. But now the ability to prove ownership is important: the creator must also register to prove ownership. The owner cannot sue or collect damages on copyright infringement without registration. If someone substantially steals another person's work or reproduces it without permission and makes substantial profit —that act of theft cuts into the originator's market. The remedy is a lawsuit for infringement. The new copyright law has been tightened up so that both registration and deposit are required if an owner wants to have the chance to sue and to recover damages.

A copyright owner has 90 days from the day copyright is claimed to register. Registration is simple—the copyright office has a bag of forms, the filmmaker fills out the appropriate one for performing arts and sends it in with a nominal $10 fee.

Deposit

Under the old system, the Library of Congress in Washington, D.C., required the deposit of two copies of film prints.[4] This proved a burden on almost everyone, so the Motion Picture Agreement was born. The Motion Picture Agreement states that instead of depositing prints with the Library of Congress, the maker may sign the agreement, and retain the prints, which are subject to recall by the Library if it chooses.

The new copyright law eliminated (in large part) this handy deposit escape hatch for filmmakers. A howl went up from the film industry, led by the Motion Picture Association of America (MPAA), and though speaking for the studios and the major independents, the MPAA marshaled the argument for all filmmakers. It cited the huge expense of making feature film prints for the sole purpose of depositing them, without the right to use the print in distribution where the print could earn money for the maker. The Motion Picture Agreement has been put back into the regulations.

Each filmmaker should determine, upon the number of films he or she makes per year, whether the loss of one print for deposit is better than the legal machinations of getting a Motion Picture Agreement. But one or the other must be done to protect the filmmaker's ability to sue for infringement. When a film is fully copyrighted (with registration and deposit) the "outs" connected with that particular film are also protected.

PIRACY: UNAUTHORIZED DUPLICATION

Film piracy is a widespread underground practice that poses an economic threat to the film business. The FBI can buy black market prints of most new American films in Cuba, the Middle East, or Hong Kong before they are released in the United States. Where do these prints come from? Bootleggers. Some lab technicians swear they've been offered up to $10,000 for a master print. Others report scavengers combing through studio trash cans for prints deemed not good enough for "legal" runs but plenty good enough for the black market.

Piracy is a massive copying where one original (whether book, magazine, film, or tape) is used as a "master" to produce duplications without limit. The copier (pirate) becomes the creator without any of the original costs or efforts, but all of the profits.

Bootlegging movies transferred to video cassettes is a big business, and big profits are made in the foreign consumption of pirated films. They are taken off the air, usually from cable television's programs of the first-run movies. It's been estimated that over $100 million per year is lost to this trade, since a cassette of, for example, *Saturday Night Fever* may run $150.

The Sony Betamax videotape recorder, primarily for home use, makes it possible now for anyone to copy programs off the air. Sony's right to manufacture the Betamax machine has been challenged in court by Walt Disney Productions and Universal Pictures. They argued that Sony is an "infringer" because it knowingly assists others by the use and availability of Betamax to infringe copyrights, from which acts Sony gains profits.[5] If Sony loses the suit, the ramifications will be sweeping. The Film Security Office was formed to combat this trade. It is a liaison between motion picture companies and law enforcement agencies and is staffed mainly by ex-FBI agents.

Piracy is being practiced not only by sleazy characters selling pornography or old features but also by "reputable" business, educational, and governmental agencies and organizations. This underground merchandising cuts a swath through the film business, from 16mm training films primarily used by corporations all the way to the most popular features.[6] Under the new copyright law, the penalties are stiff: as high as $25,000 in fines, a year in prison, and loss of all equipment. A second offense is a felony.

To suffer economic loss because of piracy can happen to anyone and points up the urgency of fully copyrighting one's work. In a landmark case,[7] Liane Brandon sued and won damages from University of California's Extension Media Center, a major nontheatrical film distributor, claiming they had pirated her film on sex stereotyping, *Anything You Want to Be*. The court held that, among other things, film titles are protected by the same laws forbidding the false description and representation of goods and services crossing state lines.

Essentially, the suit complained that the University of California had repeatedly attempted to buy prints to rent from New Day, distributor of the film, and had been refused. At that time, Far West Laboratory produced three short films on sex role stereotyping (by Gloria Golden and Lisa Hunter), one of which was titled *Anything They Want to Be*, which was subsequently distributed by EMC even though the Far West film bore a striking similarity to Ms. Brandon's.

The decision of the courts lists all the various aspects by which piracy is judged.

> [T]he offending Far West film clearly constitutes "goods" and admittedly has traveled in interstate commerce...I rule the findings of a *decrease in plaintiff's income* from her film concurrent with the increase in defendant's income from the Far West film proves the actual damages caused by defendant's use of the misleading title...I find that defendant *acted deliberately* with an awareness of the similarity of titles, subject matter, theme, presentation, running time, and price range of both films before it entered into the Distribution Agreement. *Because of this* deliberate pirating of plaintiff's property, I rule that plaintiff is entitled to injunctive relief, damages and an accounting...[8]

PLAGIARISM

Filmmakers should be acquainted with this facet of the law if only because of the vital part words and writing play in the creation of films. Plagiarism can occur in the use of the language, incidents, or plot. Plagiarism cannot be avoided simply by changing a few words around. But there are uses of copyrighted material that do not constitute infringement. Other authors' materials may be used as background when reconstructed by one's own sequence of events, or by one's own story. (As one wag once said, "If you use someone else's material for a work of fiction, that's called plagiarism; for nonfiction, that's called research!")

Background or source material, for example, abounds on Thomas Paine, all of which can be brought to bear in one's own biography. Such biographical material may be used verbatim if permission is received and credit is given. If whole paragraphs are used, payment may be required as well as credit and permission. In all cases, the route is through the publisher. All works of any kind, such as manuscripts or private letters, are covered by common law copyright until such time as they are published. If—on publication—they are not copyrighted in the statutory fashion, they fall irrevocably into public domain.

MUSIC RIGHTS

Music is rarely free. For this reason, a film's budget must include not only the cost of recording the music in most cases but also the costs of clearing it—that is, getting the proper permissions. Most particularly, no filmmaker should use any music from any record without prior written consent from both the copyright owner and the recording company that released the album and in many cases from the featured artist. Filmmakers must seek permission to use practically any kind of music, and even with professional help, the permissions can become unbelievably complex.

To put copyrighted music on a film's sound track, permission must be received from the copyright owners of the music on the *usage* and *timing* of the music within the planned context of the film. A classic case[9] was that of the film *The Life and Times of the Happy Hooker*. The producers used the Mickey Mouse fan club tune for their film without permission and "out of context," as anyone might suspect. Disney claimed that it was copyright infringement, and Disney was upheld in court. Had the producers sought permission to use the tune, they would have been refused because of the planned use and the context.

Next, worldwide *synchronization rights* must be secured which give the filmmaker the right to record the music on the film's sound track—in other words, the right to synch the music with the picture.

Both these permissions vary, depending on the medium. In the case of television, performance clearances must be obtained from the copyright owner, who must determine whether the use of the music is available within the planned television context. Such permission may be obtained from BMI (Business Music Inc.,) or from ASCAP (American Society of Composers, Artists and Performers), agencies that, in turn, pay royalties to the artist whenever the work is reproduced. If the performance clearance is permitted, negotiation takes place for the synch rights of the television program, usually to run for five years, worldwide. If the use in question is for a TV "Movie of the Week," negotiation would also cover a two-year option for the foreign theatrical rights (excluding the United States, which is treated separately).

Then there are the *broad rights*, which are analogous to the "ancillary rights" of a film (see Chapter 7); these include pay TV, subscription TV, cable TV.

For a theatrical film, performance rights must be negotiated with the copyright owner for the U.S. theatrical performance rights (since U.S. exhibitors do not take out ASCAP protection). Then the worldwide synch rights and the broad rights are negotiated.

The Harry Fox Agency in New York City represents music publishers and negotiates the synchronization rights for those people who wish to use copyrighted music. In Los Angeles Mary Williams Music Clearing House functions as the name implies: they will negotiate all legal clearances, performance rights, adaptations, and special uses. The filmmaker simply states what music she/he wishes to use, and the Mary Williams organization takes it from there. For most independent films—short or long—creating original music or obtaining cleared library music is by far the better route.

Cleared Music is that which a filmmaker purchases for set fees (costs depending on the length of a selection and ultimate use of the film). Such libraries contain all kinds of music—popular, classical, single instrument, or full orchestra.

Original Music, of course, is the score (or "track") a filmmaker purchases from a composer; the resulting music is later recorded in a sound studio with musicians specifically for the film.

Such tracks may be composed of *public domain music*, but which music is actually public domain and which is not can be a land loaded with mines for the unwary filmmaker. It is true that the original music of Bach is in the public domain, since it was composed hundreds of years ago, but a record of Bach fugues is not in the public domain. To use Bach even for an original sound track—recording the sheet music in a studio—the filmmaker would have to go back to the "pure version," for between the time Bach wrote the fugue and the present, many arrangers have copyrighted their own versions. The filmmaker cannot even pick a song like "The Foggy Foggy Dew"—a very old English folk song—out of a song book and record it as it appears in the book for it may be a special arrangement or contain lyrics copyrighted by the book's editor specifically for that book. The answer for the filmmaker: if the slightest doubt lingers about the origin of a song or arrangement, go to one of the many experts in the field of music clearances and check it out.

DEFAMATION (LIBEL AND SLANDER) AND THE RIGHT TO PRIVACY

Just as filmmaking moves across the spectrum of creative rights (music, literature, art) so it can also move from libel to slander to invasion of privacy. Who may be filmed and who may not be and under what circumstances lifts the lid of a filmmaker's Pandora's Box.

Both libel and slander suits can be brought against filmmakers. *Intent* is of paramount consideration here, just as *use* is the linchpin for invasion of privacy.

Defamation is the printing or publication of words or images which defame a person's character, hurt his/her business, or hold a person up to ridicule. Libel is the printing of *written* words which defame; slander pertains to the *spoken* word, which brings harm to a person's reputation. The stricter penalties usually fall on the side of the libel since the printed word has, for us, a permanence the spoken word does not.[10]

Spoken words on television and radio have been judged at times libel and at other times slander. It is generally believed that the 1960 *Sullivan* v. *New York Times*[11] case opened the door to a deterioration of protection from defamation for public officials. Public officials have a limited ability to collect libel and slander damages unless "reckless disregard for the truth" or "intentional falsity" can be proved. Since then, the legal thinking reflecting *Sullivan* has been brought to bear on private citizens—for example, no damages may be won unless reckless disregard for the truth can be proved. Recently, the Supreme Court narrowed the limitations of just who is and who is not a public figure. Mary Alice Firestone won her suit against *Time* magazine for printing that her husband (tycoon Russell Firestone, Jr.) had divorced her for adultery. The final decree did not mention adultery. *Time* countered on the more traditional grounds that their article was "without malice" and that she was a public figure, a known socialite.[12]

Privacy is similar to defamation and copyright in that it focuses on the use of an image—or likeness—of someone else. The determining factor for the legal ramifications of the situation is: to what use will the image (name or likeness) be put?

The right to privacy is the right to be left alone. Invasion of privacy concerns the relationship between the filmmaker and the subject being filmed or interviewed. Violations include eavesdropping, public disclosure of private or personal facts, commercial use of the subject's name, use of the face and/or voice without permission, and libel and slander.

Here, too, public figures do not have as great a right to privacy as those who are not famous or notorious. They have, indeed, relinquished the right to privacy that ordinary citizens enjoy. But when public figures are alone or on private ground, they have the same right to privacy.

There are many cases of an entity or person charging a filmmaker with invasion of privacy. Walt W. Rostow sued Peter Davis for invasion of privacy before the latter's feature-length documentary *Hearts and Minds* was released in 1975. Rostow lost his claim, the court citing that he is considered a public figure. Suit was brought against Paul Grey's film *P.I.N.S. (Persons In Need of Supervision)*, a 24-minute documentary depicting the life of young boys at a home for "problem children" in New York state. The case was eventually thrown out of court, but that it was brought at all indicates filmmakers' vulnerability in this area—especially social or point-of-view documentary filmmakers.[13]

Such suits reinforce filmmakers' need for good releases and knowledge of the law. Even if won or eventually settled, suits are expensive to fight. Institutions zealously guard their inmates' right to privacy often with little regard for the public's right to know. In some cases, the institutions are upheld when suit occurs. The cutting edge is that the public has a right to know, which, under the Bill of Rights, cannot be abridged except when "reckless disregard" of the truth can be proved. Usually, the public interest to receive information is favored over the individuals' rights or desires for privacy.[14]

A filmmaker's best protection is knowledge of the law in these areas; after that, rely on good sense and instinct. When a filmmaker thinks the camera is intruding on someone, a privacy suit may result. The only protection is to get a release. A release is mandatory if the image is to be used for advertising or trade purposes, for example, a television commercial or anything that in *any* way could be construed to sell a product. The classic example of invasion of privacy —and the circumstance from which the first written law in this matter arose—was the use without permission of a little girl's face to sell oatmeal soap.

For educational films, or films about newsworthy events, the chances are very high that releases are *not* needed, *unless* the resulting use of the image will be offensive. For normal photography of people for a film intended to educate or in some way convey current events, the chances are very high that no invasion of privacy can be maintained.

Releases must always be obtained for fictional works. The only time a release is not necessary is if a person cannot be recognized. Therefore if a filmmaker photographs someone from a sufficient distance so that the person cannot be identified, a release is not necessary. Still photographers often distort recognizable faces in the backgrounds of their photos to make people who are photographed at random unrecognizable. The point is that if a person cannot be recognized, an invasion of privacy suit cannot be brought.

The group photograph is sometimes a protection against suits. A relatively famous case involved a photo of men in the New York Public Library at 10:00 A.M. reading the *Daily Telegraph*, a New York City newspaper known for recording horse races. The picture was published in another newspaper next to an article which declared that, in effect, the people who read the racing sheets were unsavory drifters. One of the individuals, who happened to be reading the *Daily Telegraph* that morning, filed a lawsuit claiming his privacy had been invaded. He lost his suit. Although the association of the photo with the article cast aspersions on the character of these people in the picture and was potentially defamatory, no one could distinguish the plaintiff from anybody else in the group. The connection between the person who complains and the people identified by the picture or the offensive associations has to be very clear for such a suit to be won. Therefore, it can be said that it is safer to film a group of people even if they are recognizable. It is only when an individual is singled out from his or her environment or activity by the *camera*, not by *events* that a release must be obtained. That's when a filmmaker is closest to potential liability for invasion of privacy.

Obviously, the best way is the safe way—and that is to get releases in any circumstance where the least doubt exists. A release constitutes permission by the party for the film-maker to use the likeness (image) and voice in a specific film. It can be a printed form or it may be an audio tape, which some filmmakers prefer over the written form, feeling that subjects are intimidated by written releases.

To get an audio release, the filmmaker explains to the person being filmed and taped what the nature of the film is, how it's being made, and how it will be used or where it will be shown. The subject must verbally grant permission to be filmed and taped, and the agreement must be taped. Obviously, the filmmaker must retain the audio release in case it is needed later.[15]

When using homes, gardens, offices, parks or other property, location releases must be secured, signed consents from the custodian or owner—or the government agency responsible, such as the Department of Parks.

All filmmakers, when signing contracts with distributors or television stations, must warrant (guarantee) that they own all rights, have, in essence, obtained proper releases to all the material displayed in the film, and that if they do not the distributor will be "held harmless." Most distributors won't touch a film unless the maker warrants such ownership. The notion is that every discrete publication of the product is offensive and is yet another wrong, so that if a publisher or distributor makes 50,000 newspapers or prints with a flagrant misrepresentation of a person's character in it, that is 50,000 different acts of defamation or invasion.

CONTRACTS

Many filmmakers take on a film sponsored by another person or organization without a contract or even so much as a letter between them describing the basic outline of the planned film. If communication between the two parties breaks down, or was never properly created, a contract becomes crucial.

A contract is an agreement (or declaration or commitment) between the filmmaker and the sponsor (or a distributor) in which both parties give up some self-interest in order to arrive at a mutually agreeable station. It is also an exchange, in writing, of promised duties. A contract need not be an inch thick to be valid. For many films, it need only be a letter of agreement outlining the title of the film, the length and gage and stock, a description of the film's content, its primary objective and audience, planned distribution and its agreed upon budget figure with a schedule of payment by date. The letter should be signed by both parties and witnessed. It should include such points as negative owner-ship. All of these major issues can be ascertained from the following descriptions of contracts and could be excerpted for a letter of agreement, which for many organizations is less intimidating than a full-scale contract.

Contracts between filmmaker and distributor have been dealt with in Chapter 5. This section explores the combustible chemicals of the production contract between film-maker and the sponsor or financer of a short film. A copy of the standard contract for such films is in Appendix B.[16] It was compiled by the International Quorum of Motion Picture Producers.

The contract should stipulate a schedule of payment on the part of the client or sponsoring organization, and a schedule of performance on the part of the filmmaker. The standard agreement between filmmaker and sponsor states:

- Upon signing of contract, filmmaker receives 33 percent of the film's budget.
- Upon presentation (or approval) of script, or upon presentation (or approval) of principal photography, filmmaker receives 33 percent.
- Upon screening of answer print (or, in some cases, interlock), filmmaker receives remaining 34 percent.

These are the major approval (or action) stages of the film: the treatment, the completion of the script, of principal photography, of interlock or answer print. It should be agreed who has approval and how "approval" is defined. Payment may also be scheduled in steps of 25 percent each, but it is obviously better for the filmmaker to have two-thirds of the budget by completion of photography than only one-half.

The advantages to the filmmaker of having "completion" rather than "approval" appear in the contract should be obvious. Some might mutter that the client has the right to approve what the client has paid for. However, by the time the work reaches the client for approval, the filmmaker has already performed and must pay lab bills or music fees. Many clients—even large corporations—are notorious for delaying approvals and therefore payments, simply not realizing the aggravation, inconvenience, and embarrassment they cause (see Clause 2 of the contract).

If a contract stipulates "approval," the canny filmmaker will sum up early meetings with clients in writing, setting out the agreed purpose of the film, target audience, and the approach to the film's subject. If misunderstandings arise in these primary areas, it is far better to clear them up before scripting and shooting begin.

Situations also arise where the filmmaker, in good faith and with all the appropriate communication, completes principal photography only to find the company liaison replaced by a new person with new ideas. At that point, payment on "completion" of principal shooting can be a lifesaver.

If clear mutual understandings of the film's goals are established at the outset and good communication between filmmaker and client has been preserved along the way, few disputes will arise. In these cases, approval is usually prompt.

"Approval of answer print" can be troublesome. One producer made a 27-minute film for the combined social services agencies of a state—each agency being represented by one person. At answer print, one agency's representative was replaced by another person who was considerably senior to most of the others. When the lights went up, this man said that he thought the film was supposed to be more about the work of each agency and not about the combined impact of children's programs. What he wanted was not a revision, but an entirely new approach to the script, and no one on the committee wanted to take him on. The meeting broke up without approval of the answer print. Fortunately, the filmmaker had kept a written record of all principal decisions relating to the film, and eventually the film was approved. Had no written record been available, had the contract not been clear, payment might never have been forthcoming at all.

The key is: There is no substitute for trust in business dealings, but conversely, there is no substitute for putting everything in writing. The one thing ignored in discussions with either client or supplier will invariably create a snag later and sometimes an insurmountable hurdle. "Not enough producers discuss all the trouble spots, and then summarize that discussion in writing," says one California filmmaker. "Burying the problem will inevitably produce conflict down the line: 'I thought that was understood!' and 'No, we never discussed that!'" The only protection is good communication. Don't dodge the hard questions or areas of doubt, but set out all issues and questions candidly. Then solidify the discussion and agreements in a professional contract.

The contract should:

1. describe the nature of the film to be made, the gauge, length, film stock, title, and number of prints.

2. contain a payment schedule and a production schedule.

3. stipulate *one* representative to act as a liaison between filmmaker and sponsoring agency who shall have full power and responsibility to act.

4. include a clause on prompt client approval.

5. stipulate that any additional work, above that originally agreed to, must be paid by the client. If, for example, the client wishes three minutes of animation to be added, the cost must be paid by the client (but if the filmmaker is clearly at fault for a delay, the filmmaker should incur the additional costs).

6. clearly spell out who owns the negative, in whose name(s) the film will be copyrighted, and who will own the outs. A controversy—sometimes reaching impressive proportions—rages about the outs and control of the negative. Many filmmakers still feel that the person or institution who sponsors (pays for) the film automatically owns the outs and the negative. The opposing camp feels as strongly that the sponsor has paid only for the finished product (the specific film print) and therefore has no right to any additional material or control of the

negative from which prints of this purchased work are struck.

The producer should be viewed as an independent contractor so that the copyright does not automatically fall to client ownership under the new provisions of "work made for hire." The copyright law awards protection of the outs and other related material to the owner of the copyright. Since the legal owner, then, would be the filmmaker, the outs belong to the filmmaker. But the argument for filmmaker control of the negative and ownership of the outs also relates to one of a filmmaker's reputation, which may ride on the quality of prints struck from the negative. A filmmaker should be regarded as the "sole source" of the prints to maintain quality control. These elements of ownership and copyright should be carefully spelled out in any contract between filmmaker and sponsor.

7. include agreements on credit: the producer should have the right to list her/his name and those of key production people in the credits. But some corporations or organizations will not agree to a producer's credit list. This is a point the filmmaker can give to gain something else.

8. describe which expenses, such as location costs, taxes, and insurance, are covered by the budget and which the producer must pay. Also, it should be clear in any contract that release print costs are *not* included in the production budget price nor is the cost of distribution, if any.

INSURANCE

If there was ever a profession in which the unexpected regularly occurs, it is film. Since the demands of each production vary, it is impossible to cite exactly what kinds of insurance a filmmaker needs each time. Also insurance for a short 16mm film is substantially different than insurance for a feature production whose script may call for fiery auto crashes.

Generally, insurance falls into a few major categories. The basic coverages include the following:

Worker's compensation is required by law. It insures everyone hired by the producer against injury or illness while working, covering medical treatments, temporary or permanent disability, even death benefits. If a producer does not have it, he or she is liable for all costs and other risky action. This insurance usually averages 4 percent of the crew's payroll.

Comprehensive liability is also required by law. Basically, this covers injury or property damage, during a production, to people *not* working for the filmmaker; use of nonowned vehicles, whether on or off camera, but does not apply to aircraft or boats. Filmmakers often need to furnish proof of this coverage to property owners before they will allow shooting on their premises. This policy does not cover damage to a property used as a "set," which is called property damage liability.

Negative insurance protects against loss of the negative (or videotape) from fire, theft, or transportation. It does *not* cover faulty stock or malfunction of camera.

Equipment insurance: A filmmaker is responsible, when renting gear, for any loss. Some rental companies will extend their insurance to the filmmaker for an additional fee; some will not but demand proof that the filmmaker has coverage. Whether the gear is rented or the filmmaker's own, it is essential to get this sort of coverage, which protects against all direct physical loss, damage, or destruction to the equipment used in a production.

Property damage liability protects property from damage while that property is in the "care, custody or control" of the production company. It is an absolute necessity when shooting around valuable objects such as in museums.

Faulty stock, camera, processing covers against damage or destruction of the raw stock, exposed film, sound track, or any problems caused by faulty gear, editing, processing, or accidental erasures. It does *not* cover the cameraperson who used 7247 and lit for 7252 or for any other error in judgment or for inexperience. The deductible for this kind of coverage is hefty.

For features, additional insurance is necessary:

Props, sets, wardrobe protects against added expenses, damage, or destruction of props, sets, scenery, costumes, or anything else of this nature when used in a production.

Cast insurance: For budgets of over $500,000, it protects against sickness, injury, and death of actors or the director, as well as all the extra expenses of temporarily shutting down a production (when an irreplaceable actor is ill), shooting around an absent player, or abandoning the picture entirely. Deductibles range from $3,500 to $12,000.

Errors and omissions: A standard part of any contract between distributor or television station and filmmaker requires the filmmaker warrant he or she owns all rights to the film. E & O insurance covers a producer for unauthorized use of titles, format, ideas, characters, plot, plagiarism, breach of contract, and against claims of libel, slander, defamation, invasion of privacy.

Just as entertainment law differs from corporate or criminal law, so motion picture insurance is unlike collision insurance. Get an insurance company or agent who is experienced and skilled in motion picture insurance. It is unwise to treat this person like a clerk; an insurance agent is a partner to the protection of the production as far as that is possible. To be most helpful, an agent needs to know the total budget, length and locations of the shooting schedule, the crew's payroll, and the size of the cast, and to have a copy of the script or story synopsis. Some agents won't want to read the shooting script, though some will, but all agents need to evaluate the script story in terms of risk in order to evaluate the insurance needs accurately and fairly. After a review of this information, the agent announces the essential insurance needed and the "nice-to-have" additional protections. Insurance will usually run 2–4 percent of the budget.[17]

NOTES

1. Edward M. Bulchis, "The Entertainment Aspects of Copyright Law," *Filmmakers Monthly*, August 1978.

2. 17 U.S.C. of PL 94-553.

3. See remarks by Jack Valenti, president, Motion Picture Association of America, *Hollywood Reporter*, 12/8/77.

4. Only one print is now required for deposit.

5. Universal City Studios, Inc., v. Sony Corporation of America, 429 F. Supp. 407 (C.D. CA. 1977).

6. See the remarks of Homer A. Porter, Los Angeles Supervisor, Federal Bureau of Investigation, in *Business and Home TV Screen*, May 1978.

7. Brandon v. Regents of the University of California, 441 F. Supp. 1086, 1091 (D. Mass. 1977).

8. Liane Brandon v. The Regents of the University of California, Action No. 76-580-C, October 12, 1977. Chief Justice Andrew A. Caffrey, United States District Court. Reprinted by permission of *Media Report to Women*, February 1, 1978.

9. Walt Disney Productions and Walt Disney Music Co. v. Mature Pictures Corp., 389 F. Supp. 1397 (S.D. NY 1975).

10. The case asserting this concept was Ostrowe v. Lee 256 N.Y. 39 (1931). See Michael F. Mayer's book *The Film Industries*, New York: Hastings House, 1973, for an excellent summary of libel, slander, and invasion of privacy, which need not be repeated here.

11. New York Times Co. v. Sullivan, 376 U.S. 254, 84 S. Ct. 710, 11 L. Ed 2d 686 (1964).

12. Time, Inc., v. Firestone, 424 U.S. 448, 96 S. Ct. 958, 47 L. Ed 2d 154 (1976).

13. See the article by Polly Wells, "P.I.N.S. and the Dramatized Documentary," in *Filmmaker's Monthly*, August 1976.

14. See ch. 19, Michael F. Mayer, *The Film Industries*, New York: Hastings House, 1973.

15. See Frederick Wiseman, "Contract Negotiations and Legal Considerations," in Judith Trojan and Nadine Covert, *16mm Distribution*, New York: Educational Film Library Association, 1977.

16. The contract is reprinted by permission of the International Quorum of Motion Picture Producers. To obtain the right to use and adapt it, send $10 to IQ, Box 395, Oakton, Va. 22124.

17. The acknowledged expert in this field is Truman Van Dyke of the Truman Van Dyke Insurance Co. in Los Angeles. Also see the article of Ron Coleman, "Show-business Insurance," *Filmmakers Monthly*, October 1976.

CHAPTER 7

Feature Film Financing

THE RISE OF THE INDEPENDENT PRODUCER

The feature film business has been said to resemble the court of the Medicis or an insulated college campus, but the best analogy is the circus. Of humble but popular origin, a circus is as varied and as stratified as the film business. Just look at the different ways producers function under the big tops: there are the high-wire financiers, such as Dino Di Laurentiis or Sir Lew Grade. On the basis of their contacts and experience, they can raise millions of dollars in a day. They may cut the big top management in on the act or independently book it around the world. Next are the packagers and the agents, jugglers and gymnasts—low on content, high on flash and sequins. The solid professionals—the producer/filmmakers—are most like the elephants: wise in the ways of the circus and somewhat bored, they know all the ropes and are regarded with the wary respect smaller beings have for larger ones. But elephants, too, can be chained if they don't behave.

The newcomers are still sweeping the floor for the most part, but occasionally they grab a unicycle or a whip and dazzle the crowd, which makes the management take a second look and give them development money. Whatever the echelon or level of expertise, all producers use essentially the same tools or combinations of tools. The difference is that while most people have access to some of the tools some of the time, a few have access to all the tools all the time. By comparison, the short film field seems a model of management and order.

That anyone outside the studios has access to independent methods of financing and distribution is largely because of the Paramount Consent Decree of 1948. In those halcyon days before the decree, studios as producing/distributing entities were inextricably bound to their own exhibition outlets. In 1945, they controlled 70 percent of the first-run theaters in 92 of the largest United States cities, and 60 percent of the theaters in smaller cities. They had an assured outlet for the films they produced. They controlled the stars, directors, and writers by contract, for the most part, and, the producers worked under salary.

In 1938, the U.S. government filed an antitrust suit against Paramount, Loewe's, RKO, Warners, and 20th-Century Fox ("the big five"), and Columbia, Universal, and United Artists ("the little three," which did not own theaters). The legal battles raged for years and ended in the U.S. Supreme Court.[1]

The philosophy behind the government's suit was that each picture should have the opportunity to seek its place in an open market on its own merits, that theaters should be able to bid competitively for films. The government maintained that collusion existed between the big five, creating a closed market to which independent producers, bookers, and theaters were systematically excluded. After more than a decade of legal haggling, the government won its case. Besides prohibitions from price fixing and block booking,* the majors were forced to divest themselves of the ownership of theaters. The result was a supposedly open and competititive marketplace for pictures. The assured retail outlet for Hollywood films made by the studios vanished forever.

The studios' position was made worse by the advent of television and the final entrenchment of powerful unions, clamoring for higher wages. The contract system disintegrated. Liberated from their iron-clad contracts, stars, directors, and writers could and did demand higher fees for their pictures. As the price of production rose, fewer pictures were made. The traditional form of the business was breaking up like a ship on a reef.

---

*Block booking is a system devised by the studios and foisted on the theaters wherein the theater—in order to get a few high-quality pictures—has to take many more klunkers. A 1978 example of block booking: it was alleged that in New York City 20th-Century Fox demanded theater owners take *The Other Side of Midnight* if they wanted to show *Star Wars*.

The result has proved to be more profound than the separation of producing studio from theater ownership. In its wake it spawned a proliferation of independent producers whose modus operandi was often "the nose of the wind," the "hit mentality", and packages. It was the most expensive crapshoot in American business.

When the old structure collapsed in the early 1950s, the producers who had earned their wings at the studios were succeeded not by other trained producers but by the deal-makers whose "hit mentality" bred the package—that magical combination of property, star, and director they hoped would guarantee a big box office gross. The least risky of all properties is the best-selling novel or Broadway musical—something everyone already knows and loves like *The Sound of Music*. Whatever its subject matter, the property now needs to appeal not only to a broad American audience, but to the world: 45 percent of the box office returns come from leases to foreign distributors.

By the 1970s, the deal had become orgasm, and the production of the film was a downer. According to one producer, "Virtually any Tom, Dick or Harry with a strong contact can be a producer. People now think that a producer's job is to acquire a screenplay, make a deal at a studio and then have somebody else make the movie." The stampede of unqualified people with contacts into feature film production, or dealers with packages, is viewed as corrosive. "In terms of a profession, producing as such compares today to taking a course from one of the shill operations on Hollywood Boulevard and then going to Vegas for a weekend of blackjack. It's no longer a professional position. If the property's right, and the star is right, your kid can produce it! That's the standard in the film business."

Producers in the full, traditional sense of the term are now quite rare. Those who remain are steeped in the profession, and their pictures are looked upon with anticipation and interest by the critics, the audience and the industry. "A fine producer," said one observer, "does not allow anything—be it the script, the color of the star's hair, the titles on the one-sheet—to escape his/her scrutiny. That kind of producer is totally devoted and committed to the film from start to finish.''

In 1949, independent producers made 20 percent of the films released by the major studios. By the late 1950s, they were responsible for 57 percent. But today, pictures for theatrical release from independents and studios combined amount to only about 75 per year (down from 750 pictures for 1927.)[2] As the production of films for theaters has declined, the production of film for television has increased. Today the networks produce about 150 pictures a year, twice that made by the studios and independent producers. CBS alone had a $70 million budget for films in 1978.

The made-for-television movie came into being in the 1960s when NBC and Universal agreed to co-produce a series of features that would first be shown on TV, *then* in theaters. Today the networks finance their own films, producing them either through the television divisions of the major studios or the large independents. As financiers and/or distributors, the studios are now as linked to the networks as they once were to the theaters.

Each picture, no matter how short or inexpensive, is a separate business. Each demands certain personnel, financing, scripting, distribution, and marketing. But only a few people in the world can raise $5 million, and when they do, it is for a once-in-a-lifetime venture that if successful, promises to be financially self-perpetuating. But in feature films, producers, dealers, packagers must raise millions for each picture, and the only perpetuating aspect of this process is that if the picture succeeds, it *may* be easier for the producer to raise another $5 million for the next picture.

The business of raising such large sums of money is largely one of contacts, finding them, using them, holding them. It is a people business. A second characteristic is that the product is ephemeral, always beginning with someone's idea and ending with the public's whims, on which the critical and financial success of the venture depends utterly.

Even given its subjective beginnings and endings, the

financial connective tissue in between makes it a business and the people treat it as such. There are only moments of creativity along the way. "Over all, I can think of no economically sane way to reform the business," said one producer. "It functions the way it functions because of the way things are, the way human nature is, the way the audience is, the way things are structured in this country. Reality has a certain momentum. A good producer, a good artist, manages to change some things for a period of time, at great expense of energy, intelligence and feeling. That's all."

THE PICTURE AS PIE

Financing a feature film today is like cutting up pieces of the pie and selling off the wedges. For instance, to get enough money to finance the picture, an independent producer might presell the U.S. television rights to a network, sell another wedge to one or more foreign distributors for advance money, sell off the novelization rights and the merchandising rights (if it appeared the film might generate T-shirts or toys), then auction off the music rights to a recording company. Having distributed those wedges, each for a price, the producer now has some leverage with a bank for the remaining budget amount (if the entire film's budget has not already been financed). Of course there are other wedges and combinations, but the idea here is that when the filmmaker sees the picture as "a bundle of rights," not a single entity the picture's budget (or more) can be raised in the United States and abroad before a foot of film is shot. Many of these financing methods can be transferred to 16mm films, and some, like the negative pickup are almost identical to financing nonfiction films through an educational distributor.

There is no one way to raise substantial sums of money for a film. Some low-budget or first features begin with a $10,000 American Film Institute grant and progress to additional grants, from, for example, the National Endowment of the Arts or a State Arts Council. Remaining negative costs can then be raised by a well-connected partner or attorney who brings in investors.

Limited Partnership

A limited partnership is a private offering to a limited number of people whose investment role is passive, e.g., they may invest money but they may not be involved in the creation of the film itself. In this method of financing, the limited partners invest a given amount of money in a film and the amounts each is required to invest may vary from as little as $5,000 to as much as $100,000. The collective sum raised provides the budget for the motion picture. In return, the investors may receive a tax deferral for the amount each has invested. If the picture makes back its negative costs, investors are repaid their investment; if the film is a whopping success the investors may receive a profit on the investment (usually split 50/50 between investors and the producer). In the case of a complete failure, the investors get a loss write-off against their ordinary income.

Since the producer is, in essence, selling shares or securities, structuring a limited partnership agreement should be done with the advice of a good attorney knowledgeable in entertainment law. Producers cannot simply rush out and beat the bracken looking for investors; it is a felony to raise money under the wrong circumstances. The Securities and Exchange Commission governs the manner of the offering and the number of investors who can form a limited partnership. Besides the SEC, all fifty states have varying laws that apply to investment offerings. For instance, in New York a producer may approach any person deemed "sophisticated" for investment purposes, but the producer must disclose everything about the risk of the investment. The total number of people who may ultimately be allowed to invest, however, is 35. In California, a producer may only approach 25 people and accept 10 into the partnership.

Making offerings for investment can be a long, arduous and expensive proposition. To make the process somewhat simpler, the SEC has listed certain exemptions which are frequently used by film producers:

- Rule 146: by filing a short document similar to a prospectus or an outline about the nature of the offering, the producer is allowed to contact any number of people to make the offering and from that group sell to the 35 final investors. Such offerings may include both the production and the distribution cost of the film.
- Rule 147 is an exemption for offerings filed wholly within one state.
- Rule 240, filed with the SEC, allows a producer to search for seed money up to $100,000.

It is as important to know for whom the presentation package of an offering will be made as it is to know to which audience the picture will be directed. Presentation packages to investors should be aimed, according to interests and concerns of the potential investors, and should include: biographies of the principals concerned, a treatment (or script or both), and a synopsis of the story, marketing study and distribution plans, pre-sale plans, income forecasts, what it is about the picture that may make it a success, helpful graphs and charts, and other films like the picture and their histories.

One producer whose production company uses limited partnership financing (under Rule 146) to the exclusion of other methods, said: "The packages are drafted by reputable attorneys and sold through financial broker-dealers with a private placement memorandum (usually twice as long as the script). My partner coordinates all of this. In the future, we envision putting larger investment packages together, allowing us to raise money for more than one film at a time. This spreads the risk and compacts the process of selling. We sell the packages for profit motives to investors—not tax shelters. We plan to be in the business a long long time."

Why do people invest in films? For the same reason they may speculate in oil or a gold mine: for money—the big hit. Most film investors can afford to lose $25,000 or whatever the price of admission may be. Some people wish to diversify their investments; only a few want to see a particular property turned into a film. Some like the challenge of a tremendous risk, having made fortunes in other businesses. And last, but no less important, it is simply more glamorous to invest in a film than a herd of steers.

When they could not get major network financing for a TV series pilot, one small production company created a limited partnership corporation just to produce the pilot. They raised their budget amount with ten investors and then optioned the pilot to a TV syndicator. The problem with limited partnerships is that no major distributor or syndicator has money invested in the film since the money has all come from independent sources. Without that financial incentive or goad, the distributor or syndicator is not as likely to sell the film aggressively and make the money back. Despite this drawback in the process, limited partnerships remain a popular and energetic method of raising independent money for films.

Tax Deferrals

Before Congress restricted the use of tax shelters in 1976, the limited partnership method of financing films was in high gear and the loopholes in the tax shelter laws were very enticing to investors. The limited partners in a motion picture pooled, let us say, $25,000 each in the venture. On the basis of this pool, the partnership could then borrow two or four times as much, so that, in effect, each partner had "leveraged" (or raised) his or her initial investment by a two (or four-)-to-one margin. Wonderfully, loans granted for these purposes were "non-recourse": no one partner was solely responsible for the repayment of the loan. In effect, the lender was "without recourse" and had to recoup the loan from the film's proceeds, the gross film rentals. The loan came due only if the picture was a hit. Moreover, the loan inflated the amount each investor could legally deduct from taxes. If a loss occurred (as it does in nine films out of ten), each partner in such an arrangement could deduct his or her inflated share of the loss from other income. In essence, the old tax shelter laws provided an All-American Subsidy for film production by using (and sheltering) the money of the rich.

Many films, including *Shampoo* and *Taxi Driver*, were financed under the pre-1976 tax shelter laws. In some cases each unit of investment cost $150,000, which brought more than $400,000 in tax deferrals to the investor.

The new tax law plugged the best of the loopholes and blew away the inflated shelters. Congress was deaf to the prolonged pleas of the industry that shelters in effect substituted for a lack of U.S. government subsidy for motion pictures, which most other countries enjoyed.

The investor's deduction is now limited to the "cash at risk"; the investor cannot use borrowed monies for leverage, as so many did before. Deductions, moreover, are spread over the life of the picture (which may be 5–10 years) not just the first year or so of production. The cash at risk, under the new law, is not sheltered as much as it is deferred from being taxed as income for a period of time. Whether the picture makes or loses money, the investor "wins" because in the case of a loss some income has been deferred from taxation. Also, investors may take an Investment Tax Credit (ITC) which amounts to 6-$2/3$rds percent against income. But the windfall days of big shelters are gone.

The big shelter investments in American motion pictures are now coming from abroad—mainly from Germany. However, this source of financing is not a recommended route for independent producers without lots of development money and a good German connection, for the entire package (script, stars, director and distribution) must be put together in advance, and must have German approval before private investors will get in.

In the United States, a scramble has ensued to find alternate ways to finance films. The next one developed as a direct result of the tax law change.

Small Business Investment Corporations

When the Congress shut off the tax shelter tap to a trickle in 1976, the movie business lamented loudly that movies were doomed. No one would invest any money in a movie if they could only get a deferral for the cash invested—that is, a one-to-one ratio. They also accused the United States of being derelict by not financially assisting this expensive form of entertainment and communication.

Foreign subsidies are available in most nations that produce films. Some nations offer direct grants through national film funds or from the general treasury (as in Mexico, Japan, Norway, Switzerland, South Africa, Canada, Italy). Such funds are financed either from "entertainment taxes" or a levy on movie tickets (France, West Germany, Sweden, Israel, Britain, Spain). In Germany, for instance a nation that heavily subsidizes the arts, cinema owners are required to return 6¢ of the price of every ticket sold to the Film Assistance Institute, one of the three government agencies which subsidize filmmakers. Other nations, such as France, have a system of aid based on box office receipts, which amounts to post-production grants as well as grants to producers by a commission in advance of production. In Italy, some assistance is available to producers whose proposed films satisfy certain standards, and also lump sums are awarded on the size of box office grosses, as in France.[3]

The questions independent producers (large and small) have asked the U.S. government is, why don't we subsidize films, too? Until recently, the Small Business Administration (SBA) has replied that they could not underwrite a business loan to produce educational or documentary films because there was no guarantee the producer would not end up in the profitable pornography business, an endeavor the government did not wish to support, or, at the other end of the spectrum, the Small Business Administration was prevented from underwriting film production by the First Amendment to the U.S. Constitution: the government could not place itself in the position of influencing freedom of speech by funding it.

Though the First Amendment has not changed, the SBA's interpretation of it apparently has. The SBA is now experimenting with a pilot program to finance films through intermediaries—Small Business Investment Corporations (SBICs)—that will, for a share of the profits, siphon SBA money to producers. The amount of the SBA's involvement may reach $90 million in three years, but the money has a matching requirement: for every dollar the SBIC invests, the government will match it with two more.

SBICs are corporations with investors who own shares in the SBIC and have collectively put up $10 or $15 million so that the corporation can attract $20 or $30 million from the government. The notion is to encourage private wealth to make money accessible to the production of films. SBICs are similar to banks, yet they function as an alternative. Though there have been hundreds of SBICs for other sorts of enterprises, this is the first time SBIC financing is available for films. There are six SBICs now in operation that are licensed to fund motion picture investments. One corporation of the six is MSBIC created to produce films that are 51 percent (or more) minority owned.

SBICs work the same way networks or studios operate: the producer approaches them with a concept, script or treatment. Each SBIC has its own set of criteria regarding the kinds of pictures it wishes to make.

SBICs cannot put up more than 50 percent of the budget of any one picture and they cannot put up more than 20 percent of its SBIC capital in one film, so their loans—for that is what they are—will not supply the total budget amount in most cases.

Producers seeking SBIC loans must be United States citizens, as well as all key above-the-line personnel on the film. But the shooting of the picture can take place anywhere in the world.

One of the purposes for SBA involvement in film production appears to be an attempt to balance the unequal position of small production companies vis-à-vis the majors. The concept behind SBIC is to offer independent and minority producers an alternative to the studios that demand total production and distribution control of the pictures they finance.

The still not fully active SBIC operations have come in for some criticism, mainly because, it's asserted, SBIC investors (partners to the government, remember) are "fat cats" who know a good deal when they see one. Reminiscent of studio domination, SBIC's may also retain "certain rights" to the films they fund, such as casting approval, crew, locations, insurance, completion bonds, distribution agreements, and content requirements which are placed on them by SBA: no pornography, politics, or religion. If strictly enforced such films as *Elmer Gantry* and *All the President's Men* would never get SBIC approval.

However, SBIC's have a primary responsibility to be open to ideas from new (and minority) filmmakers, and they may provide—with the government's help—an alternative method of financing films in this country.

Banks

Never to be confused with investors, banks are simply lenders who look on motion pictures in exactly the way they scan requests for machinery loans. Banks want guarantees that the film will be completed, that the money loaned will be returned, plus interest, and that the packager or producer requesting the loan has collateral. Such collateral can take various forms and may be based on the track record of the person requesting the loan; the assignment of distribution contracts on previous pictures or the cash flow already coming in to the producer from previous pictures; the "rights" the producer has sewed up on the present picture, such as contracts for the star, the award-winning director, the best seller on which the film is based, or, more frequently now, contracts of a pre-sale to television or with foreign distributors.

When a producer or producing entity receives a loan, the producer now has a partner whose only concern is getting the picture in on time and on budget so that the loan and the substantial interest charges can be recouped. To fulfill both these responsibilities, the producer gambles on her or his judgment that those key people selected will perform as contracted, whether above or below the line. Most banks will not loan any money to mount a film since they consider the entire venture too risky. The few who do will only loan to producers who have a substantial and successful track record. But in those cases, it is often the bank that forms the link between a pre-sale contract and the total budget amount that the producer needs.

Television: Pre-Sales and Development Deals

There are two ways to sell to television: one is to get network financing in advance of a picture's production and prior to theatrical release _(pre-sale)_, and the second is to get a _development deal_ with a network for a film or a pilot primarily for television consumption.

Pre-Sales: Networks want those pictures that thematically match or complement their "air" or that promise to be blockbusters in the theaters which will attract a large TV audience.

Since pre-sales can climb into the millions of dollars for a single film, the successful negotiation of a pre-sale contract to network television indicates an excellent chance of repaying a bank or investors. A producer may take the script, and the star's and/or director's contracts to a network to negotiate a pre-sale of U.S. television rights for, say, $4 million. Depending on the strength of the package, the producer can get ten percent down or the total license fee in advance. In this case, let's say that ten percent or $400,000 is supplied on the signing of the contract, the balance when the film is finished and after it has aired. Banks have a hearty respect for a pre-sale-to-television contract, and it is possible for rarified echelons of producers to get a loan for up to $3.5 million on a $4 million TV pre-sale.

Development deals for television movies or programs (e.g., not for theatrical release) vary widely. The networks have slush funds of millions of dollars to spend on development. Hundreds of scripts or ideas are submitted to them every year; 50 to 60 scripts are developed, and 20 pilots made for only two or three open spots on the air.

Networks do not usually entertain program ideas from unknowns. When conceiving an idea for a Movie of the Week, or a TV series, it is far better to go to one of the established television producers. If they like the concept, they will package it, and with their leverage at the network, present it. But the creator of the idea should retain ownership of the material. What the networks, including PBS, and the large independent producers who supply the nets with programming wring their wrists about is the amount of material submitted to them that has no reference to anything currently on TV. Any writer or producer wishing to submit ideas for Movies of the Week, or for series would be well advised to analyze their concepts to see if they relate in some way to the "tone" or the "style" of current programming. Networks feel they know what the television audience wishes to see and, like hothouse flowers, the stories they buy for development are carefully selected and nurtured.

If a network likes a concept (which, in most cases, should have national appeal), the network will advance development money for the preparation of a script to the producer who submitted it. This money is usually doled out in thirds: first draft, second draft and final. When the script is approved, the producer seeks film commitment money, which again comes in thirds.

Unlike seeking financing from other sources or from TV pre-sales for theatrical films, development deals for television are made on the basis of an idea or a short outline (a presentation) usually accompanied by a strong, lively verbal pitch. Sometimes only the latter is made before anything appears on paper.

The written presentation form to propose a 90-minute Movie of the Week is similar to the treatment outlined in Chapter II, but there really is no set form, though it should contain these elements:

● Describe the premise of the picture clearly and simply

● Describe the leading characters and how they interrelate

• Describe the settings and locations: what they look like, where they are

• Outline the story of the film that the characters are entangled in (or stories, if a series)

• If possible, describe the production plan: if it will all be made on a studio lot, or shot in Alabama, say so.

Some producers feel that the increase in the amounts of pre-sales is emerging as a protection to independent producers. But fewer and fewer television programs are made, the product flow into syndication—TV's form of self-distribution—decreases. Therefore, the big syndicators like Viacom will need more programs and films, and they may begin financing that material themselves. That sort of money from the syndicators is called "back-end" money; promises or contracts of back end financing from a syndicator can assist producers with the negotiations of front end money—the license negotiations with the networks. Of course, for some producers it is possible to make a low budget TV movie solely on the license fee from the network, but the advent of back end syndication money is beginning to play a significant role that may increase.

The TV rights of theatrical films represent a distributor's insurance against a box office flop, therefore the distributor almost never gives up the television rights to a film. If a pre-sale to television has already been made by the producer, the distributor may not wish to distribute the picture, for the money from the TV pre-sale has already been spent on the negative costs and will provide no insurance whatever if the picture dies. Then again, if the picture turns out to be successful, and the pre-sale rights have already been negotiated the distributor cannot negotiate a higher license fee from the network. So, like life, pre-sale of the TV rights has its good side and its bad.

At this point, the producer has $3.5 million from a bank, having pre-sold the television rights for $400,000. The film's budget is $8 million. Now the producer looks abroad.

Foreign Distribution Sales/Foreign Financing

Selling off foreign rights is a rapidly increasing method of financing a film whether it is to be financed by bank loans or by investors. Money may be raised from foreign distributors by selling off the distribution rights territory by territory on the basis of a country's percentage of the world market (3 percent of the world market equals 3 percent of the budget, which becomes the distributor's price for participation); or, the foreign distribution rights for the world may be sold to a single large distributor for a much more substantial price.

A portion (up to half) of the production budget, or the below-the-line costs for a picture can also be raised by tapping into foreign subsidies or foreign tax shelter investors, usually by shooting all or part of the picture in the country supplying the money. Private investment firms in Germany are now large and regular investors in U.S. films. Banks and/or investment groups looking for shelters often have large sums of "blocked" money that can only be invested if the production work is performed in that foreign country.

Some nations, such as Australia, are deliberately structuring their tax laws to entice American film production. Australia's new tax law will reduce the amortization* period from 25 years to 2 years. The ratio of investment write-off remains one-to-one. The Australian Film Commission partners up to 50 percent of the negative cost on films that it feels will appeal to Australian audiences.

Let us say that the producer raises $2 million in Australian tax shelter investment money. She or he now turns around and sells off the foreign distribution rights, getting a letter of credit that stipulates the distributor will pay $2 million for all foreign distribution rights upon delivery of the picture. In the same way the producer used the TV pre-sale

---

*The span of time during which investment can be written off against income taxes.

contract, the producer can now use the distributor's letter of credit as collateral for a loan.

Such letters of credit from, say, a foreign distributor's bank to the producer's bank (or from the studio's bank if financing has been supplied by that route) amount to an inter-bank exchange, indicating that in the ledger in the sky the producer has achieved $8 million to make a movie.

Financing a film today is almost like an auction— especially so with the sale of the worldwide distribution rights. The film _Meteor_ was auctioned off on the basis of a brochure, a story synopsis, and contracts, and sealed with handshakes at Cannes in 1975. The wedges of the pie went to Nippon Herald ($1.5 million for the Japanese distribution rights), Stockholm Film ($300,000 exclusive Scandinavian rights), NAZ Film, an Iranian distributor, for $87,500. Run Run Shaw got exclusive South East Asian rights for his contribution to pre-production costs, to which was later added $2.7 million for a 20 percent interest in the profits. U.S. and Canadian rights went to American International Pictures for $2.7 million. Warner Brothers got the rest of the world for $4 million. Except for $25,000 from NAZ, no other money changed hands.[4]

Pre-sales can also be made to foreign publishers, TV and recording companies. But piecemealing a film's rights all over the globe is not done in an afternoon on the telephone: it takes months, and sometimes a couple of years. It can be nervewracking and exhausting and it always requires capital to sustain the effort. It also requires credibility between the seller and the buyer: the latter must be confident the former will do what is promised. If all goes well, however, the producer is welcomed back to the bank and can now use the first picture as collateral for a second one, proving the old Hollywood adage: "Major money for a film is advanced for those films which have profit potential. A film has profit potential if it is made by and with people whose _last_ film made a profit."

Ancillary Rights

The age of the independent producer can most clearly be

seen against the emerging importance of a picture's ancillary rights. Once producers regard their picture not as a single entity but as a pie whose pieces as pieces are worth money, it will be immediately apparent that, besides those mentioned, a picture has other attributes that can be sold off: novelization rights of the script (to be published simultaneously with the picture's release, the book's cover identical to the film's one-sheet), or the marketing of zap guns, posters, towels, T-shirts, plus the TV syndication rights or sale to pay TV.

These and other pieces of the pie are called the ancillary rights, and may include the licensing of the music rights to a recording company to produce an album of the sound track (rights which can be sold up front to help finance the film). Most major studios now have their own LP labels, for sound track albums of recent film releases are equaling or surpassing the gross of the films from which they sprang. The *Saturday Night Fever* sound track sold some $285 millions' worth of records world-wide by July of 1978. But by the same date, according to the distributor, Paramount, the film's gross was only $110 million. Obviously, such profits can only be reaped if the music appeals to a wide popular market, those who normally purchase LP's.

Novelization rights to films are proving to be more and more lucrative, and the producer should not sign them away to the distributor if it is possible to retain them, but retention of these (or other ancillary rights) by the producer may impinge upon the quality of the distribution deal. Distributors argue that if they retain all ancillary rights each can be co-ordinated with the others to help make the film more successful financially, and to insure that those people with the expertise in marketing—the distributors, of course—are the people in charge of the total campaign. Behind this argument is the distributor's wish to cushion the fall of a film dud: if the box office is miserable, the distributor wants control of TV rights and syndication and other rights to make up for the debt incurred during the theatrical distribution fiasco.

It is a powerful argument, but the distributors do not need the entire pie. It is essential that the producer work closely with the distributor whose expertise is invaluable in the marketing and coordination of the ancillary rights, for there is no question that films suffer from chaotic or haphazard scheduling of the ancillary rights.

Pay TV, whether over-the-air or cable is emerging as a promising domestic outlet for films and as a potential producer. Low-budget feature filmmakers should not ignore this market, even though it is still limited. A sale of a film to Pay TV runs between $100,000 and $300,000. Pay TV may buy films directly from the producer, but more usually from newly formed programing firms that create, acquire and distribute pay TV fare. Time, Inc., for example, owns the largest of these, Home Box Office, whose subsidiary, Tele-mation Program Services, supplies pay TV programing to most of this nation's subscribers. 20th-Century-Fox and United Artists own Hollywood Home Theater; and Viacom, Inc., owns Showtime, to name just a few.

The robust promise of cable and pay TV is that films and programing will be aired at smaller, more specific audiences. Therefore the independent filmmaker, whose film about an old woman and her dog, which would have slight chance of being distributed theatrically, may have a much better chance to earn back part of its negative costs on cable.

Cable is beginning to produce its own product, a field of activity that may open up opportunities to those filmmakers who do not have the credentials to work on studio features or at the networks. In effect, electronics and satellites are producing a potentially powerful fifth network or produc-tion/exhibition house.[5]

Studio Financing and Negative Pick-Ups

Studios are also connected to banks by an umbilical cord called the line of credit, which is that annual amount a studio may borrow from a bank—usually many millions at a preferred rate of interest. Credit may be secured by the studio's product line or cross-collateralized by its various pictures. The success of the pictures for one year can determine a studio's cash flow for the next year.

A negative pick-up is a standard financing agreement between an independent producer and a studio. The studio guarantees the negative cost of the picture, payable on delivery of a "reasonable facsimile" of the script when the film is finished. Usually the sum is an advance to the filmmaker against a percentage of net or gross on the box office receipts. In return, the studio picks up most major distribution rights to the film. In a sense, the studio is performing the function of a bank. On the basis of the negative pick-up contract, the producer may borrow against it at a bank, using the contract with the studio as collateral for a loan to finance the picture. Or, the producer may also raise independent money, since a negative pick-up contract has a salutory effect on investors, guaranteeing either distribution, negative cost reimbursement on delivery, or both.

Negative pick-ups can become extremely complicated. The major dispute that can arise circles around how closely the finished film resembles the original script. The producer's agreement is to deliver a film based on a script, usually with certain stars and a certain director, which the distributor approves. But changes always occur during the shooting or editing of any film. Too many deviations from the approved script may cause the distributor to reject the finished film. Therefore, the contract between the producer and the distributor should clearly spell out the concept, the expected technical quality, and the film's content. If the film's concept is amorphous or subjective, the producer runs the risk of not having the finished film approved.

So the negotiation of a negative pick-up contract should be approached with care and with the professional assistance of a good entertainment attorney. Also the same lines of communication described between client and producer (Chapters 3 and 7) in the nonfiction field, with at least informal stages of approval, are worth keeping in mind here.

In negative pickups, producers often receive "a piece of

the action"—profit participation. The best piece is a percentage of the gross film rentals which distributors receive from exhibitors because, combatants report, it is harder to "play with" this figure, compared to the net figure. Besides, it is bigger. In the game of subtractions from the gross to determine the net, a percentage of the gross is usually better.

But most people do not get a percentage of the rentals' gross or participation in ancillary rights. Most people are "net players" who share in a piece of the profit _after_ costs, not in the gross film rental income. An array of costs and fees above the break-even point may be attributed to the picture: the negative cost, 30 percent distribution fee, 25 percent overhead charge, interest on loans, legal fees, prints (charged at retail though bought at discount), foreign taxes, all advertising, and promotion. These are the costs that have created the formula that a picture must make back 2.5 to four times its negative costs just to break even.

The exorbitant rise in costs gnaws at the core of producing and filming in Hollywood. Negative costs rose 178 percent in the four years from 1975 to 1979—the average cost of a major picture in 1979 is $5.3 million. The stars and the unions are normally blamed for the rise, yet it's hard to point at greedy crews when their salaries are compared to the staggering stars' fees: Reynolds and Nicholson get $2 million up front; Brando, Redford, McQueen, and Newman get between $2 and $4 million. That's not all: they also expect and receive sizable perks plus location expenses of up to $2,500 a week. The truth is that money is simply squandered on the production and distribution of major motion pictures made in this country. The more expensive it is to make and distribute a picture, the longer it will take to reach the break-even point, and profit—on which net participation is hinged—is determined only after the break-even point has been reached.

Therefore, the major disadvantage, aside from the studio rejecting the finished film because it is not up to "technical standard," is that the producer is usually in a "net net" position with no influence over the studio's release of the picture, and at the mercy of high distribution fees and charges. Therefore, as a hedge against the film becoming a big box office hit, a producer should build into the contract increased percentages of the profit if the film's income exceeds certain levels.

If the studio's facilities are to be used, a $2 million dollar picture may cost $3 million. The producer must become a signator to the unions, shooting at union scale rates; studio sets are charged at very high rates; the studios also charge for legal, accounting, and administration costs (all usually accumulated in a percentage of the overall budget).

The latter costs are analogous to the percentages charged by the nonprofit museum or university that serves as the filmmaker's pipeline to the foundation, receiving indirect costs over and above the film's budget.

In negative pick-ups particularly, but in other forms of financing as well, the studio's concern is to keep the film from going over budget. If a producer can guarantee completion of the film on budget, he or she stands a much better chance of receiving the needed financing.

A studio, or any group of investors, may require a *completion bond,* which is a kind of insurance that guarantees the studio (or investors) that the film will be completed on time and on budget. The guarantor, a third party, puts money at risk, betting on the producer's ability to bring the picture in as scripted. For that service, the third party charges a percentage of the total budget. The guarantor's risk is that if the film is not completed as contracted for, the guarantor will have to kick in whatever sums are necessary to finish the film. In that event, the guarantor has the license to fire the director, change locations, and adjust any aspect of production to finish the film.

Large investors often require a bond before handing over their money to producers of a picture. A firm or individual in the completion bond business becomes a link between investors and producers, overseeing every expense, no matter how small. Bonds can reach $3 million for high-budget pictures and can cost the producers hundreds of thousands of dollars. The purpose of the bond is to make sure the film comes in on schedule, and it also provides a cushion should the production run over-budget.

The advantages of a negative pickup are that the producer need not piecemeal the film around the world and instead receives all the film's financing from one source. Distribution is almost certain and upon delivery of an acceptable picture to the studio, the producer knows she or he can bail out the investors.

Only a few can finance their films through the studios—the largest production and distribution institutions in this country. The studios say they are looking for new material, and to some extent that is true, but they are really looking for fresh material from experienced agents and producers who they recognize as professional and credible. The amounts of money for a single, middle-range picture today are so huge that few studio executives are likely to take chances with people they do not know.

To reach anyone at a studio with a script (treatments are not enough) and to get it read takes an agent or a high powered friend with a studio contact. When an agent or attorney submits a script to a studio, the writer does not have to sign a submission agreement because a neutral third party has entered into the submission. Otherwise, the writer will usually be required to sign a submission agreement which gives the studio the rights to the property. (The legal implication is that if the studio or producer makes the film from the submitted script, he or she is liable to the writer for the full value of the subsequent film.) If, after the submission agreement has been signed, the studio decides to produce the picture, in most cases the submission agreement will be ignored and proper payment made to the writer.

Submitting completed films to a studio for distribution is quite a different matter. In these cases, the studios are on the hook only for the distribution costs, not for the negative costs as well. Also, unlike a script presented by an untried or unknown, studios have something concrete to evaluate: a finished film. But here, too, the picture for the newcomer is not rosey for the studio must be simply crazy about the finished film, must instantly perceive its commercial value before sinking $2 to $3 million into the marketing of it. However, there are more cases of studios picking up completed films than reading and buying a script that came in the mail.

Stock Sales and Loans

Individuals who shun, or have no hope of, financing through banks or a studio can raise the negative cost by incorporating for the life of the picture and offering stock or profit participation to friends and/or family. The advantage is that no taxes are owed on the recoupment of an investment *loan*, though such investors may not write the cost off (since it is a loan) as they can in limited partnerships. Such "friendly" investors are less likely to ask for a string of guarantees from the producer than "arm's-length"* investors. The profit repayment schedule to such investment lenders, or stock owners, is a 50/50 split between lenders and producer, after the negative costs have been recouped.

In any case, a producer has only so many ways to inspire investors or lenders to put money in a very risky enterprise: securities (collateral of some sort, such as the film's copyright, or previous distribution contracts, which provide the producer with a certain cash flow, or subordination of all rights of all other creditors until the loan is repaid), profit participation of the gross or net proceeds. But friendly investors, known to the filmmaker, usually are not particularly interested in collateral or profit incentives; they are interested in helping the filmmaker or seeing a particular film made. However, it is tidier and more responsibly professional for the filmmaker to offer profit percentage after recoupment of negative costs.

It is extremely difficult for filmmakers of limited experience to raise money through the major sources described. They must fall back on raising it from independent sources

---

*Investors who are independent of and in no way related to the filmmaker.

or developing less conventional avenues by adapting traditional methods.

The only basic step in the financing of features that has changed since the 1950s is the radical overhaul in the tax laws. Other aspects of financing have become more prominent, such as foreign markets and increased value of the ancillary rights. Other than those, the parade is much the same: a filmmaker has a powerful contact, a pre-sold or original property, or even a star; development money is sought that will permit the writing of a script; the filmmaker or a representative then proceeds to make a production deal from any or several of the sources mentioned, and the film is born. These methods are not significantly different from the financing of a short film except that the choreography is more complicated, and the budget and the risk are higher. But it can be readily seen that the financial worth of a feature film (or feature-length documentary) is estimated by its parts: the U.S. and Canadian markets; the foreign distribution markets, the domestic and foreign television rights; the nontheatrical distribution; and various ancillary rights, which, in a few years, will include lucrative cable TV, video cassette, and videodisc licenses.

NOTES

1. See Chapters 15 and 16 of Tino Balio, *The American Film Industry*, University of Wisconsin Press, 1978, for an excellent summary of this phase of the film business.

2. It is doubtful that anyone knows for sure just how many films are annually produced in the United States, since no one is actually counting all the independents' productions. Some people have estimated that in 1977, 64 percent of all movies made were backed by independent money.

3. From the Motion Picture Association of America.

4. See Jerry Cohen and Ronald L. Soble, "*Meteor*—How A Movie Came to Be," *Los Angeles Times*, July 2-4, 1978.

5. See Chapter 10 for a fuller discussion of pay TV.

Recommended for further reading: Mitch Tuchman has written two excellent articles that relate to areas covered in this chapter: "Post-tax-shelter Hollywood Has a New Mogul: Uncle Sam," *Film Comment*, November 1978 and, "Helter Shelter," *Film Comment*, January/February 1977.

Pauline Kael's essay "On The Future of the Movies" in *Reeling*, New York: Warner Books, 1977.

Janet Weissman, "A Few (Thousand) Select Words on Film Financing," *Action*, published by the Director's Guild of America, March/April 1978.

Donald C. Farber and Paul A. Baumgarten, *Producing, Financing and Distributing Film*, New York: Drama Book Specialists, 1973.

The Director's Guild of America has produced tape cassettes of their Film Financing Forum, April 1978. Inquiries should be addressed to David Stewart, Special Projects, DGA, Los Angeles.

CHAPTER 8

Feature Film Distribution and Exhibition

DISTRIBUTION MAKES THE DIFFERENCE

Just as in the 16mm field, the most important aspects of theatrical distribution are a filmmaker's realistic assessment of the film up for distribution and, on the basis of that, selection of the right distributor. No contract, however fair, can make up for a producer's sloppy analysis of the film and its placement with a distributor who doesn't understand that film or who has no track record marketing that sort of film. One well-known independent producer, with a string of award winning films—features and documentaries—recently complained that his last five pictures were indecently distributed—which they were. But even a casual glance at the pictures shows that in each case the producer displayed no overall sense of the sort of film he'd made: the Academy-award winning, feature-length documentary went to a major studio distributor with a very poor track record for that kind of film and no visible sympathy or understanding of the subject matter (hence little awareness of the target audience); another feature-length documentary with an international potential few pictures enjoy, went to a small, independent U.S. distributor that knew next to nothing about foreign territories. This producer had a talent for placing films with distributors who could not handle them properly.

It is widely agreed that theatrical production and distribution "can be hazardous to your health."[1] But it is least unhealthy for those filmmakers who study the procedures, movement, and design of the distribution-exhibition systems and learn how they work, instead of allowing themselves to be at the mercy of the industrial stratum of this business, which is nowhere more forceful than in the marketing and distribution of films.

When choosing· a distributor for a feature film, filmmakers can apply the same criteria suggested for the 16mm arm of this field: the distributor must be financially solvent, with enough capital to invest in and maintain the marketing of the picture; the contract must be evaluated carefully in terms of percentages, rights leased, net or gross, and so on and, in features, should never be negotiated without an attorney; the distributor must show evidence of solid experience in the business; and, crucially, the distributor must understand and respond to the sort of film being offered.

Most independently produced theatrical films are marketed through the studios, which are wholesalers of pictures, leasing them to subdistributors or to retailers (the theaters) who sell to consumers (the audience). Though from this description, this may look like other businesses, it is not. The difference is that the film has to be completely paid for in advance. If the product were glass jars, the manufacturer might make a few thousand and if they did not sell well, discontinue the effort. But to make a feature film takes millions of dollars, and it must be paid entirely before the single end product—the film—can even be seen.

Moreover, this is one of the few businesses that depends for its cost and profit return on a *lease* of the product. For instance, wholesalers of jars sell 100 to the retailer, collect the payment and, from that amount, pay the maker and their costs. The risk of the sale passes on to the retailer, who must make the wholesale cost back plus profit. But in the feature motion picture business, the "price" is not set and the product is not "sold." Indeed the ultimate "price" depends upon the head count in a number of theaters scattered throughout the world over a period of years. That "price" depends also on the accuracy and honesty of a crowd of intermediaries between producer and audience. It is a curious way to run a business.

THE PRODUCER'S INCOME: A PERCENTAGE OF THE CLOUDS IN THE SKY

Financially, the producer's goal is to recover the negative costs of the film, to make a profit, and, on the basis of that record, to go on to make another film. To ensure a fair return, a producer must know as much as possible about the various permutations of the distribution contract. Though such knowledge will not guarantee the recovery of the negative cost or a profit, it will put the producer closer to that goal.

One of the first questions to arise is this one: is the film-maker better off getting a distribution deal before the first frame of film is shot, or is it better to wait until the picture is in the can? Distribution up front gives the filmmaker the assurance that the picture will be distributed in some fashion. But unless the contract clearly stipulates a certain amount of money will be spent on advertising and prints, and unless the distributor likes the final film, the filmmaker has no guarantee regarding the *quality* of the distribution. If the filmmaker waits until the picture is finished, there is no guarantee anyone will like the picture, let alone distribute it. However, if three distributors love the film and compete for the distribution rights, the filmmaker, having no single distribution contract, is in a much better position to get favorable terms.

There are two major kinds of producer/distributor splits: gross or net. In the first, a 50/50 or 40/60 split is made on the gross rentals with no deductions for prints, advertising, or promotion, all of which come out of the distributor's 60 percent share. Though on the surface this looks better for the producer, a recent study[2] points out that, not surprisingly, this sort of split does not "motivate distributors" to spend as much money on advertising and promotion as when the costs come out of the producer's share. It also appears to provide a less lucrative return to the producer unless the film fails to make back at least two-to-one on the negative costs. However, this split on the gross simplifies the notoriously complex (and, some charge, crooked) bookkeeping and accounting to the producer; with a gross deal, the producer does not have to check the distributor's expenses since they are not deducted from the producer's percentage.

Net deals are much more common. The standard distributor's fee has been 30 percent to 40 percent of gross receipts paid from the exhibitors, plus costs, but in recent years to attract independent product, distributors are taking fees of 25 percent and even less, as well as advancing print and advertising costs, which are later recouped by the distributor over and above the percentage fee. Such deals may also have sliding percentage scales so that if the distributor's fee begins at, say, 25 percent, it may drop in stages to 15 percent after certain gross levels have been reached.

On a net deal, a producer normally begins to receive money on a picture after the cost of the negative has been recouped, after payment of the distributor's fee, and after charges for advertising, promotion, publicity, print costs, legal fees, and any interest due on loans. That is why a producer with a percentage of the net rarely sees any money.

The potential sources of revenue from a film come from its U.S., Canadian, film rentals, and foreign sales and TV and ancillary rights. Therefore, the need to define which rentals or rights will constitute the film rental gross is as crucial here as it is in the nonfiction field. Does the gross include money from the sale to television or foreign distribution, or from novelization and other ancillary rights leased off by the distributor? In other words, which markets' income define the gross? If any markets are excluded from the calculation of the gross percentage to the producer, the producer should not pay for the cost of distribution in those areas. If the deal is net, the producer must know which costs and fees will be deducted from such gross sales to constitute that net.

A producer's gross should be calculated on the film rental gross the distributor receives from the exhibitor, which will eliminate payment of double distribution fees by the producer. Otherwise, there can be an expensive miscalculation by the producer. The payment of double distribution fees may result when the distributor uses a subdistributor. If the term "gross receipts" has not been carefully defined in the contract, it may mean the "gross receipts" received from a subdistributor, who subtracts his or her percentage from the exhibitor's gross receipts, and from that remaining amount, the distributor then subtracts his or her percentage.

Producers' "war stories" accuse the major U.S. distributors of many evils, some exaggerated, some not. The recounts of the rapes should only stand as warnings about the distribution business; they should not serve to persuade independent producers into going into other lines of work.

In their roles as distributors, the studios are charged with promoting those films in which they have a financial interest at the expense of those in which they have smaller or no financial interests. Producers also aim this charge at the networks. Distributors are accused of exorbitantly padding their expense accounts, costs that are deducted from the distributor's gross and therefore shrink the producer's net percentage. Filmmakers have been known to pay for distributors' mistakes: if a producer's film is successful and profitable, distributors may charge the distribution costs of less successful films against the hit.

Depending on the distributor or the contract, filmmakers may have no control over the way the film is to be marketed, the tenor of the ad campaign erected for it, or the terms the distributor negotiates with the exhibitor (exclusive, limited, multi), the kinds of theaters booked, or the time of year the picture is released. The initial box office failure of the now cult classic *Harold and Maude* can be attributed to the studio that had booked a number of theaters during the Christmas holidays in anticipation of releasing *The Godfather*. *The Godfather* wasn't ready. *Harold and Maude* was, and it went into 2,000-seat theaters where it promptly flopped.

There is almost no way for a filmmaker to know if the film has been "block booked"—that is, leased at a lower price to an exhibitor as part of a package of films so the exhibitor will be forced to take weaker films the distributor is having trouble handling. Consequently, when the film is billed with another of the distributor's pictures, the filmmaker will not know if the costs the distributor claims have been charged against the film are true costs. Distributors and exhibitors frequently withhold money owing from the profits of a picture: the exhibitor delays payment to the distributor and the distributor delays disbursements to the producer. Needless to say, no interest is paid on the money held up.

THE DISTRIBUTOR VS. THE EXHIBITOR

The old patterns of theatrical distribution and exhibition started to break up after 1950. The distributors have survived well, but the theaters have been on the downslope ever since. For the filmmaker the handwriting is on the wall: theatrical exhibition alone will not be the hefty source of financial return it once was compared to television, foreign sales, and burgeoning ancillary rights.

Distributors not only function as "designers of the product" but as the merchandisers, creating the "selling strategy," the materials, the budget, the media placement and advertisements, the promotion and publicity methods, the pricing terms. But distributors are fond of reminding producers that they (distributors) are not in control of their own destinies, since they are prohibited by law from franchising or having partly or wholly owned subsidiaries at the retail (theater) level. They are also prohibited from establishing a retail price; therefore the theater ticket price cannot be based on the cost or quality of the production being offered.

The exhibition of films in the United States is now widely regarded as a seller's market in which the distributors call most of the shots and get the terms that are to their advantage. The reversal of buyer's to seller's market has occurred in less than a decade. The Hollywood studios are simply not producing the same number of pictures they once did.

As far as the majors are concerned, the United States is divided into about 25 geographic centers, with offices linking the studios and their films with the exhibitor in that area, taking out trade ads and creating mailings, marketing strategies, and advertisements—all designed to interest the exhibitor in the film. After this barrage, negotiations for the picture are opened and solicitations sent out concerning the availability of the new film and the distributor's suggested percentages. The exhibitors then "bid" on the picture. All of this takes place long before the picture has been seen by anyone, and none of it is initiated until the distributor creates "a marketing plan" that consists of (1) identifying for exhibitors and themselves just what kind of picture they have on their hands, (2) timing of the release date, and (3) to which kinds of theaters it should be released.

Identifying a picture involves a fairly simplistic labeling process: is it an art film, a mystery, a thriller, an adventure, a Western, a children's picture? The release date concerns the time of the year: for instance, Christmas and Easter are good times since people attend a lot of movies around the holidays.

There are three possible theatrical release patterns: the *exclusive engagement*, used when the distributor feels that the product is risky (a new director or an art film). This pattern relies on good word of mouth and usually calls for a low advertising budget. If the picture proves successful in the one house chosen for it, it may be distributed more widely. If not, it will die there.

Exclusive runs in a geographical area used to guarantee theaters a certain protection and an edge over the competition. But in a seller's market, where the costs of advertising have skyrocketed, exclusive offerings from the sellers (distributors) have drastically decreased in order to amortize the advertising dollar: it costs the same to advertise a picture playing in one theater as it does in 20, but a multiple release obviously increases the profit.

A *limited engagement* seeks different focal points in the market. While this pattern does not overextend the picture, it assures filling the small number of houses chosen for it so a profit can be made.

A *wide, multiple-saturation release*, the third market strategy, is for well-known films, re-released or repeat films, or films the distributor knows are no good. The last instance calls for blitzkreig ads to entice the crowds of people into the theater before the bad word of mouth gets around.

Another factor in theater decay is the profit split between distributor and exhibitor: it used to be 40/60, or some split similar to that, but it is now 90/10, the 90 percent going to the distributor. The active distrust distributors and exhibitors have of each other is industry legend and quite unlike most close and necessary arrangements between wholesaler and retailer in other businesses. Part of the antagonism stems from the fact that the distributor and the producer are dependent upon a portion of the cash box office receipts to get their own costs back as well as a hopeful profit. Under those conditions, the honesty of the house count becomes a prime issue. Exhibitors are accused of all sorts of finagling, from upping the cost of the house nut (a stated theater overhead figure that is the first cost to be deducted from the box office gross) to "palming" and "bicycling" to faking invoices for advertising.

The ticket taker "palms" a ticket simply by not tearing it in half. The ticket is resold to a second, even a third patron, and the house makes the unreported difference. Fake billing involves the collusion of a friend who submits phony invoices for advertising never run. Since the distributor often pays a percentage of the advertising, the exhibitor has, by this method, picked up a tidy sum. "Bicycling" is moving a print leased for one theater over to another (usually a neighborhood or drive-in) owned by the same exhibitor, where it plays for the sole profit of the exhibitor.

"In the distributing companies I was involved with," said one worker, "there was no theft, per se, from the producer. We would load the expenses a little bit—especially if we had a winner—like every single phone call, every bit of time, nickels and dimes. But, it's common to send phony reports to the producers until they finally send an auditor in. Where distributors get the producers is in the expenses; they can drive you crazy with that. As far as exhibitors' stealing—that goes on all the time, unless you're dealing with a major chain, and then you're still being stolen from, but his cashiers are stealing from him! With the smaller independents [theaters], it's the old story of being at the wrong place at the wrong time. For instance, if the exhibitor has an IRS bill that he's got to pay—where does he get it?—outta the box office—where else?" Essentially, the theft is from the producer: the less the distributor makes, the less the producer will eventually regain.

The inventiveness of exhibitors in retaining as much of the gross as possible is legendary. One drive-in exhibitor charged the distributor a rental fee for each sound box and deducted the costs from the gross owed. As a hedge against what they are sure will be fraudulent box office reports, some independent distributors rent the print for a set fee to small theaters: "Many times we ship a print C.O.D. for the rental charge," said one small production and distribution organization. "It's the only way you can survive the theft. It's more prevalent where there's a lot of Mom and Pop operations which are left over from the days when anybody who had a field had a drive-in. They'll show any junk they can get their hands on and the only way to get payment out of them is to send the print C.O.D. One guy, who paid $100 for a three-day date thought he was buying the print! When he finished the showing, he'd throw it in a storeroom. We finally discovered he had 150 prints in there! Another time we sent a print for $500 C.O.D. and after weeks, the print was returned to us for $1,000 C.O.D.!"

The issue that sows so much distrust is that no one—not even the theater owners—ever know what the box office gross really is. The producer never knows whether all the distributor's costs registered against the gross are true, any more than the distributor knows if the house nut, deducted by the exhibitor from the box office gross, is true or inflated, or whether the stated weekly gross is true or half of what was actually taken in.

Distributors have sued exhibitors for underreporting box office receipts; recently, a well-publicized case was brought by a Texas theater chain, L.C.L., against ten major distributors.[3] It was the first real court test of the distributors' practice known as box office checking, the hiring of a firm to check on the box office receipts so the distributor has some objective idea of what is being taken in. The court upheld the distributor's right to retain a checking firm on percentage engagements. The L.C.L. theaters were found guilty, in a countersuit, of underreporting the box office receipts.

Distributors reason that obtaining advances or guarantees from the exhibitor is the only protection against dishonest counts. But more and more frequently, distributors' solicitations for bids from exhibitors do not require a set amount of front money, leaving exhibitors free to bid the amount and terms they feel will win the contract. The small independents, however, must compete with such giants as General Cinema, which owned 791 theaters in the United States at last count. The amounts such outfits can afford to bid in guarantees and advances cannot possibly be matched by small independent exhibitors.

However, the size of the bid does not always count, as the owner of a 500-seat theater discovered when he bid $20,000 for *Julia*. A bid means the theater owner will guarantee that the studio (distributor) will receive the amount of the bid from the receipts. This theater owner also offered an advance of an additional $10,000. The picture ended up going to a theater owned by a chain that not only bid less but had a much smaller house.[4]

The uproar over blind bidding (not to be confused with block-booking) has created the widest schism between distributors and exhibitors, who are now gearing up for national anti-blind-bidding legislation. Five states have already enacted such laws (Ohio, Alabama, Louisiana, South Carolina, and Virginia). Ohio has also outlawed advances and guarantees.

In blind bidding, exhibitors must bid on a film six months to a year before the film is released—therefore long before anyone can see it to judge quality or sales potential. In place of the film the exhibitors get a letter from the distributors which solicits bids describing the film's stars and director and states the minimum playing time for the film (a run of 10-12 weeks is typical) and a suggested distributor's percentage, usually the 90-10 split.

The studio distributors defend the practice as a way to control the exhibitor since the distributor cannot set a price. It is believed that advances or guarantees of, say, $100,000 for a picture encourage the exhibitor to protect that investment by promoting the film with additional publicity that would not occur if the exhibitor had no money at risk in it. They also point out the short time between finished film and release date. To let a film lie around on the shelf for six months while bookings and screenings are set up for bids would cost astronomical amounts in interest alone.[5] Requiring a guarantee on a film exhibitors have never seen does not make for sound business judgments, in the opinion of the National Association of Theater Owners (NATO), which has pointed out that no one has to pay for a meal in a restaurant before being allowed to look at the menu or eat the meal.

Since distributors demand terms that call for their right to have either a straight cut or a percentage—whichever is greater—the exhibitors say they have been forced to fall back on their popcorn. The concession stand *is* a money maker, and exhibitors have retaliated against excessive distributor demands by cutting the price of the ticket so that patrons will spend more money on candy—a source of income not shared with grasping distributors.

"The three- and four-theater complexes that have replaced the old Goliaths have produced a new level of thievery which is probably beyond comprehension," says one Hollywood executive. "What most of those operations do is pool the receipts so that you never know what the count is for any specific film. They have *Jaws* in one theater, *Dance Gorilla Dance* in another, *Julia* in a third, and suddenly—one's light and one's heavy. The skimming is notorious. Distributors who do not have direct access to the cash get theirs in other ways—usurious loan charges, blind bidding, guarantees, and overblown advertising and publicity expenses."

A newer development is filmmaker financing (for example, George Lukas's financing of *Star Wars II*) and selection of independent distribution companies instead of the majors. Added to that development is expanding foreign investment —"especially from Arabs," says one observer. "We may see more stringent and more organized accounting systems; hence the business may have to become a little more legitimate. But there's still going to be the exhibitor who, if he has a $10,000 night, can report $9,000. However, this goes on everywhere—restaurants sell 50 dinners and report that they only sold 40. Supermarkets sell 1,000 cases of peaches and somewhere along the line it's only 900."

One Hollywood film investor said, "As a part of the future of distribution, the day may come when heat-sensitive cameras will be installed in every theater to measure the number of bodies in the house in segments of 12 minutes at a time. A factor will be arrived at so that at the end of any given day, a distributor (and producer) will know to a tenth of one percent how many tickets were sold in any particular theater. Should this come about—the hardware is available for it right now—the icing techniques that start at the box office would cease. Too many theater owners rip off the subs and the subs rip off the distributors and the distributors rip off the producers. It's a matter of common knowledge that a great many distributors keep two or three sets of books that eventually withhold millions of dollars from the rightful owners—the producers and backers."

FROM EXPLOITATION TO MARKETING

"When I entered the industry in the late 1950s," said one advertising executive, "people were presidents of advertising, publicity and exploitation, and there was a certain basic honesty about calling it 'exploitation'." Exploitation covered a variety of activities: putting signs on street corners late at night, or loading a leopard on a flat bed truck and taking it around to advertise a jungle movie. "Now we call that promotion, and it's become a big business in the motion picture industry. All three—advertising, publicity, and promotion, thanks to Madison Avenue and the research firms—fall under the term 'marketing'. So now *we* have Vice Presidents of Marketing just like the big guys at J.C. Penney's and U.S. Steel." Now in marketing meetings one rarely hears the words "film" or "audience"—it's product and consumer, integration of tools and function, interaction of the marketing process, components, profiles, design of product.

Before the advent of monster marketing, advertising and

promotion were not considered very important for producers to know. As one advertising executive said, "When a producer finished a musical, he looked at the poster and said, 'Hey, looks nice,' and went on to the next movie because the studio *owned* half of the theaters in the country and the musical went right into those theaters, and then it went off to play in the theatrical holdings overseas. So the producer didn't have to promote the picture—all he had to do was create the product." But, following the Paramount Decree, when the studios were divested of their theaters, marketing expenditures increased explosively "to get people into the tent." Now, the producer has not only to create the film but to create it with an eye on participation in the eventual marketing.

In fact, this busines is only just learning how to market its films, and the wheels that turn in the movie world haven't caught up with the titles. Integration of the advertising, promotion, publicity, and research functions has moved the marketing of a picture from a secondary to a dominant function. The product, however, remains unique because marketers are selling "motion and images, the residue of which is only memory, unlike hairspray."[6]

Advertising

About $500 million was spent to advertise pictures in one recent year in the United States and Canada. Most of this money was spent in newspapers—which is odd when the marketers admit that most people who go to movies do not read newspapers any more; they watch television and listen to radio. Of a total advertising budget 5-10 percent is spent on radio, a smaller percentage on magazines, and the rest goes to television (after newspaper expenditures). Some producers are even working in reverse, coming up with an advertising campaign first, then developing a film idea for production.

Publicity

As in weaving a fabric, each strand must have a relationship to the whole and add to the total effect or pattern, so as a marketing ingredient, publicity must be entwined with advertising and not go marching off by itself. Publicity is defined as directing public attention to a movie at a certain time or in a certain space. The goal here is to create a continuous program of "news" information from the time a film property is acquired to the premiere. It is also a form of brainwashing or preconditioning, so that when the picture is finally released, the consumer feels familiar with it, yet curious and tempted. Publicity is not paid for in the same way an ad is bought. The cost lies in flying the nation's press to see a screening of the film and enjoy a party so they can write about it and interview the stars. In short, publicize it. It is the unit publicist's job to keep this river of news, interviews, and behind-the-scenes notes flowing.

Promotion

Promotion is the final act in the marketing drama and is often a stunt of some sort, calling attention to the movie without the aid of the press, TV, or radio. It is the parade led by an elephant, or the large white rabbit in the department store window. It has developed into the sale of the novelization rights whose cover imitates the film's ads. Promotion may include all the merchandising of such items as shower curtains or T-shirts or records of the sound track. Originally created to promote the film, these items in some cases become a bigger income producer than the motion picture.[7]

Market Research

Market research, the last of the four marketing elements, and the newest, may well prove to be the most powerful. Research is supposed to evaluate public reaction to potential advertising designs *before* millions are spent. The 1978 box office gross in the United States and Canada was $2.7 billion. One-fifth of that—half a billion dollars—was spent to get the $2.7 billion. Market research seeks to lower that investment and one way to do that is to find out more about the audience, of which very little is known. The marketing research that develops may very well influence which movies will be made simply on the basis of which movies are deemed "marketable." The fate of the "unmarketable" or "special" film of the future, as far as theatrical release is concerned, has never been so clearly spelled out.

Research is not yet very highly thought of in Hollywood, but its reputation is improving. Hollywood has always believed it knew what the public wanted and that research on the same subject was redundant and inaccurate, but the Westwood section of Los Angeles near the UCLA campus has never infallibly reflected Wisconsin or Utah preferences.

Some of the studios are putting a toe in the waters to test audience preferences in the same way other industries do. And clearly other methods have to be found "to get people into the tent." In 1948, theatrical admissions were four times what they are today. It is estimated that 50 million regular moviegoers are 12-34 years old, single, living in cities or suburbs, have what is called an "upscale" character (slightly richer, better educated, and more mobile than the norm), yet they are not an elite group in society; on the whole they lead active, open, "hip" lives.[8]

Movies are seasonal—for instance, late April is a very poor moviegoing time, late June is good, Christmas and Easter are excellent. People usually go in pairs or in groups; less than 2 percent attend alone. Audiences want convenient, local outlets, since most people will travel only up to four miles and no farther for a movie. Therefore, the location of theaters has real bearing on box office grosses.

But very little is known about why people go to movies. It is "an emotional experience," which may explain why it is called a word-of-mouth business. But research so far indicates that people do not make emotional choices about which movie to see; that decision appears to be a rational one of selecting movie A over movie B.

Keeping in mind that theatrical attendance is down nationwide, it's easy to see why marketing may have a profoundly significant effect: a $10 million picture *must* bring in about $34 million to break even. On an average it costs $2.9 million to launch a picture, about $1.2 million in radio and television, the rest in newsprint. The more money spent on the marketing plan, the more conservative the campaign becomes. The price of a ticket is increasing, but only gradually and hardly at the pace of production/advertising costs. Though the theaters are screaming for "product," when their cry is analyzed, they don't mean just any movie, they want blockbusters.

If theaters formed the only retail outlet, the future would look dim for a diversity of films. But by 2000, it will probably not matter how a picture does in the theaters, once cable and pay TV, videodiscs and cassettes are exhibiting as well as producing, for these technologies will help filmmakers target special audiences—something theatrical releases cannot today.

The major reasons filmmakers should be involved—to the greatest extent possible—in the marketing of their pictures include the following:

- Marketing, in its present form, often lacks imagination and is usually conservative in its approach;
- Marketing, at present, is wasteful and expensive, and thus the fear increases of innovative campaigns;
- Economics have and will continue to determine which pictures are feasible theatrical risks, and which pictures the marketers only *think* are feasible. Both beliefs are based on, so far, very small and shallow samples from which an entire marketing campaign approach is determined;
- Limited audience research may consist of no more than two sneak previews. In addition, the previews may be inappropriate: for example, studio marketers are famous for previewing an intimate "art" film to an audience that paid to see a Clint Eastwood picture.
- No one yet knows why 60 percent of the potential audience does *not* go to the movies.

The system does not seem to be working very well since only one picture out of ten makes back its negative costs.

Producers have long charged that the studios know how to market Westerns, sex films, comedies, and musicals, but that everything else stumps them. Robert Altman's experience with *McCabe and Mrs. Miller*, which was promoted as a kind of sleazy Western, could not have been more typical: treated as though the film *was* what the promotions said it was, it opened in a 1,700-seat house in New York City and died. It was not until it was re-"programmed" and reissued that it found the audience for which it was made. (Tom Laughlin had the same experience with *Billy Jack* until he wrested control of the picture's distribution away from Warners by suing them.)

As far as theatrical release is concerned, there appears to be little apparent effort to develop new molds to market special films. Paramount made an attempt with Terence Malick's *Days of Heaven*, released in 1978. Given contemporary cubist marketing practices, the campaign selected for it, exclusive runs, and visually beautiful advertising singularly free of hard sell and hype, was moderately successful.

But marketers are not going to look at the problems of marketing special or different films creatively unless the filmmakers push for it. And any filmmaker who spends a year or so making a film, ought to spend time concentrating on how the film is to reach its intended audience. Whether feature or documentary or industrial, a film needs to be aimed and particularly promoted. The quality of the film's promotion has a great deal to do with the number and kinds of opportunities a filmmaker will have later to produce more films. A filmmaker's responsibilities do not end with the final cut.

FOUR WALL DISTRIBUTION

Four-walling refers to the producer/distributor leasing a theater outright for a specified period of time, footing the bill for advertising and promotion, and often supplying ticket takers and cashiers in the leased theater. The return from the box office is not split with the theater, if the producer is four-walling, and not split with the distributor. Four-walling requires an enormous capital outlay for theater rentals (usually many months in advance) and blitzkreig advertising on radio and television.

One of the major influences left from the four-wall balloon is the switchover from print to saturation television/radio advertising of motion pictures. Before anyone ever heard of four-walling, television and radio commanded very small percentages of any distributor's advertising budget. With four-walling (and particularly the success of *Billy Jack* in the early 1970s), the emphasis changed. But that's about all that is left of four-walling, which is simply no longer a viable means of distributing films, except for the two remaining independent companies, Schick-Sunn Classic and Pacific International. Nevertheless, a legend about the efficacy of four-walling hangs on especially in the hearts of independent filmmakers—and though several independents rode the four-wall wave in the late 1960s and early 1970s, a recent comparison between four-walling receipts and 90/10 deals shows that the latter result in a better return to the distributor.[9]

Four-walling has become synonymous with "G" pictures the whole family can enjoy. And that's the kind of picture Schick-Sunn Classic and Pacific International turn out: *Wilderness Family* and *Grizzly Adams*. Far more heavily than any other producing firm in the business, they rely on computer read-outs and survey pretested market concepts, analyzing moviegoing habits and demographics.

A precise, predetermined relationship exists between picture content and audience for such producer-distributors as Sunn Classic. Before releasing its pictures, Sunn researches neighborhood profiles and TV spot-buying patterns to ameliorate the high risks of filmmaking. Sunn Classic insists they are in the business to help filmmakers by setting up parameters within which they can choose to work or not, as they wish. Now that marketing, and its attendant maid, research, have gained ground in the majors, the heritage of four-walling may be much more than the use of television spots to advertise motion pictures.

WORLDWIDE DISTRIBUTION

The importance of planning for and achieving good foreign distribution of an American film is vital since 40-60 percent of each film's gross now comes from overseas. At the end of 1978, United Artists received about $20 million in rentals from Japan alone. For smaller, independent distributors, to whom a $50,000-$150,000 profit per picture is enough, foreign sales can make the difference between staying in business or going under.

Foreign distribution deals are made in the U.S. with representatives or at the Cannes Festival, or at MIFED, Milan's October festival, where distributors and producers arrive laden with reels and promotional materials.

Each territory has a slightly different character, which must be taken into account. The best foreign markets for U.S. pictures are England, Italy, Germany, France, Japan, and Spain; next best are South Africa, Australia, Brazil, Mexico and Scandinavia. Others, such as the Middle East and Central America and Africa constitute poor markets for U.S. pictures. The criteria for judging what constitutes a good market: the number of people who go to the movies in a nation and the amount they pay for the ticket. The cost of launching films in foreign markets is just as high as in the United States. In 1978, $2 million was spent to advertise and promote *Death on the Nile* in Japan and 50 percent of that went to TV spots.

Major U.S. distributors that own their own theaters in foreign countries have an assured outlet, much as they did in the United States before 1948. Independent producers should realize that those pictures in which the distributor has a financial investment will be favored in its own theaters. For example, a distributor may make a rental agreement with its own theater in, say, Spain for a lower percentage of the gross paid to the distributor; the distributor will subsequently pay the producer less on the distributor's net. But, in essence, the distributor has retained 100 percent of the profits from its wholly owned exhibition operation. If the distributor makes $100,000 from a film shown in a theater the distributor owns, and the deal is 60/40—the distributor automatically gets 100 percent since the firm owns both. This makes producers' payments less because the distributor does not have the economic incentive to bargain hard for a 90/10 deal.

In such cases a producer should see that the contract with the distributor calls for safeguards to insure "arms-length" arrangements between the distributor and its overseas theaters so that it receives advantageous terms. In as many instances as possible (except in small territories), producers should make sure the picture is distributed all over the world for percentages, not fixed fees.

NOTES

1. *Motion Picture Laboratory*, vol. 19, no. 4, 1977.

2. See Lee Beaupre's "Industry" articles in *Film Comment*, July-August 1978.

3. Columbia, Paramount, MGM, 20th-Century Fox, Warner Brothers, Buena Vista, United Artists, Universal, Allied Artists, and Avco; *Hollywood Reporter*, June 18, 1976.

4. *Los Angeles Times*, June 21, 1978.

5. See David Lee, "The Booking of 'Superman', et al...". *Los Angeles Magazine*, December 1978.

6. Richard Kahn, Senior Vice President, World Wide Marketing at MGM, speaking at the FIC/USC Film Marketing Seminar, Los Angeles, December 1978.

7. For *Grease*, the Travolta/Newton-John single "You're the One That I Want" hit the Top 10 six weeks before the film opened: Ivor Davis, "Read The Book, See The Movie...," *Los Angeles Magazine*, June 1978.

8. Excerpted from a speech by Robert Cort, Vice President and

General Manager, Advertising, Publicity, Promotion at Columbia Pictures, FIC/USC Film Marketing Seminar.

9. See Lee Beaupre's "Industry" article on four-walling in *Film Comment*, September 1978.

For an excellent overview of some curious film business practices, see Harold J. Salemson and Maurice Zolotow, "It Didn't Begin with Begelman: A Concise History of Film Business Finagling," *Action*, published by the Directors Guild of America, July-August 1978.

CHAPTER 9

Independent Features and Documentary Films

The financing and distribution of low budget independent feature films has always been a personal and professional miasma for the filmmaker, and the reasons for this are readily apparent from the preceding chapters. Rarely do filmmakers embark on their first feature with a mentor or previous experience or learned standards of action against which they can gauge their production and distribution plans. As one filmmaker said: "Artistic control is half the problem; financial and honest accounting is the other."

This chapter presents the experiences of independent filmmakers—how they financed and distributed their features (or 90-minute documentaries), where they made their mistakes, where they triumphed, what they would do differently.

In the episodes that follow, it will be clear that the filmmakers saw their films as entities separate from themselves—either sooner or later—and that distance allowed them an essential analytical capacity. They combined and adapted facets of the money-raising/financing/selling process according to their analysis of the film—which leads directly back to the first law of financing: the availability, the amount, and the source of money depend wholly on the scope and nature of the picture (Chapter 3). For the successful ones, their role vis-à-vis the film did not end with the final cut but extended through the selection of the distributor and the promotion and the marketing of the film, in short, through the entire "life" of the film.

METHODS OF FINANCING

The independents who are finally able to finance a feature, or feature-length documentary, usually share one or more of these characteristics or qualities: (1) They have previously made one or more short films that won a pile of awards and gave them a "credibility"—which means that people will entertain proposals for a new, more ambitious film; it does not mean that money is automatically forthcoming. (2) They have graduated from a prestigious film school and though they may not know much more about the making of feature films than anyone else, they have made powerful contacts. (3) They are independently wealthy or have personal access to large amounts of money which they will use initially on the financing of the film. (4) At some crucial point, either just before the financing of the film or during, a mentor or partner joins them. This partner's role is usually financial. The partner may be an accountant or lawyer who becomes interested in and committed to the talent of the filmmaker or the specific film to be created; a person of inherited wealth who has credibility in the world of cultural fund raising; or a banker or major corporate executive with credibility in the business world.

One filmmaker said that his mentor/partner (though not a corporate partner per se) literally raised all the money and made his first Academy Award-winning, feature-length documentary possible. (Before then, he had made only short industrial and educational films.) "Beginning with the pressures of running over budget, compounded by the problems of distribution, aggravated by my brashness and his inexperience, great difficulties developed but through it all, his opinion of the film never waned. While every other investor (pre-Academy Award) felt uneasy, he knew it was good. When it won the Oscar, of course, all the others echoed, 'I knew it was great all the time.'" From this business mentor, he learned about structuring limited partnerships for the raising of speculative capital and how to recruit sophisticated investors. "I began to see the endless possibility of producing films of my own design and creation, rather than the direct contract films of the corporate client."

A filmmaker's survival, especially in the early days, depends on the ability to stay in production. The logical answer then is for someone else to raise the money. After ten years, one filmmaker found a partner who brought to the enterprise 12 years of financing and banking credentials in a large investment firm. "No way can I see a man of his experience and financial success selling documentary budgets of only $75,000 to clients. So while he is clearly the answer we have worked years to find, those years just may have been required to qualify us for his interest." They have since formed a new corporation that finances, produces, and distributes their own feature films. All the money raised is by a form of limited partnerships as a profit incentive, not shelter investment.

Since the nature and scope of the film determine the source of the money, those films that appeal to a broad audience and reflect basic American myths and values will have an easier reward; money for such films can be raised through limited partnerships with the kind of credentials described above. What if the film is critical of this country's morality or ethics, or its subject is highly controversial? What if the format is not a dramatic story but a 90-minute documentary?

"There are two problems with raising money for films," said one filmmaker who had recently completed his first 90-minute documentary, which was then in theatrical distribution. "It's like geometry: the less money you have, the harder it is, in geometrical proportion, to get it. The first thousand is as hard to get as the last $10,000. Second, while raising the money, you never discover what you did wrong. You only know you didn't get the money." This filmmaker believes that some films have a better chance of being funded if the film has a reason for being—if it promotes some social change, raises a provocative issue—as well as holds out the promise, if not the reality, of making money.

"In such situations, you really need to have two people— the hard-headed film-oriented producer, and the artistic, socially oriented temporizer, such as the fundraiser."

The fundraiser plans the approach to the investors, often helps write the prospectus, uses a network of friends and associates, and, in some cases, creates a "respectable" façade for the venture on his or her own reputation and belief in the picture. Such a person can make the difference in the financing or fundraising of a film, and filmmakers should be aware at the outset that some person is needed to fill this role—with competence, concern, interest.

Once the venture becomes identified as profit making, the next issue to be confronted, as always, is the filmmaker's credibility to potential investors. "If they really believed that they would make money by investing in the film, they'd go out and mortgage their homes because there is no risk involved. But they don't think you can carry it off, and besides that, there *is* considerable risk. These two factors make it a bad investment. Our job was to convince them that the film would make money, it would promote social change, and we could carry it off. Once you've done that, you've broken the barrier."

One feature-length documentary began with a small group of investors in a limited partnership arrangement. The budget was under $100,000. But they very shortly realized they had a tiger by the tail in terms of film content and a much larger film than initially conceived. To make a feature-length documentary, they recapitalized for a below-the-line budget of $250,000 and went back to the original investors to get their permission to open up the partnership, which they received. They pre-sold the national television rights to PBS for $50,000 and then got $50,000 in non-recourse loans from a bank. "Even though we had a competent banker who believed in the film and a contract for the television pre-sale, it isn't at all easy to get loans from a bank without a spectacular history with them." The film organization retained all rights except U.S. TV, on which PBS had a three-year option.

They needed $150,000 to complete the budget for the film, and it was at this point they found a fundraiser. "I don't think we could have possibly raised the money without her. Her role in our venture was absolutely vital."

Raising money is as involved as making a film. "For me, the experience was like building a dam, learning where the leaks are, and the stress points, where to put the big rocks, where the small ones, until the water level rises."

This filmmaker and his filmmaking group designed everything the potential investor saw or heard. The proposal, which took six months to write, contained a story synopsis, the social implications of and reasons for the film, the various distribution plans (theatrical, nontheatrical, television), other marketing plans, credentials of the filmmaker, limited partnership papers, plus dozens of letters extolling the filmmaker's work.

Even with an excellent proposal and sample footage, they didn't get any money for a long time. "All that proved was that I could write proposals and make some films. We had to convince them that the proposed film would work, and that was extremely difficult because we didn't have a film, we had an idea. If we had had the film, we could have raised the money—the irony all filmmakers face."

Overcoming this common "Catch 22" lies at the heart of raising money. In sponsored or information films, the obstacle is surmounted by selling a communication process or a solution, not a film per se. In features, the filmmaker is selling a tax deferral, or an investment, or an exhilarating gamble, or, less often, a message of value to millions. This filmmaker used video, which demonstrated to potential investors that the embryonic film would have impact.

"You have to design the process of raising money in such a way that no steps backward are ever left open to the investors. For example, book and record clubs insist that members send the card back *not* to get the record. We printed cards for each potential investor invited to a screening, which said we'd be calling them in the next few weeks to ask their reactions to the film. They had to "X" *out* a box if they did *not* want to be called. They also had the option of suggesting other people to contact, which they were asked to write on the back of the card."

He advises that to raise money in this fashion, filmmakers should always start with the people they know. "They will feel bad if they can't give you any money, so ask them for something they can give—names of other people who might be interested, or hosting a party at their house for the screening, or mailing out proposals on their stationery, or making calls for you."

Filmmakers need to be persistent and well organized. "You have to call a lot of people ten times before you can get to them. Be courteous but insistent. I can't think of a single instance when someone was turned off by persistence as long as it's elegant persistence."

Through the process of fundraising itself, the filmmaker must build a record of competence and commitment. "If you say you're going to do something, such as call or put something in the mail, do it that day. People are looking for reasons to back off. The filmmaker/money raiser must be on deck 100 percent all of the time."

Timing: "People are most fired up directly after they have seen footage and heard the filmmaker talk. You have a better chance of getting more financing two minutes after the presentation than five minutes; a better chance the next morning than a week later."

All the legal paperwork must be completed before any dollars can be raised, and the packets must be available at the screenings. "You have to be ready to receive the money. Our basic proposal was 40 pages. The investor's packet was over 100 pages long: it included the contract, a tax letter that guaranteed certain tax write-offs, etc. We found the most likely investors were either very wealthy people (those who don't have to reinvest their salaries to expand their own business or prepare for old age), and the professionals who simply don't need every dime they are making—like the single psychiatrist who makes $50,000 a year and owns his/her own home, the BMW, and the boat. What else can be bought? A film!

"I personally make the gamble of the investment clear to every investor. I did not want anyone investing who would be hurt, so my standard line was that if you cannot afford to lose the money, do not invest. And that became a moral protection for me. The irony of fundraising is that people do not give you money unless they believe you don't need it. Desperate people will not raise any money. The more discouraging I was to investors about the likelihood of them ever making their money back, the more likely it was that they would invest."

The first one or two films a filmmaker creates are critical tests of financial and professional competence, and it will never be as hard to raise money again—even if the films are not box office blockbusters. Brian de Palma's first film, *Greetings*, was financed by family and friends—$20,000 in cash, $23,000 deferred. The second, *Hi, Mom!*, was financed by a small company for $100,000. Having proved he could make films, he went on to produce *Obsession*, among others.

But it begins with analysis, knowledge of financing methods and distribution routes, and an impetus to begin. Once started, "Don't rely on anybody but yourself."

METHODS OF DISTRIBUTION

To cope with the myriad problems that constantly arise in distribution, filmmakers need to know (1) the basis on which an intelligent evaluation of distribution selection can be made (the same criteria noted in Chapters 5 and 8); (2) which audiences the film will primarily appeal to, and which are secondary; and (3) the route the money takes from the box office back to the producer and the investors.

"My biggest complaint about distribution was feeling up front that we are going to be cheated. What kind of happiness is that?" mourned one feature producer. He is not alone. It is the rare filmmaker who reports a prosperous and contented relationship with a distributor. Invariably, the advice to filmmakers is to "get your money up front"—that is, get an advance on the picture to guarantee a distributor's continued interest in doing a credible job on the film. Few feature distributors know how to market "special product," films that cannot easily be tagged "Western" or "thriller"; most low-budget first features or documentaries fall into the "special product" category. Distributors are even less enthusiastic about handling such troublesome product because they know the filmmaker, unlike MGM, does not have a string of films coming along to back up the box office failure of the first one. The successful release of a 90-minute documentary is almost unheard of.

"One of our films would probably not even have been made if we'd known more about the distribution situation of feature documentaries. The film won a Gold Medal at the Atlanta International Film Festival, but then ran up against the fact that there is virtually no market for feature documentaries. The television market is also extremely limited. The number of feature documentaries that have made money can be counted on one, maybe two hands. Most of those have gotten more publicity than box office bucks."

Furthermore, independent films compete at the box office with those films financed by the distributor. It is natural, if not commendable, that distributors push the films in which they have 100 percent financing above those in which they have no money or a small advance.

The deal most frequently offered to an independent filmmaker is a small percentage of the distributor's net ("the infamous net deal," as Martha Coolidge rightly dubs it[1]) and a 50/50 split of the advertising and *no* advance. Screenings for distributors can tie up prints for months. The distributor's reactions: they love the film but can't distribute it, the audience is too small, and the film doesn't fit into an established slot in the marketplace—or does not appear to, to the distributors.

The filmmaker then turns to small independent distributors and faces a new set of problems: lack of capitalization, staying power, and influences with the exhibitors. Small distributors cannot offer large advances or major advertising campaigns. They don't have the capital. They may not even have enough to sustain distribution of the film. And, they have no clout with the theaters because they do not have and cannot guarantee the "product flow" in the same way Warners or Universal can.

When every distributor in town turns the film down or offers ridiculously low net deals, filmmakers generally start to distribute it themselves or showcase it by entering it in festivals where it will be "noticed" and hopefully acclaimed. This gambit can make distributors take another look, but it rarely improves the first offer. To showcase it at festivals means that a filmmaker needs to budget money for pre-distribution or distribution costs of both 16mm and 35mm prints plus travel and hotel costs; if a film is accepted by a festival and shown, the filmmaker must be on the spot to meet distributors and hustle interest in it.

Besides the obvious pitfalls created by certain curious business practices already recounted in Chapter 8, sub-distributors and even distributors have been known to collect from the exhibitor and then file for bankruptcy, leaving the filmmaker with virtually no recourse to recoup the owed amounts.

One filmmaker contracted with an independent but highly successful distributor to market a feature-length documentary that promised wide audience appeal. The filmmaker was no neophyte and fought for all the rights he could get during contract negotiation. The film was released and enjoyed a substantial success. Just before the payment that would pay off the negative costs, the distributor filed bankruptcy. The filmmaker now couldn't get the money owed or retrieve the negative and prints. Depending on the terms of the contract, filmmakers have watched helplessly as a distributor—under perfect legal cover—continues to distribute the film using the prints already purchased, the proceeds going not to the filmmaker, but to creditors who stand first in line for repayment.

"Having made and never received my first million dollars in this business, I know a lot about distribution of independent features. My film made something in excess of $7 million (some reports say $10 million) on a budget of about $400,000, and the patient, benevolent backers of that film are still waiting for a remaining $200,000 on their $400,000 investment."

In light of his experiences with distribution, this film-maker would like to see an industry arbitration board working between producers (especially independents) and distributors. "The board should be able to examine records and consider grievances promptly, without the costly process and questionable justice of the courts." Since he does not think the majors (being the distributors) would ever agree to such a board, and because of his previous experiences, he has already formed his own distribution company. Funding for the distribution of all pictures created by the organization is built into the original financing of the picture. "Though limited, we are confident this type of distribution will ultimately be in our economic best interest. The prestige of major distribution does not buy bread for the table. With independent distribution of a producer's own product, we conservatively figure the film can make the same profit on half as many tickets."

One filmmaker who released his first feature-length documentary in the fall of 1978 decided to distribute the documentary himself when he learned that no organization would touch the theatrical distribution unless assigned the nontheatrical rights, as a hedge against the high risk in the theaters. He booked it into a small San Francisco theater under a four-wall arrangement for a fourteen-week run. Besides the cost of a publicist, and the theater's overhead (the nut), the expenses were totaling about $40,000; all promotion and advertising, $30,000; the cost of the 35mm blow-up prints, $28,000.

"Tremendous sums are involved in theatrical distribution, and often decisions have to be made instantly by sheer intuition," said this filmmaker. "For instance, the size of the daily newspaper ad has to be selected days in advance. This decision involves thousands of dollars. If the audience for the film is shrinking, do you increase the size of the ad to reverse the trend, or do you decrease the size because you have less revenue? You can never spend enough on advertising and promotion, for there is a direct relationship between what you spend and what you get. Unless your campaign is completely inept, more dollars spent on advertising will always mean more dollars at the box office. During our distribution period, I felt like an ambulance driver with an application into medical school being forced to do brain surgery in some sort of epidemic of my own causing."

The film next opened in New York City, an act said to be *de rigeur* if a film is to receive any national distribution offers. There he got a standard 90/10 deal, which, in some ways, as he pointed out, is similar to a four-wall arrangement except that the producer is not liable for the costs of the house should the gross fail to cover them. However, a 90/10 is only satisfactory if the producer actually receives the 90 percent, after house nut, from the exhibitor, which the filmmaker so far has not.

The reasons for a New York opening can only be described as archaic. New York does not set any preference patterns in terms of "average" audience, and it has been proved beyond doubt that the tastes of people in Kansas are not the same as those of New York filmgoers. New York openings are important for reviews in New York papers and national magazines. Nevertheless, national booking offers are usually based upon the first week's (or first few weeks') *business* done in the New York run because "that's the way it's always been done," as any film distributor will tell you. Therefore a filmmaker opens in New York City, hoping the first week is good enough so that the distributor will offer a fat advance and a fair split.

This filmmaker benefited from the "New York syndrome," since his first week, at $20,000, was good. He received a $10,000 advance and a $10,000 advertising guarantee from a Los Angeles theater. "The making of this last deal is a very good example of the importance of timing in theatrical distribution. The name of the game is quick decision. The figures fell off fast after our first week in New York: and the second week was only $12,000. I made the agreement with the Los Angeles booker at the end of the first week; we were both betting on futures. If the gross had gone up or held, he would have made a good deal because he would have had exclusive rights to a hot film in his area at a good price. Since the grosses fell, I made a good deal because we'd have been offered much less, had we waited."

At this point, he decided he could not, for a variety of reasons, continue the theatrical distribution himself. The major reason was "exhaustion," a filmmaker's perennial companion. "Not only can you never spend enough money but you can never do enough. There is always another poster to put up, another critic to coerce...another community leader who didn't get a free pass." The current distributor has both theatrical and nontheatrical rights; one house should handle both rights because the 16mm and 35mm distribution must be coordinated. If a film has played nontheatrically in a small university town, a successful theatrical engagement there is stupid since college students and teachers will form both audiences. The usual practice is to hold up the nontheatrical until the theatrical bookings have run their course.

The new distributor offered a choice of terms:[2] 50/50 split with costs off the top (equal sharing of the distribution costs, the 50/50 split on the net after costs) or the filmmaker could have 30 percent of the distributor's gross, the distributor paying the costs from its 70 percent share. They chose the 50/50 "net" deal, feeling that they could keep in closer touch with the costs and that since the filmmaker was sharing costs, the distributor would be more inclined to spend what the film really needed to promote it.

Distribution is as important as production and production as important as financing. In light of these lamentable examples, it may sound like a hopelessly impossible goal to suggest that a filmmaker should try to make a distributor a partner in the enterprise, rather than assume the relationship will be one of adversaries. Distributors suffer from a bad reputation—largely deserved—and filmmakers have a tendency to move in hard and fast when first dealing with them, anticipating the worst. The worst is all too easy to receive, but since the filmmaker will probably not have the legal right to overrule the distributor's marketing decisions, a good working relationship should be sought. How else will a filmmaker be able to convince a distributor of alternate advertising plans, or to reexamine the marketing approaches? At the beginning that's better than demanding impossible advertising budgets or radical departures in marketing techniques.

The filmmaker's goal while negotiating with a distributor is to see that a reasonable and specified amount of money will be spent on advertising and promotion, for, once money is spent, the distributor cannot just open the picture and walk away from it. It is just as important to put a ceiling on those expenditures if the filmmaker's deal is a net one, because the distributor's fee and the marketing costs are deducted.

Sales policies vitally affect the pattern of expenditures, how much will be spent, and when. Therefore, every sales decision will affect the ads, which affect the gross, which affects the filmmaker. And *that* affects the filmmaker's next picture.

It is estimated that even hit pictures reach only 15-20 percent of their potential audience. Since no one knows why the other part of the audience doesn't go to the theaters, foreign distributors and the sale of ancillary rights become especially significant to independent filmmakers. Collectively, these rights, such as cable and video cassettes and now videodisc should be seen as important as theatrical and nontheatrical distribution rights, if for no other reason than that they cater to specialized markets which theatrical distribution cannot afford to and apparently is not able to reach.

"I was brainwashed to believe you can't distribute your own picture!" one independent feature producer said. "So I went to a couple of old pros and I said, 'Can I distribute my own picture?' And the answer was 'Yes!' Our picture is specialized, so we're going to give a lot of tender, loving care. By distributing it ourselves, everybody will get an honest count, and we'll know exactly where the bugs are. I'm tired of working for people who rip me off. I'm going to call my distribution company Bumble Bee. Know why? The weight of a bumble bee's body and the size of its wings says it's aerodynamically impossible for that little bee to fly! They've been telling me I can't distribute my own shows—we'll see about that."

NOTES

1. See Martha Coolidge, "I've Made the Film; Now What Do I Do with It?" in Judith Trojan and Nadine Covert, *16mm Distribution*, New York: Educational Film Library Association, 1977.

2. A competent, experienced person in entertainment law or distribution and marketing practices should examine the contract before the filmmaker signs.

Special thanks to Peter Adair, Mariposa Film Group, San Francisco, for his permission to quote from "Distributing *Word Is Out*," a report by Mr. Adair to his investors, © 1978, Peter Adair.

CHAPTER 10

Vid Lib: Will It Set Us Free?

THE NEW MEDIA

The technological developments of the years 1970–80 have lit up the film/video/communications landscape of the 21st century. It is full of promise and excitement. This coming-of-age for communications has been dubbed "narrowcasting" instead of broadcasting, a term that points up the fact that the future may well be an era of individual viewer choice, viewer participation, and programs made for small, specialized audiences. Never before has that been economically sane.

A filmmaker's agony begins with the need to prove that a large audience exists for the film (in order to gain financing) and ends with the despair of trying to reach that big audience.

Currently, a film or video program must appeal to a wide audience: features aim for people ages 12 to 35; a TV program that reaches a paltry five million is a dismal failure. The need to make films for mass audiences has a chilling effect on financing and on distribution, not to mention the filmmaker's originality—very few ideas can promise and deliver audience appeal in the millions.

It is generally believed that the future of videodisc, video cassettes, and other developments will economically thrive *not* on reaching mass audiences but on reaching "special interest" audiences—"affinity groups," as they have been called—largely because multiple channels of distribution will be widely available. To be able to reach smaller groups on a sound economic basis is precisely what filmmakers of all kinds need. With disparate means of distribution, film may become more like a raw material for communication than a medium in itself capable of reaching its own audience through its own distribution, something it has never done well or specifically.

The major technological developments are video cassette, videodisc, satellite transmission to cable and pay TV systems, optical fiber, and digital recording. Add to these a major political development—the proposed revision of the 1934 Communications Act—and the communications revolution is in high gear.

The Federal Communications Commission (the FCC) has always looked upon cable TV as an ancillary service to network broadcasting instead of a medium in its own right. If restrictions on cable are lifted (as proposed) and if American Telephone and Telegraph (AT&T) is allowed to enter this sector of the communications field with the use of optical fiber, the "wired nation" will become a firm reality. Optical fiber transmits signal by laser light instead of electronically, thus increasing the band width (the "space for encoding and transmitting") astronomically. Such a means, coupled with cable networks and/or satellite transmission, increases the capacity of channels to bear many signals and two-way signals. The more channels there are, the more specialized the programs they carry can be. If the new regulations allow, as present cable TV fears, AT&T could very well end up supplying each home not only with a phone service but a wide-band, multi-channel link to the world of services (TV-newspaper, TV-banking, shopping, and schooling) plus entertainment and news programming.

It has been estimated that by the year 2000 all of television will be as selective as anyone could wish; "ad hoc" networks, connected by satellite, will be beaming programs to those geographical areas or homes for which the program was expressly created and intended. Once markets are recognized as varied, instead of homogeneous mass, the filmmaker/communicator/producer's role becomes diversified, expansive, and creative. Perhaps, for the independents, economically sound at last!

The present period is one of transition, moving from a focus on mass audience to special interest audience. As more and more people pay to get "on the wire," the risks of innovative special programming will decrease. As they do, the opportunities for filmmakers rise.

Producers and critics warn that what counts is imagination, not hardware. And that is true. But it is the hardware that will allow imagination a broad sweep of methods from 8mm to holograms, which will inexorably lead to a communication center in every home with literally hundreds of channels available from cablevision.

CABLE TV

Cable TV (CATV) began as a means to bring television to tiny communities that, because of geographical obstacles, could not receive it over the air. Cable service proved so good, in fact, that a small rural town in Vermont could often receive New York City programs more clearly than people got them in Manhattan. More important, cable TV allows subscribers to receive many channels (instead of just a few) and makes it possible for impulses to flow in two directions: viewers can select or reject programming and "talk back to the television set." One out of five homes is now wired to cable. It is estimated that by 1981, cable will have penetrated 30 percent of the nation's homes, which means that in some areas 60-90 percent of the homes will be on the wire. The average cable operation in the United States has 2,000-3,000 subscribers. Only 20 systems have 10,000 subscribers or more.

Cable television franchises are granted by municipal governments to CATV corporations, which bid for the hotly contested rights "to serve" an area. The city usually receives an advance plus a sliding percentage of gross CATV earnings. The main uses of cable are the redistribution of existing signals; the importation of distant signals (which would not be available to the viewer regardless of the terrain); and the origination of television programming. Coaxial cable can carry many channels per cable. To get extra channels above the usual "free" 12, the viewer now has the option to pay for additional programs.

THE PAY TV WINDOW

This additional program service comes "by air or by wire." The statistics on subscriptions jump around wildly, but there were probably about 2-2.5 million people watching pay TV in 1978 (up a million from 1977), and there will probably be 3 million or more by the beginning of 1980.

There are three ways to transmit the programs: (1) to bicycle (physically carry) the tapes, which takes an origination facility and programmers, (2) by microwave transmission,[1] (3) by satellite to earth, which is less expensive than MDS (multi-distribution service) microwave but requires the cable operator to install an earth station (a 30-foot dish that costs about $90,000) to pick up the signals.

There are two kinds of pay TV services currently being offered: *per program*, whereby a viewer pays a nominal monthly charge and then pays a small amount for each film she or he wishes to view that month; or *subscription service*, whereby the viewer pays a higher monthly cost and can receive the whole program package at no additional charge. The concept behind subscription service is that people will watch films they probably wouldn't watch if they had to pay extra or go out to a theater. It also negates the programmers' need to promote heavily each film to get people to pay for it— the cost is included in their monthly fee. The kinds of programs currently being offered are entertainment specials, sports, and films. But it is the chance to see, conveniently, uncut, uninterrupted films that sells pay TV to subscribers, not sports (so ably handled by the networks) and so far not the entertainment specials.

But as exhibitors, pay TV people toss a hundred movies on the screen per year. Any film must be promoted to some extent, and films for per program services need a lot of promotion. It's the old problem of how to get people into the tent, only this time it's how to get people into the living room to turn on the channel.

Pay TV looks on itself as an exhibitor, not a distributor. The vast majority of pay TV is offered by the cable operator who purchases a packaged program service from a program supplier, such as Showtime or Home Box Office, the two largest. Suppliers provide the operator with a program guide and a schedule and may even deliver the ¾-inch video tape.

An example of an area with competing programming services is Los Angeles. Theta Cable's Z Channel in the western part of the city has about 50,000 subscribers. Teleprompter owns 50 percent of the Z Channel, which gets its programming from Hollywood Home Theater.

In addition to Theta, there are two over-the-air pay TV services in Los Angeles, ONTV, (owned by American Subscription TV) and SelecTV, the new rival system (owned by National Subscription TV). ONTV had 100,000 subscribers by the end of 1978 who paid $19.49 per household per month, plus an installation fee and a deposit.

SelecTV is a "pay-as-you-go" TV per program service that began in 1978 but had still attracted only 6,000 subscribers by 1979. The cost is $6 per month, plus between $1 and $3 for each program that the viewer selects to watch. Since viewers can select programs, this system of pay-as-you-go TV can be said to supply producers and programmers with an index of current viewer tastes. SelecTV's computer logs the number of people who watch (and pay for) each program.[2] It might be more accurate than Nielsen.

The battle is joined for a market share of the potentially lucrative pay TV and cable industry. Nearly every studio in Hollywood has a pay TV or cable subsidiary: Hollywood Home Theater (a program supplier) is owned by Fox and United Artists; Paramount owns Hughes TV Network; Broadcast Entertainment Subscription TV (BEST) is a subsidiary of Universal Subscription TV; United Artists and Columbia own Cablevision, Inc., and so on.

One of the most innovative systems is QUBE, owned by Warner Cable, a subsidiary of Warner Communications. QUBE began as a two-way, talk-back cable experiment in Columbus, Ohio, and it now offers 30 channels of programming: religion, sports, courses from history to yoga, Nickelodeon (young people's satellite network), opera, first-run films, community programs, pay TV specials, and soft-core porn—all with the added two-way feature, which, some believe, will alter the relationship between receiver and sender. Warner Cable has just added its former major rival—Coaxial Communications Cable—in Columbus to its corporate galaxy. This will make QUBE one of the largest cable systems in America (69,000 subscriptions) and will increase QUBE's franchise area to 177,000 homes.

Time, Inc., is a major investor in cable and pay TV.[3] Time-Life owns Home Box Office, which was formed in 1972 and claims 1.7 million subscribers for its satellite pay TV programming service. Through its subsidiary, Telemation Program Systems, it supplies 80 percent of the nation's cable viewers with programming. About two-thirds of its programs are produced in house, the others farmed out to independent producers. Home Box Office has recently initiated Take 2—a family-oriented, satellite-transmitted, pay TV channel so that HBO's cable *affiliates* may offer one or both services to a household. Retailing at $4–$6 per month and available by mid-1979, Take 2 is a demographically targeted pay TV program service of G and PG pictures, off-network G's, music, comedy, variety, children's shorts—no R movies and no sports. Home Box Office will produce the programs for Take 2. Looking at the 500 affiliates HBO declares they have, a filmmaker will quickly perceive something approaching a network. It has been estimated that when linked to a satellite, such a system could reach 15 million people by 1985, which would give them the financial leverage to compete with the networks for major films and sports.

Viacom, Inc. owns 50 percent of Showtime Entertainment, the second largest pay TV programmer; Teleprompter, the nation's largest cable TV operator, owns the other 50 percent—a purchase said to have reshaped the pay TV industry. The immediate impact was twofold: Teleprompter dropped its long-time affiliation with Time's Home Box Office and now subscribes to the programs offered by Showtime; and Showtime suddenly had a great deal more money to spend on production. This programming service currently puts out two pay TV specials per month, each budgeted at about $75,000. It also purchases programs and films from Columbia's and Warner's cable suppliers, as well as "pre-buying" and/or financing programs ("software") from independents.

In 1979, Showtime and Home Box Office—the two national pay TV programming services—announced they would produce about 60 made-for-pay-TV shows between them, many from independent producers. Development deals with the major studios have begun for pay TV feature production. Moreover, the studios are eager to develop ways to promote their own films on pay TV—especially those films that have not been theatrically successful (hence, the rise in the value of a film's ancillary rights).

The growing program appetite for first-run movies tailored for the pay-TV window has not been fully recognized by independent producers, who still think in terms of making films for theatrical distribution.

Independent producers can finance shows and films for pay TV through pre-sale guarantees (averaging $150,000-$250,000); occasionally they can pick up total financing. Some producers are pre-selling pay TV rights solely on the basis of scripts, which may become much more common in the 1980s. Such pre-sales are similar to a negative pickup: the finished film should resemble the script, as approved, and should contain the cast and production team stipulated. Therefore, by selling off the pay TV, foreign theatrical, first-run syndication rights, it is now possible to cover the negative costs of a low-budget ($1-$3 million) film.

All pay TV outfits say they are willing to analyze theatrical films from independent producers, and many are interested in packages of short films, which are what ICAP is trying to promote for filmmakers on Cable TV (see ICAP, Chapter 5).

The acquisition departments are expanding. It is estimated that $25 million has been spent in 1979 alone for *first*-run pay TV program development, and that by 1981 some programming suppliers will be buying the TV distribution and exhibition rights to 40 features a year *prior* to production. All program suppliers for pay TV are looking for ways to broaden the audience base by appealing to specific age groups, ethnic, and geographical regional tastes. For instance, the stated target audience of Showtime's specials: people 25–49, and the over-55 group.

In developing a specialized audience for special programs, the issue of quality emerges: Americans are used to multi-million-dollar network programming, and such productions have become the reference frame for quality. Many low-budget and foreign films simply do not have slick production values, though they may have plenty of other values. Once a large number of subscribers are wired to pay TV services—such as 50 million—the specialized audience may emerge. At present Woody Allen's *Interiors* is not economically viable for 105 people in New Mexico and 105 more in Oregon, but that doesn't mean a solid audience doesn't exist nationwide; it means that pay TV isn't yet wired to enough members of the *Interiors* audience. No matter how geographically scattered, they may total 500,000 by 1990. When wired and paying $3 per foreign film or unconventional feature, they constitute a $1.5 million market.

Furthermore, producing for pay TV does not require rehashing old formats; pay TV appears to be looking for new formats of any length (since this medium's programs do not have to fit into broadcast TV's time limits) and may prove to offer innovative programs by all kinds of producers.

Payment varies for already completed feature films that have been made primarily for theatrical release. Usually, pay TV outlets license the films for a percentage return of the gross subscriber revenues received to the producer or distributor, which is similar to theatrical distribution. Income to the producer or distributor of a film can range from 10¢ per subscriber for the pay TV run, up to 55¢ or 60¢, even 75¢ for major films like *Jaws*. The average return price is 35¢; therefore, at the pay TV window a film can earn $100,000 to $500,000, depending upon what kind of film it is and how large the pay TV audience is.

To some extent, independent producers will suffer from the same problems here that they do on the "outside" with theatrical distribution: a studio can give a pay TV programming service a package of pictures, each picture at a different rate, the package averaging out to 35¢; but two independents peddling their first or second low-budget picture do not have a string of films to average out the lows and the highs.

Though small at present, the pay TV window promises to provide the independent short and feature film producers with an alternate source of income for finished work or planned work, alternate audiences and markets, audiences and distributors for special, controversial, or unconventional films that would never succeed in the theaters, and opportunities to create original programming.

For producers, it's a good idea to remember the Darryl Zanuck press conference in the early 1960s. One of the reporters asked, "What do you think about the invasion of television into the profits of the movies? Will it cause the demise of the movie business?" And Zanuck, with his ten-inch cigar, floored everybody when he expansively welcomed TV: "I'll finish my film on Friday, and on Saturday it will be shown in the homes of America on large screens, and by Monday, the cost of it will be returned and I'll be on to the next. It will be a new world."

The effects on theaters will probably not be good. Generally, the fear is not that theatrical revenues will decrease but that many films will not be shown in theaters at all. These apprehensions have boosted exhibitors' irreversible craving for block busters—since, they feel, no one will go out to see an ordinary film when they can see it at home in a matter of weeks or a few months. But it must be kept in mind that in the 1950s the motion picture business was terrified of the threat television posed. But TV proved to be an economic boost when the studios began collaborating in the production for home screens, which they are now doing for pay TV as well.

Because of their appeal as the big-screen, group event, the ultimate effect on the theaters may be to preserve them only as places to see the premieres of multi-million dollar pictures in the same way one sees New York musicals or plays today—at one theater, not at many. Though one well-publicized report predicted that cable TV would drive the last theaters out of business[4], others have noted that the advent of strong pay TV response in a geographical area has stimulated movie attendance. In any case, the experiences of going to a theater and watching television are just not the same, and the demography of the audiences is different. Certain audiovisual programing that imitates features simply will not work on pay TV. It is a new medium with new program demands, and that's the way producers should perceive it.[5]

GETTING ON THE BIRD

One of the reasons for the rosy predictions for pay TV growth is the concomitant growth in satellite technology. The ultimate effect of satellites on TV will be to justify the use of the visual media as ways to communicate between large and small groups, for satellites make multiple uses possible. For instance, by 1980, Holiday.Inn predicts they will serve 100,000 rooms nationwide with "free-to-the-guest" satellite-distributed pay TV. Programming will be provided by Fanfare, a Houston-based pay cable network affiliated with Hollywood Home Theatre (the joint subsidiary of 20th-Century Fox and United Artists that programs Los Angeles' Z Channel and others).[6]

There are two kinds of satellites: one is a fixed, low-level satellite service of multiple channels beaming into *large* earth stations, which require local distribution by TV broadcasting or by wire. The second is a high-powered, expensive satellite broadcasting service that beams into small earth stations whose antennae (or "dishes") may be only 10 feet across, and a lot less expensive to purchase and install. A satellite channel, leased by a programming service, is called a transponder, which is a device that receives a particular

kind of signal and retransmits it in a different mode—
rebroadcasting it, in other words, in a larger pattern.

The growth in earth stations (to receive satellite transmissions) owned by cable operators is phenomenal: there
were 77 in 1976; by 1978 there were about 700. Satellite
transmission is cheaper than cable; therefore the demand for
satellite space has burgeoned. RCA is launching a third
satellite in late 1979, and plans a fourth Satcom in 1980.

Satellite transmission brings a great many benefits to
filmmakers, distributors, and exhibitors. "I think it's possible that major chains of theaters will also be wired to
receive satellite broadcasts of feature films," said one producer's representative in Hollywood. "The day of the motion
picture that requires 500 to 2,000 prints is rapidly coming to
an end. The tremendous costs of selling those prints by our
antiquated present-day selling techniques need a long hard
look."

The satellites are beginning to make the creation and
distribution of alternate programming economically possible, and the cost to distribute by satellite is going down as
usage goes up. Satellite-distributed signals are one-third the
cost of terrestrial networks.

Reduced cost means increased access. Access means
more markets opening up and the need for more programming. More programming means more work for producers,
writers, musicians, and so on. Once the technology develops
to the point where small groups can afford to plug into a
satellite service, they can distribute whatever program they
have to whomever they wish. The national "ad hoc" networks
—small groups with common interests such as birdwatching
or filmmaking or dentistry—could conceivably set up a
program on a particular subject at a particular time. It would
be possible for independent filmmakers all over the United
States to punch up a channel fed by satellite and watch the
Edinburgh Film Festival one week, the Columbus Festival
another, and MIFED from Milan on a third.

Conversely, it is already *possible* to see daily packages
of industrial films beamed by satellite to certain cable

systems by both Modern Talking Picture Service and Association Films, as well as independently made short films in some areas. Satellite service not only gives the films a distribution not possible before but also gives short film producers with access to these cable systems an unprecedented chance to see what is being made. When the service gets cheaper and broader, the same can be true of experimental films, children's films, or programs of interchange between Spanish-speaking American teenagers, and South American teenagers.

The global village has arrived.

21st-CENTURY BOOKS

Videodiscs

The problem with films and television is that the programs go by at their own pace—not the viewer's pace. If a viewer was enthralled by the dark implications of an Antonioni film or confused by the way the carburetor functioned as explained in a self-help film, the only recourse available was to wait for a replay or sit through a second show. That is why film, though educational in the general sense, has never been considered as effective a "teacher" as a book, where the student can read a paragraph over.

Videodisc is an amalgam of these two disparate media; now anyone can read a film. Disco-Vision went on sale to the public in December 1978. The players are manufactured by Phillips and distributed through Magnavox; Music Corporation of America (MCA, the parent corporation of Universal Pictures) manufactures the discs and provides the programming from its vast film and television library.[7]

Unlike video cassettes, videodiscs do not record anything; they are strictly a means of distributing and exhibiting prerecorded material. Disco-Vision is just what the name implies: a disc bearing a program or film's words and pictures, which, with an attachment, can be played through a

TV set. The playback unit, which looks like an ordinary phonograph turntable, attaches to the VHF connector on a TV set by a cord. Similar to a stylus and an LP record operation, a laser beam picks up both sound and image from the disc (optically, not electronically) and translates the prerecorded material on the disc into sound and pictures through the TV set. Each disc currently contains up to 60 minutes worth of programming.

The discs are said to be virtually indestructible: repeated playing does not wear them out, they won't break, and they can be handled by jam-sticky fingers. The machine is capable of "random access": slow motion, fast forward, reverse, and the cinematic "freeze frame." Any section of the disc can be found automatically and immediately, like finding a page in a book, simply by "calling up" the frame index number. Since it is self-pacing, viewers can repeat a section (like a book) until they understand it; the slow motion mode means that if the viewers don't quite see how that dance step was made, it can be replayed frame by frame. It has a dual (and discrete) sound track system, so that foreign film discs can be bought in both English and the original language, or language discs can be had in both.

The factory cost to manufacture a 60-minute disc is remarkably low and the finished product is far less expensive to buy than to rent a 16mm film. It is also much easier to play. So far, videodisc programming consists mainly of feature films. But how many times does one want to watch *Casablanca* or *Saturday Night Fever*? Therefore, it would appear that once the hardware is accessible to a broad spectrum of consumers, the opportunities for producers of special programs—short or long, radical or traditional— become as varied as for the producers of books or records. When the market for continuing education and self-improve- ment is developed, the disc may prove to be one of the greatest learning tools since Gutenberg. It has been proposed that Disc-of-the-Month Clubs could regularly supply the film buff or the film professional with an affordable disc library of short films, documentaries, features, and educational programs. Such a concept extends easily to any professional field or amateur interest.

With videodiscs—and to some extent video cassettes—independent filmmakers finally have access to a cheap distribution and exhibition system to reach specialized, small audiences. When it is possible to sell the finished "film" product for a couple of dollars to a lot of people, it is much more possible to get the "negative" costs back. The film- or tape-to-disc business begins to look very much like the record or paperback business.

Once the disc technology is going, filmmakers will not be stuck with "$300 pressings." The process of production and distribution for small audiences becomes economically feasible. If only 5,000 discs are sold for $3 each, the risk of making back the cost of production decreases because the risk of sale is as small as the price, compared to the risk of a sale for $250 per print. Many more people can buy a "film" disc for $3 than are able (or willing) to buy one for $250.

As a medium, videodisc can survive on runs of discs as small as 10,000 and can therefore afford to appeal to small groups of people with special interests, such as French cooking or how to tune a car.

Though few people are creating programming specifically for videodisc, MCA is developing a rate card for the mastering and replicating of the discs on a lease, purchase, or per-show basis for producers. When the consumer's unit cost comes down to a few dollars, the incidence of unusual or even radically experimental subjects rises. There may only be a million people in this country who really want to see a short film on azalea cultivation, and of that million, perhaps only 15,000 would actually buy such a disc for $5, but that's a gross of $75,000. If the film cost, via videotape, $5,000 to produce, $1 each to master and dupe, and another dollar each to print the cover sleeve, the economics of marginal or experimental programming can readily be seen. The marketing of discs as opposed to the marketing of films has a staggering potential: discs can be sold in any drug store, bookshop, record store, or supermarket. Unlike 16mm films, discs can be mailed out anywhere cheaply and quickly.

"We are champing at the bit for the day when technology permits sponsored films to reach huge audiences," says one industrial film producer. "Videodiscs and satellite access will give our medium a vastly bigger contact with mass audiences, and inexpensively. When our sponsors can give away a videodisc of a show the way they give away Christmas records at gas stations, our industry will be riding high. And when we can share satellite time inexpensively to reach stations ready to tape free public service shows, we will be out of the minor leagues."

Just in terms of economics, format, and ease of distribution alone, the arrival of the disc in conjunction with cassettes will place individual learning and entertainment on a previously unknown and specialized level. If this promise is fulfilled, the programmer, the producer, will be in a prime position.

Video Cassettes and Tape Productions

Consumer access to video cassettes the size of pocket books, bearing either prerecorded programs or blank tapes for consumers to use as they will, promises solid contributions in the electronic information revolution. If the price of the home playback system can be made low enough, preprogrammed video cassettes can rival the paperback textbook trade, though it appears that they will not be as inexpensive as the videodisc.

The market in video cassette use is booming and has wide applications for industry, government, the military, schools, and home use. They are easy to play and easy to record: simply put a small box in a big box and press a button. Like discs, they are much simpler to use than super 8 or 16mm: no projectors, no loading or threading problems, no screens to set up or take down.

Video catalogs and libraries of existing tapes for industry and educational use are springing up as the tapes proliferate; a Videotape-of-the-Month Club is starting. Video cassettes are reaching every kind of "special interest audience," and the industry as a whole is growing so fast that no one has an accurate reading of what the market is worth or what its rate of growth is. So far, the major video cassette recorder manufacturers are Sony (Betamax), Matsushita's Video Home System (VHS), Quasar's VX2000, and Sanyo's V-Cord System.

One distributor evaluates video and the educational and sponsored short film this way: "Film will continue to parallel videotape and other electronic formats for a long time. We will see film as a primary educational, motivational, entertainment medium, until the technical integrity of the video-projected image onto the large screen, in front of 100 people, can match that of the 16mm projector. However, where quality is *not* the prime concern, and where it is more convenient for the user to play back electronically, video will be used."

This distributor and others believe that since so much material will be coming by satellite over the air, school systems will want to be able to record, as well as playback, on their electronic systems. Therefore, while they may very well end up with dual systems—cassette and disc—the duplication may seem unnecessary. Though homeowners may not build libraries of visual material, the schools and libraries probably will.

When it comes to creating original programs, however, videotaping has several advantages over shooting film: principally time, economics, and ease of operation. Using tape, a major TV production can now be turned out in about half the time and for 60 percent of the cost, of film. Taped programs no longer suffer in terms of quality, and almost no viewer can tell, during broadcast, what has been taped and what has been filmed. Transfers from tape to film are now excellent, and the editing gear for tape has improved enormously.

Many people connected to this field readily see the day when most programs for television will be taped, but the changeover is slow and is usually attributed not so much to the equipment or the cost of changeover as to the attitudes and habits of producers and directors and the lack of appropriate contracts with unions.

"By the late 1980s, no one in his right senses will run a negative through a camera, and then pray that nothing happens to it in transport, in processing, in conforming, in printing, in the vault," said one producer. "Once a good, small video camera is available to us, and excellent tape-to-film transfers are available *widely*, why bother with negatives? But taping techniques will be cinema techniques—not television techniques. This has also started, with tape productions being made 'the cinema way' with one camera lighting every shot as though for film, etc., then editing on tape and later going to film."

Digital Processing

After the turn of the century the video library may also contain digital-processing products—a technology already possible but not yet developed for consumers. This is a process by which a half hour TV program or film—in color with sound—can be recorded on and played back from a 3-by-7-inch card. The cards can be duplicated as easily as photographs. A feature film can be recorded on an 8½-by-11-inch card, duped for less than a quarter, and sent through the mail like a letter. The playback hardware for consumers may cost $500. Think about that the next time a projector puts new perfs in your new print, or you have to send ten prints of an hour show by Air Express.

One of the results of these technological developments is finally to put the filmmaker in touch with specialized audiences; the converse is that individuals will be able to make media choices among really different material. The estimated population of the United States is 210 million. If one 200th, or about a million people will pay $2.50 each to see an opera over pay TV in one geographical region, that's a gross income of $2.5 million to pay for the programming, the feed by satellite, and the promotion. Conceivably, the opera could be syndicated to other program suppliers that serve other areas. Until now, to create any program or film for a mere million television viewers has been economic folly. But if 500,000 people pay $5 for a videodisc on skiing twice a year, that's an annual gross of $5 million.

To filmmakers, the value of fragmented audiences (ethnic, age, or interest) should be obvious. People have always had different media needs, and filmmakers have always wished to create different sorts of films. But there was no distribution system to get special films to special audiences on any regular or economically sane basis. Mass media never fulfilled viewers' or makers' needs. Now the technology for distribution and exhibition will help link the producers and the audience in a synergistic connection that promises an extraordinary and mutual fulfillment. Whether that promise, in terms of film or program content, will become a reality is quite a different matter.

NOTES

1. Multi-distribution service (known as MDS) is a type of microwave transmission now being used by pay TV program distributors indirectly with cable TV systems or directly into the home in 40 U.S. cities, including New York and Los Angeles.

2. For an analysis of these systems, see John G. Watson, "Battle of the Airwaves," *Los Angeles Times*, November 29, 1978.

3. Time, Inc., recently bought the nation's second largest cable TV owner-operator, American Television and Communications Corporation (ATC). ATC has submitted a subscription TV (STV) application to the FCC along with designs for an STV encoder and decoder box for technical approval. They plan a mix of movies, sports, and specials.

4. The Arthur D. Little Report, 1978.

5. Director's Guild of America Seminar, "The Impact of Video on the Film Industry," 1977, Los Angeles. Eight cassettes of the seminar's proceedings, moderated by Gene Youngblood, can be purchased from Convention Seminar Cassettes, 13356 Sherman Way, North Hollywood, Calif., 91605. The series is excellent in all respects.

6. *Hollywood Reporter*, December 8, 1978, Los Angeles.

7. RCA has a competing system in development, Selecta-Vision, but it may not be marketed until 1981. Selecta-Vision differs from Disco-Vision in that the sound and picture signals are picked up by a diamond stylus.

Special thanks to the Director's Guild of America for permission to use "The Impact of Video on the Film Industry"; and to Ed Swanson of Modern Talking Picture Service.

Foundation Grants*

NATIONAL

1. The National Endowment for the Arts (NEA) is an independent agency of the U.S. government. It supports a number of programs, most of which are only available to nonprofit, tax-exempt organizations: grants to Media Arts Centers, Video Artists Fellowships, Aid to Film and Video Exhibition, In-Residence/Workshop Programs (which enable organizations to invite nationally recognized filmmakers and videomakers for stays of various lengths of time), production of film and video and radio work, and archival programs.

The grant categories which it supports (or assists in support) for individuals are the *American Film Institute*, the *Independent Documentary Fund for Public Television*, and the *Short Film Showcase*. Of this group only the first may be applied for at the Endowment. (See separate listings for these.)

The Media Arts Program of the Endowment also makes grants to individuals under the "Production" and "Services to the Field" categories. Generally, grants are made only on a matching basis: for every dollar the applicant requests, he or she must show a matching source and amount of money. This means that in most cases, the applicant supplies one half of what is needed, NEA supplying the remaining half.

Limited funds are also available to film and video makers under other NEA programs, such as the Music Program (Dance Film/Video) and the Education Program, which has a Film and Video Component.

Filmmakers should write the Endowment for their substantial and informative brochure "Application Guidelines, Media Arts: Film/Radio/Television," which supplies all detailed information regarding the programs, as well as application forms and budget sheets. Address requests to:

---

*Adapted from a list compiled by Ernest Nukanen, San Francisco State University.

Grants Office, National Endowment for the Arts, 2401 "E" Street, NW, Washington, D.C. 20506.

2. The National Endowment for the Humanities assists groups, institutions, and organizations that seek to identify, develop, and produce television, film, and radio programs in the humanities. The humanities include history, archaeology, comparative religion, philosophy, language, linguistics, literature, jurisprudence, history and criticism of the arts, ethics, and aspects of the social sciences.

The Media Program: Films and video programs must show a substantive and clearly defined use of specific humanities resources (published scholarship, archival materials, field research and artifacts), as well as the direct collaboration between the appropriate scholars in the humanities and highly skilled, experienced media professionals.

Five basic kinds of grants are provided: *Planning*—to explore the relationship between scholars in the humanities and media organizations; *Research and Development Grants* —for applicants who have a specific plan for a media program related to the humanities; *Pilot Grants*—for those who have completed one or more scripts for a TV, radio, or film series designed to examine a specific subject in the humanities; *Production Grants* for a single film or TV program or limited radio series, or for those who have completed a pilot and wish funding for the series; and *Acquisition Grants* for existing programs or films designed to advance an understanding of knowledge drawn from the humanities.

The Endowment provides three kinds of grant support: (1) outright grants for certain program costs; (2) gifts and matching grants; and (3) combined grants (composed of both outright and matching). The Endowment has a cost-sharing requirement which asks that in some cases applicants must contribute to the costs of the film or program to the extent possible. Such contributions may be in-kind or in cash.

Grants are awarded on the basis of the applicant's proposal and as approved budget. All rights to the material remain with the grantee, but half of any royalty or net proceeds in excess of $200 must be returned to the Endowment until the amount returned equals the sum of the Endowment's original support.

Once you have received your copy of the guidelines booklets and have determined that your film or video program falls within general guidelines, you should send a preliminary inquiry describing the film or program. This should be done at least six weeks before the deadline for formal submission. Write to Media Program, Division of Public Programs (Mail Stop 403), National Endowment for the Humanities, 806 15th Street, NW, Washington, D.C. 20506.

3. The American Film Institute. This program assists filmmakers working in animated, documentary, experimental, or narrative films. The grants, annually, run up to $10,000 per filmmaker. For further information contact, The American Film Institute, 501 Doheny Drive, Beverly Hills, Calif. 90210.

4. The Independent Documentary Fund for Public Television. For both film and video makers, this grant program is administered by the Television Lab at WNET, Channel 13, in New York City. Its purpose is to encourage the production of documentaries for public television by independent producers. There is no restriction on subject matter or format other than acceptability for broadcast on PBS. Write to Television Lab, WNET, 356 West 58 Street, New York, N.Y. 10019.

5. The Short Film Showcase. A program administered by the Foundation for Independent Video and Filmmakers in New York, it distributes completed short films by independents to commercial theaters throughout the United States. In effect, the Showcase purchases a nonexclusive option for theatrical distribution from the filmmaker for up to $2,500 for three years. For information: The Foundation for Independent Video and Film, 99 Prince Street, New York, N.Y. 10012.

6. The Revolving Documentary Fund. Administered and granted by the Corporation for Public Broadcasting under new guidelines (available by the fall of 1979), this fund is for the production of documentaries of quality and impact over a broad range of subjects. Proposals from independent film-

makers and from PBS stations are accepted. About $1 million will be available to the fund. For information on applications and guidelines, write: The Revolving Documentary Fund, Television Activities, Corporation for Public Broadcasting, 1111 16th St., NW, Washington, D.C. 20036.

7. Step-Up Completion Fund. This fund, administered by PBS from granted CPB funds, gives modest amounts (approximately $200-plus per finished film minute) to permit completion of films or video programs specifically for national PBS broadcast or to bring completed work up to broadcast quality. It was originally developed at CPB so that locally produced programs suitable for national airing could be made available and pays for such things as tape transfers and talent fees. PBS taps this fund to fill out its programming schedule. The average "buy" is about $12,000. Contact PBS Programming, 475 L'Enfant Plaza, SW, Washington, D.C. 20024.

Before any application is made to PBS, it is helpful to write for a copy of its "Independent Producers Guide," a booklet that lists the various programs and methods of application.

STATE RESOURCES

1. State Arts Councils. Most states now have a council that administers state grants to the arts. The councils are frequently more closely in touch with the arts needs and artists of a state than national foundations and are therefore an excellent source. Though some state councils do not place film and video in the ranks of the arts (making the grants in these areas small), many (California, New York, Oregon, Louisiana) are active supporters of film and video makers. Most councils meet on a regular basis throughout the year at the state capital. In addition, state arts councils often know of other state funds available to film and video makers and often prove to be excellent sources of information in this area.

2. State Humanities Committees. Each of the fifty states and Puerto Rico have state-based committees that work with the National Endowment for the Humanities on the state level. Many of these committees give grants for media production. They are, in essence, re-granting NEH funds to local, nonprofit organizations for programs of civic, business, labor, or community concern where they relate to the humanities. A list of these organizations may be obtained by writing the National Endowment for the Humanities.

3. Private Foundations, State. Each state has a few foundations that make grants to residents for film or video production within the state and on subjects of concern in that state. Use the research avenues suggested in Chapter 2 to determine which foundations within your state make grants to media.

PRIVATE FOUNDATIONS AND OTHER SOURCES: NATIONAL SCOPE

1. The Film Fund was created by independent filmmakers and video producers, distributors and community activists and funders to support the production and distribution of quality films, tapes, and slide programs on social issues for social change. It is a tax-exempt, national organization. The granting cycle is yearly. It gave $126,000 to 22 applicants in 1978. Contact for guidelines: The Film Fund, 80 East 11th Street, New York, N.Y. 10003, or 308 11th Street, San Francisco, Calif. 94103.

2. The Foundation for Independent Video and Film, Inc., 99 Prince St, New York, N.Y. 10012. This foundation grew out of the Association of Independent Video and Film Makers (AIVF), a national nonprofit association. Comparatively new, its goals are to give increased support to independently produced film and video work.

3. The Arca Foundation gives grants for educational programs that are geared toward population control and stabilization. The foundation is considering proposals for educational films that emphasize population stabilization,

nutrition, and nontraditional education. Frank D. Dobyns, Executive Director, Arca Foundation, 100 East 85 Street, New York, N.Y. 10025.

4. The Robert Sterling Clark Foundation takes a very broad approach to philanthropy, considering proposals for projects of great diversity. While most of its giving is centered primarily in New York City, grants are given nationwide. The foundation tends to support well-established groups with traditional programs and funds many of the same organizations each year. Mr. Robert F. Higgins, Executive Director, Robert Sterling Clark Foundation, 100 Wall Street, New York, N.Y. 10005.

5. The Arthur Vining Davis Foundations are actually three foundations which function as a single philanthropic institution. Since 1965 a major portion of the grants by the Foundation have been made in the fields of private education, medicine, and religion. Recently, public television programming has been added as a principal area of interest, with grants going to motion picture production and acquisition. The Arthur Vining Davis Foundations, 1714 South Biscayne Boulevard, Miami, Fla. 33131.

6. The Ford Foundation has supported motion picture production along with several film training programs through its Division of Humanities and the Arts. Grants are given to organizations as well as filmmakers of national reputation. The foundation is also very active in supporting educational television through its Noncommercial Television Grants Program. The Ford Foundation, 320 East 43rd Street, New York, N.Y. 10017.

7. The John Simon Guggenheim Memorial Foundation offers annual fellowships to men and women of high intellectual and personal qualifications who have already demonstrated unusual capacity for productive scholarship or unusual creative ability in the fine arts. The fellowships for film and video artists include support for production expenses. The fellows are usually between thirty and forty-five years of age. The John Simon Guggenheim Memorial Foundation, 90 Park Avenue, New York, N.Y. 10016.

8. The Edward W. Hazen Foundation supports a number of cross-cultural projects between Asia, Africa, and within the United States. The foundation focuses on higher education in developing nations, student values and concerns, and pioneering efforts to understand and improve higher education in the United States. The Hazen foundation supports films that promote respect and understanding between the races and ethnic groups of our nation. Dr. William L. Bradley, President, Edward W. Hazen Foundation, 400 Prospect Street, New Haven, Conn. 06511.

9. The Jerome Foundation. The majority of the foundation's grants have gone to support the development of talented filmmakers, the showing of new films, and documentation and publication in the film field. Grants to individuals and to organizations range from $2,000 to $300,000. The foundation meets quarterly to award grants. Mr. A. A. Heckman, President, Jerome Foundation, West 1052 First National Bank Bldg., St. Paul, Minn. 55101.

10. The Robert Wood Johnson Foundation is the second largest foundation in the United States and is devoted exclusively to the field of health care. The foundation is giving high priority to demonstration projects, including health training programs. Grants are awarded for educational films that contribute to health care awareness and training. Miss Margaret E. Mahoney, Vice President, Robert Wood Johnson Foundation, Forrestal Center, P. O. Box 2316, Princeton, N.J. 08540.

11. The Lilly Endowment has traditionally worked to promote religion, education, and community development since its creation in 1937. The foundation is currently taking a more community-oriented approach to funding by supporting innovative programs in education, the arts, and self-help community groups trying to alleviate the problems of inner-city life. The Lilly Endowment is also underwriting numerous Corporation for Public Broadcasting telecasts. Lilly Endowment, Inc., 2801 North Meridian St., Indianapolis, Ind. 46208.

12. The John and Mary R. Markle Foundation has been

giving grants that deal with all aspects of the communications media. Support has gone principally for scholarly research in the media and for acquisition grants to Public Broadcasting stations. Occasionally grants are given for media production purposes. One aspect of the foundation's program is to try to find ways in which the media can be used to benefit groups of the population—that is, children or minorities. Mr. Lloyd N. Morriset, President, John and Mary R. Markle Foundation, 50 Rockefeller Plaza, New York, N.Y. 10020.

13. The McGregor Fund supports seven areas of interest: education, health, welfare, the humanities, science, international affairs, and religion. While most of the fund's activities are centered in Michigan, grants are given nationwide. Most of the grants for motion picture production are for educational films. Mr. Cleveland Thurber, President, McGregor Fund, 2026 Commonwealth Building, Detroit, Mich. 48226.

14. The Andrew W. Mellon Foundation is one of the largest general-purpose foundations in the country with assets of over $636 million. The foundation prefers to support established organizations whose accomplishments are widely recognized in their field. Cultural projects received $11.5 million in grants in a recent year, including support to museum, libraries, and conservation organizations. Many of these grants are for public education purposes, including educational films and Corporation for Public Broadcasting telecasts. Paul Mellon is the only surviving foundation donor and exerts a great deal of influence in making grant selections. His major interests are in arts and humanities, archaeology, mythology, psychology, and literary criticism. Mr. John E. Sawyer, President, Andrew W. Mellon Foundation, 140 East 62d Street, New York, N.Y. 10021.

15. The Sydney Meyers Memorial Fund is administered by the Museum of Modern Art in New York City and gives annual awards to purchase and/or subsidize movies made by deserving film artists. The Sydney Meyers Memorial Fund, Museum of Modern Art, 11 E. 53rd St., New York, N.Y. 10019.

16. The General Mills Foundation gives grants in the areas of education, civic and cultural affairs, and health and

welfare. The foundation considers applications for film projects that are aimed at educating the public in these areas. Grants are given in communities in which General Mills is a corporate citizen. Mr. William R. Humphrey, Jr., Vice President and Executive Director, General Mills Foundation, Box 1113, Minneapolis, Minn. 55440.

17. The John D. Rockefeller 3rd Fund was established in 1963 by John D. Rockefeller 3rd to support cultural exchange activities between the United States and the countries of Asia extending from Japan through Afghanistan. The foundation's Asian Cultural Program regularly funds film projects that document the traditional Asian visual and performing arts. Grants under the Asian Cultural Program are made to organizations and also to individuals in the form of fellowships. Grants to individuals are made only when the applicant has had special preparation in the Asian arts field. Mr. Richard S. Lanier, Director, Asian Cultural Program, JDR 3rd Fund, 50 Rockefeller Plaza, New York, N.Y. 10020.

18. The Sears-Roebuck Foundation. Recently, the Sears-Roebuck Foundation has added cultural activities to its list of programs receiving support. Most of the grants in this area have gone to the performing arts. Another new emphasis of the foundation is support on all levels of education. Mr. Edward L. Quinn, Vice President and Executive Director, Sears-Roebuck Foundation, Dept. 703, Sears Tower, Chicago, Ill. 60684.

19. Alfred P. Sloan Foundation. The principal interests of the Alfred P. Sloan Foundation are to resolve social problems by supporting the development and application of new knowledge in science, technology, engineering, economics, management science, and cancer research. Recently the foundation has expanded its program to support media technology in education and is considering proposals for educational films and television. Alfred P. Sloan Foundation, 630 Fifth Avenue, New York, N.Y. 10020.

20. The Tinker Foundation gives grants to produce films that contribute to respect and understanding of Ibero-America. The foundation regularly funds filmmaking crews to produce ethnographic documentaries on Latin America.

Most organizations receiving support are educational institutions, museums, and public broadcasting stations. Tinker Foundation, 645 Madison Avenue, New York, N.Y. 10022.

APPENDIX B

STANDARD MOTION PICTURE PRODUCTION CONTRACT

© MCMLXXVI INTERNATIONAL QUORUM OF MOTION PICTURE PRODUCERS

This Agreement is made at _____
this _____ day of _____ 19____ between _____
_____ whose address is _____
_____
hereinafter called the Client, and _____,
organized and existing under the laws of _____
_____, and hereinafter called the Producer, for the purpose of producing a
motion picture under the following specifications, terms and conditions.

Clause 1   DESCRIPTION
The Producer shall make and the Client shall buy a sound color motion picture with the working

title of _____

on the subject of _____

which when complete will run approximately _____ _____ minutes and is to be photo-

graphed on _____ stock and prints are to be made on _____

_____ stock.

Clause 2   PAYMENT
In consideration for this motion picture the Client shall pay _____,
hereinafter called the Contract Price, according to the following terms:
_____ percent on signing of this Agreement
_____ percent on completion of script
_____ percent on completion of principal photography
_____ percent on Client approval at interlock showing
Invoices are payable net within 10 days of receipt. No discounts or commissions are allowed.

Clause 3   PRODUCTION/APPROVAL SCHEDULE
The parties agree to cooperate and work in a prompt and businesslike manner to complete this
motion picture, if possible, in accordance with the following schedule:
Treatment or script by _____
Client approval by _____
Photography and recording by _____
Interlock showing by _____
Answer print by _____
Client approval by _____
Release prints by _____

Clause 4   SERVICES
The Producer shall provide all services, materials, technical personnel and equipment necessary
for the professional completion of this motion picture, and as are called for in the approved script,
except as to services, materials, technical personnel and equipment furnished by the Client.

Clause 5   QUALITY STANDARDS
The Producer agrees to perform under this Agreement in accordance with the trade standards and
ethics of the International Quorum of Motion Picture Producers and with the quality standards of
the Producer's work as previously exhibited to the Client. The Client agrees that he is satisfied
with the professional competence of the Producer.

Clause 6   LIAISON REPRESENTATIVE
The Client agrees to appoint one liaison representative who shall have full power to act for the
Client, including prompt and final approval of work at all stages, binding upon the Client. The
liaison representative shall be available to the Producer and responsible for the Client's technical
and policy decisions during photography and recording.

Clause 7   PRODUCER COOPERATION
The Producer agrees to minimize interruption or inconvenience to the Client during the Producer's
work and to complete his work in a prompt and business-like manner.

Clause 8 CLIENT COOPERATION

The Client agrees to provide the Producer with such reasonable assistance as is necessary for completion of this motion picture, including but not limited to script research; arranging photography and recording in locations under control of the Client; loan of products, technical equipment and properties; expert assistance, and making Client personnel available for appearance in this motion picture. Client agrees to provide for safety of producer personnel when in locations under Client control, and in such cases as the Client knows unsafe conditions exist, he shall notify Producer of such unsafe conditions with sufficient advance notice for Producer to take remedial action.

Clause 9 APPROVALS

The Client agrees to correct and approve the Producer's work promptly upon submission, and where corrections are required, the Client shall be specific and constructive so that the Producer is able to make corrections promptly and professionally.

The Producer shall obtain approval of the Client, which shall not be unreasonably withheld, at the following stages:
    A. Completion of treatment or shooting script
    B. Completion of storyboard or key drawings for animation, if any
    C. Interlock showing
    D. Delivery of answer print

Clause 10 ADDITIONAL WORK AND COSTS

A. All photography and recording necessary for completion of this motion picture are included in the Contract Price. Additional photography and recording ordered by the Client to be performed during production of this motion picture are to be charged to the Client. Such additional work would include photography and recording ordered by the Client prior to script approval and not needed in the motion picture, and extra footage for television commercials, archives, publicity, scientific study and sales.

B. The Producer shall make such reasonable changes as the Client may request without charge. If, in order to comply with additional Client changes, the Producer must depart from the previously approved work and specifications and incur additional expense as a result, the Client shall reimburse the Producer. However, the Producer shall make changes at his own expense if they are the result of his own unsatisfactory work or his material departure from specifications.

C. If the Client fails to provide facilities, personnel, properties or other requirements at the time and place agreed between the parties, thereby increasing costs to the Producer, the Client shall reimburse the Producer.

D. The Client agrees that once he has accepted one phase of work and authorized the Producer to proceed to the next, he may not revise or order revision of earlier approved work unless the Producer agrees to do so, in which case the Client will reimburse the Producer the costs of such revisions.

Clause 11 RIGHTS

A. The Producer shall obtain all rights to dramatic, literary, artistic and musical work and performance necessary for the completion of this motion picture and its uses as defined in Clause 13 herein. The Producer agrees to obtain releases wherever practical from professional talent performing and speaking in this motion picture. The Client agrees to accept responsibility for legal clearance for photography and recording of personnel and locations under its control.

B. Originals and negatives of this motion picture are to be owned by the _____
Production materials are to remain in the custody of the Producer for storage and making of prints in accordance with Producer's standards. Provision of additional prints and special versions of this motion picture shall be commissioned only from the Producer.

C. The securing of rights for this motion picture by the Producer shall not be construed to comprise rights for the Client to use such performance, work, likeness or name in any other manner.

D. Producer shall have the right to own and use prints of this motion picture for his own library, reference and demonstration.

E. The Producer shall accept responsibility for securing at his expense copyright protection for this motion picture in Producer's name as a means of protecting both parties against outside infringement.

Clause 12 WARRANTY

The Producer warrants that his own creative work shall be original and subject to legal protection as such, and that this motion picture shall not violate or infringe on any copyright or patent right.

Clause 13 USES

A. The Client shall use this motion picture only for the following purposes:
(Strike out uses not applicable)
      Theatrical
      Non-theatrical
      Television

And in the following geographical areas _____
The Client shall not exhibit the motion picture for other purposes or in other areas without first obtaining written consent from the Producer and paying for any additional rights or permissions necessary.

B. The parties agree that neither party may resell or syndicate this motion picture or any part of it without prior written consent of the other party.

C. The parties agree that stock shots may be used in this motion picture and scenes from this motion picture may be used as stock shots in other motion pictures.

Clause 14   SCREEN CREDITS

Producer shall have the right to include in the titles of this motion picture his own name and the names of his chief production personnel, and seals or insignia in accordance with the Producer's obligations to labor unions or other organizations.

Clause 15   PRINTS

The Producer shall supply, free of any claim, lien, charge, mortgage or encumbrance, except as

mentioned in Clause 21, one answer print of this motion picture and _____ release prints. If no release prints are provided as part of the Contract Price, release prints will be supplied by the Producer to the Client in accordance with the following schedule of prices and quantities:

_____

_____

The above prices are based on a running time of _____ minutes and laboratory prices prevailing on the date of this Agreement. Should the length and completion date of this motion picture vary from those specified, the above release print prices will vary accordingly.

All prints shall be mounted on standard reels head-out, packed in standard cases, marked by title and fitted with head and tail leaders.

Clause 16   INDEMNITY AND INSURANCE

A.   Producer and Client agree that both parties shall maintain normal insurance protection against all claims during production of this motion picture. The Producer agrees to take reasonable precautions against damage and loss but cannot be responsible for damage or loss to property owned or supplied by Client that is involved in this motion picture.

B.   The Client indemnifies the Producer against all actions, civil or criminal, claims or demands other than those covered by Clause 11 herein, which may arise out of the sound or picture content of this motion picture or any exhibition of it. The Client further indemnifies the Producer against claims resulting from use of Client products, services on locations during production of this motion picture, and against claims resulting from motion picture footage, photographs, art or recordings furnished by Client for use in this motion picture.

C.   The Producer indemnifies the Client against all actions, claims or demands arising from dramatic, literary, artistic or musical rights obtained by the Producer for this motion picture.

Clause 17   TAXES

The Client agrees to pay all applicable taxes on all billings hereunder.

Clause 18   TRAVEL AND ACCOMMODATIONS

The Producer agrees to pay for all travel and accommodations for persons in his hire for this motion picture, and the Client agrees to pay for all travel and accommodations of Client personnel who travel in connection with the production of this motion picture.

Clause 19   SPECIAL PROVISIONS

The following special provisions are agreed to and initialed by the parties: (Entries here may cover such matters as famous-name talent, multiple sponsorship, currency adjustment, distribution, duplicating masters, music score details, number and identity of locations, and public print sales. If none, write None.)

Clause 20   INDEPENDENT CONTRACTOR

The Producer warrants and agrees that in all transactions relating to this motion picture he is an independent contractor and that all contracts and arrangements, including those of employment, shall be made by the Producer as principal and not as an agent for the Client.

Clause 21   TIMELY PAYMENT

A.   In the event the Client fails to make timely payments, the Producer shall have the right to suspend production until due payment is received. However the Producer must resume immedi-

ately on receipt of such payment plus service fee not to exceed _____ percent per annum on balance due, plus such collection costs. arbitration and legal fees as have been expended.

B.   The Producer is required to complete and release this motion picture and related materials immediately after receipt of all due payments. The Producer shall have a lien on all prints and other tangible property related to this Agreement until all payments are made by the Client to the Producer.

Clause 22   DELAY AND TERMINATION

A.   Delay by the Producer in production of this motion picture due to war, fire, embargoes, strikes, laws, lockouts, government orders, industrial actions, illness, accidents, laboratory failures, public disaster, Acts of God or other cause beyond his control shall not give rise to any claim against the Producer.

B.   In the event of unreasonable delay due to the above causes, the Client shall be entitled to terminate this Agreement subject to payment of all costs incurred and commitments made by the Producer to the date of termination, inclusive of overhead, plus 10 percent of such costs. Where such total amount is exceeded by the amounts already paid by the Client hereunder, the difference shall be immediately reimbursed by the Producer to the Client.

C.   If at any time the Client wishes to abandon production of this motion picture for any reason whatsoever, the Client may do so by giving written notice to the Producer and paying the Producer only the amount of profit which would have been due had the motion picture been completed and for costs of production incurred or committed by the Producer prior to date of termination. Immediately on receipt of termination notice, the Producer shall acknowledge and agree to termination, end all work, commitments and expense in the best financial interests of the Client, and submit to the Client within 30 days of receipt of termination notice a detailed and final claim.

Clause 23   ARBITRATION

Any dispute or difference arising hereunder shall be settled by arbitration within 60 days of receipt of written notice by one party to the other. The dispute or difference shall be referred to a single arbitrator to be agreed between the parties. Failing agreement, each party shall select an arbitrator and they together shall select the single arbitrator to settle the dispute or difference.

Clause 24   BANKRUPTCY AND LIQUIDATION

Either party to this Agreement shall be entitled to terminate this Agreement by written notice to the other party if that other party shall become bankrupt or have a receiving order made against him or shall present his petition in bankruptcy or shall make an arrangement with his creditors or shall have an execution levied on his goods or, being a corporation, shall go into liquidation (other than in connection with a plan of reconstruction or amalgamation) or have a resolution for its winding up or have a receiver appointed.

Clause 25   ENTIRE AGREEMENT

This instrument sets forth the entire agreement between the parties, all prior negotiations and understandings are merged herein, and no change or addition shall be of any effect unless in writing and signed by both parties.

In witness whereof the parties have executed this Agreement this _____

day of _____ 19 _____.

CLIENT _____

SIGNED BY _____(SEAL)

TITLE _____

PRODUCER _____

SIGNED BY _____(SEAL)

TITLE _____

WITNESSED BY _____

Production Budget

Date _____

_____ (Production Title & Number)

Type of Film _____

1. STAFF

Producer	$
Director	$
Asst. Director	$
Researcher/Writer	$
Production Mgr.	$
Production Asst.	$
Script/Continuity	$
Secretary	$
Tech. Asst./Consultants	$

   subtotal _____

2. CREW

Cameraperson	$
Assistant Camera	$
Soundperson (Mixer/Recordist)	$
Sound (boom)	$
Gaffer	$
Asst. Gaffer	$
Grip	$
Assistant	$
Graphic Artist	$
Props	$
Still Photographer	$

   subtotal _____

3. TALENT

Narrator	$
Actors	$
—wardrobe	$
—makeup	$
Extras	$
Other	$

   subtotal _____

PRODUCTION BUDGET, p. 2

Date _____

_____ (Production Title & Number)

4. EQUIPMENT RENTAL	# of days	$ per day	Total
Camera Gear			
Sound Gear			
Lights			
Props			
Editing Equip.			
Studio			
Other Special			
Subtotal:			_____

5. SUPPLIES	# of rolls	$ per roll	Total
Film Stocks			
¼ Inch Tape			
Videotape			
Mag. Stock			
16mm			
35mm			
Subtotal:			_____

6. POST-PRODUCTION	# of ft	$ per ft	Total

A. *Processing Picture*

Type _____
Type _____
Type _____
Workprint
Coding
Transf. Mix to Optical
Answ. Print
Interneg. or CRI
1st Trial or Check Print
Release Prints
Reels and Cans

subtotal _____

B. *Sound*

Recording (a) Music (b) Narration
(c) Other
Transferring/Resolving
Sound Mix (Dub)
EQ
Rerecording
Interlock Projection
Sound Effects

subtotal _____

PRODUCTION BUDGET, p. 3

Date _____

_____ (Production Title & Number)

6. POST-PRODUCTION, cont.

    C. *Music*

        Original Score
          Composer
          Musicians
          Other
        Cleared Library Music
        Other: Rights Clearances,
          Worldwide
          Television
          Broad
        Miscellaneous

                        subtotal _____

    D. *Art*

        Titles (main/end)
        Layout Design
        Animation
          simple
          complex
        Other

                        subtotal _____

    E. *Editing*

        Editor
        Asst. Editor
        Conforming/Negative Cutter
        Sound/Music Editor
        Other

                        subtotal _____

PRODUCTION BUDGET, p. 4

Date _____

_____ (Production Title & Number)

7. PRODUCTION EXPENSES

A. *Travel* Research/Writing Production Crew	# of trips	cost	total
B. *Other Travel* Car Rentals Truck Rentals Helicopter	@ per mi		total
C. *Per Diem* Research/Writing Production Crew Other	# of people	days @	total
D. Releases			

subtotal _____

8. ADDITIONAL EXPENSES

A. Options

B. Storyboard
    Artists and Supplies

C. Opticals

D. Shipping, Trucking

subtotal _____

9. TOTALS FOR PRODUCTION

Staff
Crew
Talent
Equipment
Supplies
Processing Picture
Sound
Music
Art
Editing
Production Expenses
Additional Expenses

(continued)

subtotal _____

PRODUCTION BUDGET, p. 5

Date _____

_____ (Production Title & Number)

TOTALS FOR PRODUCTIONS, cont.

Overhead (Messenger, Copying, Office, Telephone, etc.)	(___%)	
Insurance	(___%)	
Legal Expenses		
Contingency	(___%)	
Profit	(___%)	
	subtotal _____	
Taxes (state, local, payroll, pension, etc.)	(___%)	
PRODUCTION TOTAL	_____	

DISTRIBUTION BUDGET

Personnel
Prints
Literature and Printed Promotion
   —writer
   —artist and layout
   —printing
Print Maintenance
Postage & Shipping
Reels and Cans
Correspondence (secretarial)
Customs/Duties
Insurance
Film Festival Fees
Miscellaneous

DISTRIBUTION TOTAL   _____

Sample Proposals:
Two Information Films

Proposals and presentations come in every shape, length, and form, but generally they follow an orderly description of film objective (or purpose), theme, audience, content (or description of the film), budget, and distribution.

Here are two proposals that reflect the basic format, though each has developed its own approach to the organization of the material—because the nature of the film at hand often dictates the various topics to be discussed about it, as well as their organization within the proposal form.

The first example is a preliminary outline for a documentary/educational film:

*Re-entry for the Woman Prisoner**
(28-minute, 16mm color)
by
Gwendolyn Stripling

INTRODUCTION: RATIONALE FOR
THE USE OF FILM

Film is today's only language, and it speaks in color and movement and sound. Film has been used successfully in every field of investigation to gain or impart knowledge difficult to attain or communicate in any other way. Film demonstrates and teaches; film engages the audience emotionally and gives the viewers a sense of participation that no other medium can do as well. Language, education, and emotional barriers present in the prison population dictate that a film be made, that no other medium will communicate as quickly or as well.

---

*All Rights Reserved, © Stripling 1978.

1. THE FILM'S OBJECTIVES

Most women are paroled from prison without knowing what will happen, or what is required of them, what problems they will surely face "on the outside." The main objective of the film is to prepare women prisoners to re-enter American society, to help decrease their fears and apprehensions of the world outside.

2. THEME

The underlying theme is a positive statement to prisoners: these women on the screen recognized the adjustments to be made and the problems to be faced. It wasn't easy. If they can do it, you can do it.

3. DESCRIPTION OF THE FILM

The film will focus on three women—one black, one Chicana, and one Caucasian—as they prepare to leave the prison system. In dialogues with each other, and with prison and rehabilitation officials, the film will show their apprehensions (which are not unfounded and must be confronted) and the various roles the women prisoners will assume in a society that they have not been a part of for years. In this vein, it will be shown to be imperative that the women recognize the attitudes and prejudices of society about women ex-convicts. To bolster the re-entry process, the film will cover job skills and employment, educational training, counseling on family relationships and social adaptations—since these are primary concerns of the parolee and the prison parole boards. In short, the film will take the three women prisoners step by step, on both emotional and practical levels, through this period to the day of their release.

4. AUDIENCE

Primary: For all women currently in prison, women about to be released from prison, and those recently out of prison.

Secondary: For the parole system, and for the public, which includes students of criminology, social welfare, women's studies, and social psychology. The film will give students a much more direct comprehension of all the problems women convicts face when released from prison. It is also directed toward various prison associations that conduct prison research and reform study, for the film will show the need for a community-wide approach to prison-related problems over which the prisoner herself has little control.

5. STYLE

Closest in form to a social documentary, the film will be shot with real prisoners—those about to be paroled from a selected California institution. It will also carry the voice-over experiences of real prisoners who have just been released, who let us know in their own words what some of the social and economic problems are that all women prisoners must face. The film must appear, in style and execution, candid, spontaneous, without artifice of any kind so that the prisoners and parole officers for whom it is primarily intended can relate to and identify with the women on the screen.

6. BUDGET

The estimated budget for all phases of production, from planning stages through post production, is $50,000. A detailed budget is available on request.

7. DISTRIBUTION AND USE

Primary: In prisons and for the parole systems. An evaluation system will be established after each viewing of the film so that prisoners can relate their opinions of the film and the information presented in it, how it applies to them and their situations. This use of the film will enable the parole officer to analyze her prisoner(s) regarding her re-entry program. The evaluation must be oral, providing more candid and open responses from the women.

Secondary: The film has a significant market in the educational and community network. For this reason, the proposal has been sent to various distributors seeking their reactions to the subject matter and its treatment. Their positive responses are attached, for it is obvious that few films on this subject exist, and none directed to women prisoners. The responses from the distributors indicate that commercial education distribution will take place. In addition, the 28-minute length, as well as the national subject matter, make this film suitable for television broadcast. The Public Broadcasting Service in Washington, D.C. has been contacted, and their positive responses are also attached to the proposal. It appears likely that the film, besides its very real and major use within the prison system, will receive a broad audience beyond. Reaching that audience is, of course, necessary to accomplish the secondary goal of the film— community awareness, community response.

The second proposal sample provides a variation of the format. The filmmaker gives a story outline at the beginning, followed by notes on audience, distribution, budget, and so on.

*Survival Run**

by

Magus Films, Inc.

*Competing in the Dipsea
Race is like competing in
life. You don't win it;
you survive it.*

    Harry Cordellos

*All Rights Reserved, © Magus Films, Inc., 1978, Two Embarcadero Center, Suite 2780, San Francisco, Calif. 94111.

THE FILM (A TREATMENT)

Fade in on a downtown San Francisco street at dawn. A blind man taps his way along the deserted sidewalk, heading toward the subway station. He carries a collapsible cane in one hand and a bright orange athletic bag in the other.

His name is Harry Cordellos. At 40, he is the country's top blind athlete. Harry takes the escalator down to the station and waits for an eastbound train. Silently, a subway glides in and Harry steps aboard, sitting by a large window. As the car accelerates, tunnel lights sweep across his face, reflecting in his dark glasses. He is lost in thought.

Suddenly, we are outside. Sunlight streams through redwood trees, illuminating the blind man. He is running along a firetrail on the edge of the forest. His dark glasses are gone, revealing eyes that appear opalescent in the sun.

As we pull back, we see him pacing alongside another runner, Mike Restani. Harry grips Mike's wrist as they climb up the mountainside. Their legs move in perfect unison. They are dressed for a marathon.

It is an odd couple. Harry is thin, tightly muscled, spidering his way up the slope. Mike is massive, chugging forward like a diesel semi, pulling his partner along.

Mike guides Harry with a verbal command as their running path changes. He gently shepherds his companion around a turn with the touch of an elbow or the squeeze of an arm. As Harry strides alongside Mike, he smiles into the wind.

We are back aboard the subway. Harry's smiling face fills the screen. In a moment, the train rises out of its tunnel into the morning light of Oakland. Another workday.

Harry mans the switchboard of a transit company. He answers phones and directs lost commuters to their destinations. But today he is thinking about something besides timetables and transfer points.

In less than a week, he and Mike are going to run the toughest race of their lives: the Dipsea.

The Dipsea course in Marin County is a mere 6.8 miles.

But it is the ultimate cross-country race. The route from Mill Valley to Stinson Beach is filled with winding stairs, treacherous ravines and gulleys, steep mountainside ridges, and thorn-infested thickets.

It is a punishing race. One-half running, one-half sheer survival. But to Mike, a self-admitted "madman" who seeks to push himself beyond the limits of his body, and to Harry, who gave up the whole notion of limits years ago, the Dipsea challenge is irresistible.

Two o'clock is quitting time for Harry. He meets Mike at Lake Merced for their daily workout, a ten-mile run around the suburban park. The pair maintains a smooth, even pace. Other afternoon runners pass and wave. Soon, Harry and Mike are swept into the group and disappear beyond the Lake House.

After the workout, both partners relax at a local diner. Over pie and coffee, Harry describes his past: a childhood of blindness, his athletic awakening ten years ago, the importance of competition in his life. Mike talks about the enormous responsibility of being Harry's "eyes".

But the conversation soon turns to the upcoming Dipsea Race. With only a week to go, the pair has to work on a running technique to get a blind man and his guide over the tortuous route without a mishap.

During this week of training, we experience with Harry and Mike the different running environments of San Francisco. On a cool, grey morning, the pair runs along the waterfront. They are joined by the tough, old men of the Dolphin Street Running Club. This motley pack heads up the wharf toward the Golden Gate Bridge for an early morning race.

At noontime, Harry and Mike jog along the Marina Green, the social center for runners in the city. This course is filled with young women in the latest running styles, pursued by young men with more than exercise on their minds. The whole world seems to be jogging on the Green today.

The evening sun silhouettes Harry and Mike as they

sprint along the ocean beach. Their days of training will soon be over.

It is Dipsea Sunday. The Bay Area is lost in morning fog. Slowly, the greyness disperses over Mill Valley as the first runners arrive. The officials expect 1,500 participants this year. Grandfathers and preteens, housewives and lawyers. Today they are all marathoners.

Harry and Mike join in the pre-run rituals: suiting up, stretching exercises, the last-minute energy food. Harry adjusts his red kneepads and pulls on his leather gloves. Now they are ready. They assume their starting positions.

The town clock strikes 9:00. The starter gun fires. The race has begun.

The runners spread out over the main street with Harry and Mike in the lead. Soon, they are all powering up the 671 steps that begin the ordeal. Mike calls out each step to Harry, who is gripping the handrail and his partner's wrist. Their legs are pumping in unison as they hit Windy Gap. Here some of the faster runners pass the two, shouting out their encouragements as they race by.

The running horde cuts across the Flying Y Ranch, scattering the frenzied horses. Mike is carefully guiding Harry through the poison oak and the blackberry thickets. Everyone is feeling the altitude. Traffic is stopped on Panoramic Highway as the first runners cross, heading down toward Suicide Hill.

This is a steep descent, covered with loose rock and soil. The front runners are struggling to control their slides. A few have taken headers. Mike shouts to Harry to shift positions. Harry swings behind his guide and grabs him from the rear, train-fashion. In tandem, the two chug down the hillside.

Mike maintains a steady flow of orders, talking Harry through each hop, step, and jump of the route. At the same time, he must establish enough footing to offset Harry's momentum. They hit the bottom of the hill in one last two-man leap and scramble off into Muir Woods, splashing across a creek with twenty other runners.

This high-speed trek continues up a nature trail through the redwoods. When they finally break out of the forest, they face the dry, baking heat of summer and a two-mile mountain ridge.

Mike and Harry break from the pack and run onto a broad firetrail that runs parallel to the actual Dipsea route. They have further to run, at a higher elevation, but navigation is easier. The pair can now run side-by-side again. From the top of Cardiac Hill, a long train of Dipsea runners stretches across the horizon, moving towards the sea like a vast migration of nomads in running shorts.

Harry and Mike have been racing for an hour now. Only two and a half miles to go until Stinson Beach. But in Swoop Hollow, a near-disaster occurs. A traffic jam of runners is clogging the twisted gulleys. Harry and Mike must step aside to let the faster ones skitter through. As they move onto the thirty degree slope, Harry's footing gives way. Without breaking stride, Mike lifts Harry into the train-position once more—a Herculean effort which transforms the two into a sure-footed quadruped again.

The final drama occurs in Steep Ravine which plunges through a rain forest. Mike must navigate Harry around a fallen redwood tree, practically carrying him over the enormous trunk. Jogging was never like this.

By this time they reach the pastureland overlooking the finish; they have been passed by over three hundred runners pushing relentlessly onward towards the finish line. But for Mike and Harry, their greatest competition remains themselves. And as they leap over the wooden fence onto Highway One, they begin to feel the adrenalin rush of victory. A victory of faith and endurance.

Sprinting toward Stinson Beach, Harry no longer feels the scrapes and bruises on his legs. He is only conscious of the cool sea breeze on his face and the chant of the welcoming crowd in the distance. "Harry, Harry, Harry!"

As the pair crosses the finish line, the chanting and applauding reach a crescendo. Their time: one hour and twenty-two minutes. A mere half hour out of first place. Mike explodes with joy, hugging Harry and swinging him past the cheering crowds. Harry smiles triumphantly. He can visualize this moment perfectly.

The applause fades. The image of Harry's smiling face dissolves into white.

We fade up into a San Francisco street at dawn as Harry taps his way towards the subway station. A new work week has begun.

But Harry is already thinking about the next marathon. A slightly modified version of the Dipsea: Mill Valley to Stinson Beach...and back.

* * *

THE AUDIENCE

Educational community (age range 15-35)

25 million runners

Roadrunner Club network in the U.S. and other running clubs

Libraries

The general public through its human interest story

Professional interest groups (schools for the handicapped, special educators, sociologists, optometrists, physical educators).

DISTRIBUTION

The following represents a basic outline of the distribution possibilities for *Survival Run*. If there is further interest in any of the alternatives offered, a specific and more detailed analysis can be submitted.

Educational Distribution

This system calls for a professional distributor and requires no additional capital for distribution. The distributor (that is, Pyramid Films, see letters attached), upon agreement to distribute the film, promotes and sells it to educational markets. The sponsor and the producer receive a percentage of the rental and sales fees. This system is excellent for reaching audiences between the ages of 15 and 25 interested in sports and human potential. The film can be shown in a wide variety of school disciplines from psychology to sociology and physical education.

Theatrical Distribution

United Artists has already expressed an interest in acquiring the film after its production to be shown in theaters across the country as a short. The sponsor can obtain wide exposure with many kinds of audiences, depending on the feature film it is playing with. There are two dramatic feature-length films on running to be released this year: *Running*, produced by Michael Douglas, and *The Golden Girl*, produced by Avco Embassy. *Survival Run* will be an extremely good complement to these films, and your company can benefit from the exposure to a running/sports-oriented audience.

Sponsored Distribution

Through this distribution system, the sponsor pays a professional distributor, such as Modern Talking Pictures or Association Films, to have the film distributed to target audiences. The sponsor chooses the geographical areas and the market segmentation he wishes to penetrate, and the distributor operates the distribution system according to these data. Although this system guarantees the sponsor's exposure to a specific cross section of the market, it represents an additional expense for prints and a service fee payable to the distributor.

Self-Distribution

The sponsor can select its target audiences and show the film as either part of a presentation to clients or by itself. Screenings would be at retail stores or local theaters with announcements being made in local media of the special screenings of the film.

Internationally

Since the film will be nonverbal for the most part, it could easily be shown internationally.

Television

Network and independent stations, perhaps public broadcasting services, could show the film as a documentary short. Specially edited parts of the film could be used as television spots.

FILM SPECIFICATIONS

Film: 16mm color
Length: Between 15 and 20 minutes
Sound: To use the full potential of the theme, the film should be nonverbal. The visuals can speak for themselves, carrying the message to the audience with an orchestration of sound effects, music, and some synch-sound of Harry Cordellos.
Locations: San Francisco Bay Area (Mill Valley, Lake Merced, San Francisco Marina, Stinson Beach, BART, and others)

PRODUCTION SCHEDULE

Pre-Production: 2 weeks
Production (filming): 1 week
Post-production (editing, mixing, and so on): 4 weeks

ESTIMATED BUDGET

The estimated cost for the production and post-production of this film is between $30,000 and $35,000. A detailed budget outline is available upon request.

OTHER CONSIDERATIONS

Theme of the Film

Survival Run is a film about Harry Cordellos, a blind athlete who runs one of the most difficult races in the country: the Dipsea, in Mill Valley, California.

The film not only conveys physical endurance and coordination of motion, but also provides the audience with a strikingly beautiful geographical background, a moving human interest story and the chance of witnessing an unprecedented event; for if the Dipsea Race is considered unusually tough by experienced runners who can see, it must seem inconceivable that a blind runner would dare to compete with them. It is evident, therefore, that *Survival Run* is in itself an astonishing story. It interrelates the national passion of running with an exceptional individual who is currently admired by the public. The theme of this film is bound to attract audiences throughout the country.

The Main Character: Harry Cordellos

For Harry, losing his sight was an opportunity to demonstrate the relativity of human limitations. His interest in athletic activities is reflected in his obtaining a degree in physical education. His visual disability has not allowed him to teach the subject on a full-time basis, but he has given conferences and served as an instructor on occasion, for several organizations.

Running is just one of the athletic activities in which Harry is involved. To the amazement of those who surround him, he also excels in water skiing, cross-country and downhill snow skiing, kayaking, hiking, swimming, horse riding and countless other sports. He is, indeed, quite a unique individual.

Harry's personality conveys a powerful charisma and, listening to his reflections on his struggle to better himself, encourages his audience to strive for higher goals.

Harry Cordellos is well-known to the running community in this country. His name appears frequently in running publications throughout the nation (*Runners World, Running Times, The Runner*, and *City Sports*, among others). Furthermore, he is the object of admiration of Dr. Kenneth Cooper's Aerobic Center and associations for the visually handicapped, such as the American Foundation for the Blind, the American Association for the Blind and The Eye Foundation. Harry is often set as an example of success to visually handicapped individuals.

His popularity among the general public is increasing rapidly. *US Magazine* recently printed (April 3 issue, see attachments) a feature story on Harry—exposure between 4 and 5 million readers. *Evening Magazine*, a television show produced by Group W, will be airing a personality profile on him in May—estimated audience of 30 million viewers in 25 markets. Also, *The Today Show*, and *Good Morning America* will be doing interviews with him later this year, and Harry's autobiography will be published in the fall. The sponsor, by having its name connected with Harry and the film, will have a guaranteed exposure during the film distribution period.

Impact

It is our consideration that Harry Cordellos will convey an image that will have a direct positive effect on the image of the sponsor and on the sales of its products. The fact that an exceptional blind athlete can run one of the toughest races in the country will certainly convey a feeling of reliability, endurance, and confidence to the audience.

The unique nature of this film, and the cinematographic quality that Magus Films is capable of incorporating into it are certain to make this movie a successful candidate at film festivals and, thus, have a very positive impact on the sponsor's public image.

National Organizations

Association of Independent Video and Film Makers, Inc. (AIVF) 99 Prince Street, NYC 10012. 212-966-0900. A national nonprofit association devoted to the support and independent film and videomakers. Formed in 1974, AIVF provides members with practical information and moral support, and seeks expanded distribution and exhibition of members' films and tapes. Monthly newsletter, screenings, presentations, workshops.

Independent Cinema Artists and Producers (ICAP), 99 Prince Street, NYC 10012. 212-966-0900. Began as the cable TV committee of AIVF and has now become a separate organization representing filmmakers with cable TV buyers nationally.

Information Film Producers of America, Inc., National Headquarters, 750 E. Colorado Blvd., Pasadena, Calif. 91101. 213-795-7866. The largest association of independent industrial and information film producers, founded in 1957, IFPA's goal is to help professionals improve their position in the industry and promote more business. Its members are people from all industry crafts (directors, producers, writers, technicians) as well as distributors, labs, and suppliers. It sponsors the CINDY awards each year, holds regional and national conferences, publishes a newsletter, and represents the independent industrial producer in the AFTRA/SAG negotiations.

International Quorum of Motion Picture Producers (IQ), International Headquarters, P.O. Box 395, Oakton, Va., 22124. 703-281-4508. A nonprofit, international network of film producers for business, government, television, and theaters founded in 1966. It assists in the exchange of ideas and information on an international scale through affiliations with member producers located throughout the world, and seeks to raise the professional standards of the motion pictures by examples of excellence. It offers members the opportunity to exchange or share personnel, equipment, or footage at any location in the world. Members include 115 motion picture companies located in 65 metropolitan U.S. areas and one company in each of 50 countries worldwide. Publishes *Quorum Quotes* on a quarterly basis, holds international conference annually, and presents the IQ One World IQ World Fellowship awards annually.

Independent Media Producers Association (IMPA), Suite 1000, 1100 17th Street, NW, Washington, D.C. 20036. 202-466-2175. IMPA is a trade association representing companies involved in the production or distribution of films or videotapes to see that the laws and regulations by the U.S. Government in Washington, D.C. reflect the needs of the communication industry. IMPA offers a newsletter (which outlines new rules and regs that affect producers), discounts on trade publications, and a Washington contact.

Women In Film, 8489 W. 3rd St., Suite 49, Los Angeles, CA., 90048 (213-651-3680). A non-profit corporation, founded in 1973, to promote equal rights for women in the industry, to serve as a clearinghouse of information on qualified women in film, and to educate the public and people in the industry about women in creative fields, discrimination and other problems women face in the industry. Monthly membership meetings, numerous workshops and presentations, monthly newsletter, membership roster. Chapters in New York, Atlanta and Washington, DC.

Selected Bibliography

Adler, Richard, and Walter S. Baer. *The Electronic Box Office: Humanities and Arts on the Cable.* New York: Praeger, 1974.

Allen, Herb, ed. *The Bread Game: The Realities of Foundation Fundraising.* San Francisco: Glide Publications, 1974.

Association of Independent Video and Filmmakers, Inc. and New Day Films. *Doing It Yourself: A Handbook of Independent Film Distribution.* New York, 1977.

Balio, Tino, ed. *The American Film Industry.* Madison: University of Wisconsin, 1976.

Bayer, William. *Breaking Through, Selling Out, Dropping Dead and Other Notes on Filmmaking.* New York: MacMillan, 1971.

Bluem, A. William, and Jason E. Squire. *The Movie Business: American Film Industry Practice.* New York: Communication Arts Books, Hastings House, 1973.

Bobker, Lee R. *Making Movies from Script to Screen.* New York: Harcourt Brace Jovanovich, 1973.

Brown, William O. *Low Budget Features.* Los Angeles: privately printed, 1971.

Butler, Ivan. *The Making of Feature Films: A Guide.* London: Penguin Books, 1971.

Chamness, Danford. *The Hollywood Guide to Film Budgets and Script Breakdown.* North Hollywood: D. Chamness and Associates, 1977.

Da Silva, Raul and Richard H. Rogers. *The Business of Filmmaking.* Rochester, New York: Eastman Kodak Company, 1978.

Farber, Donald C. and Paul A. Baumgarten. *Producing, Financing, and Distributing Film.* New York: Drama Book Specialists/Publishers, 1973.

Hampton, Benjamin B. *History of the American Film Industry.* New York: Dover, 1970.

Klein, Walter J. *The Sponsored Film.* New York: Communications Arts Books, Hastings House, 1976.

Lewis, Jerry. *The Total Filmmaker*. New York: Warner Paperback Library, 1973.

London, Mel. *Getting into Film*. New York: Ballantine, 1977.

Mayer, Michael F. *The Film Industries: Practical Business/ Legal Problems in Production, Distribution, and Exhibition*. New York: Communications Arts Books, Hastings House, 1973.

Sklar, Robert. *Movie Made America*. New York: Random House, 1975.

Smith, Ralph Lee. *The Wired Nation—Cable TV: The Electronic Communications Highway*. New York: Harper and Row, 1972.

Taylor, Theodore. *People Who Make Movies*. New York: Avon 1967.

Trachtenberg, Leo. *The Sponsor's Guide to Filmmaking*. New York: Hopkinson and Blake, 1978.

Trojan, Judith, and Nadine Covert. *16mm Distribution*. New York: Educational Film Library Association, 1977.

Index